Marlyn's
Garden

Marlyn's Garden

Seasoned Advice
for Achieving Spectacular
Results in the Midwest

Marlyn Dicken Sachtjen

CHICAGO
REVIEW
PRESS

Library of Congress Cataloging-in-Publication Data

Sachtjen, Marlyn Dicken, 1925–
    Marlyn's garden : seasoned advice for achieving spectacular
results in the Midwest / Marlyn Dicken Sachtjen.
        p.cm.
    Includes index.
    ISBN 1-55652-208-8
    1. Gardening—Middle West.   2. Landscape gardening—Middle West.
I. Title.
SB453.2.M53S23   1994
635'.0977—dc20   93-40712
                                                                          CIP

© 1994 by Marlyn Dicken Sachtjen
All rights reserved
First edition
Published by Chicago Review Press
814 North Franklin Street
Chicago, Illinois   60610
Distributed by Independent Publishers Group
Printed in the United States of America
5 4 3 2 1

To Bill
Always so helpful, so loving, and so much missed.
The life we shared was good and our children
helped to make it rewarding:
Leah (Gerry), Steve (Shari), and our
grandchildren, Staci, Scott, Danae, Jeffrey, and Karl.
Each has been a blessing.

Acknowledgments

EACH of the following played a role in some form or fashion towards this book becoming a reality: Deon Prell, Pam Wolfe, Jack Ferrari, Mary Evert, Dorothy Camper, Marian Mooney, Joanna Reed, Gwen and Panayoti Kelaidis, Deborah McGown, and R. Bruce Allison. Thanks of course to Ray Evert for writing the Foreword and to the Thomsons for proofing the botanical names.

Many gardeners and gardens have touched me over the years, though none so much as Joanna Reed's, Ruth West's, and Virginia Umberger's.

A special thank you to these friends who have responded to my repeated pleas for help: Jim Madar, Joe Gilbert, Karl Sachtjen, Dennis Tande, Lois Kinlen, the Hogans, Schumachers, Fryes, and Reillys, and especially to Linda Matthews for leaving the flavor and my personality intact. Thanks.

Contents

List of Illustrations

Foreword

MARLYN'S *Garden* is a thoroughly delightful, comprehensive, accurate, and informative guide, written specifically for the Midwest gardener by the creator of one of the Midwest's truly remarkable gardens. There is no other book like it. It is just what I would have expected from Marlyn, and it should be required reading for gardeners everywhere.

Continually experimenting, Marlyn has created a garden that is unique in its arrangement and combination of plants, many of which are found nowhere else in the Midwest. Although she advises new gardeners to begin with plants that are "tried and true" in their area, she also encourages gardeners to experiment, noting that many plants "will surprise you with their adaptability." Complete lists are provided of all the plants included in Marlyn's garden, along with sources.

Marlyn's garden and *Marlyn's Garden*, the book, are alike in that both are full to bursting. Moreover, Marlyn's personality—unconventional, enthusiastic, and tireless—is reflected in both. The advice she provides is both down-to-earth and sweeping, telling us how to prepare the soil and work with the weather ("All gardeners must be prepared to deal with extremes; we can't trust averages"), how to dig our planting holes, cook our home-grown green beans, and at the same time how to get rid of massive, overgrown conifers or gut a backyard and transform it into a meadow or prairie.

Marlyn emphasizes conservation and naturalizing throughout the book. In addition to being one of the most energetic and creative persons I know, Marlyn is also a master of time. She has carefully organized her garden with low maintenance in mind, utilizing lots of bulbs, grasses, and large perennials and letting them naturalize. Marlyn has begun to replace her vegetable garden with a sanctuary of trees and shrubs, late-flowering perennials, and fall-blooming bulbs. Her Moonlight Garden and Desert Garden are low-maintenance gardens at their finest. The "gardening naturally" approach, which includes the planting of seeds directly in the garden year-round, is only part of Marlyn's maintenance strategy.

Marlyn's innovative approach to propagation and unique plant combinations make her garden so unusual that people volunteer to work with her in the garden to learn her techniques. Readers of *Marlyn's Garden* will have the advantage of her knowledge and experimentation without having to travel to Madison to work with her. Read and enjoy.

Ray F. Evert
Katherine Esau Professor of Botany and Plant Pathology
University of Wisconsin, Madison

Marlyn's Rules

1. Hand water, especially new plantings. Carry water from the faucet or, if you have a big garden, keep large water tubs full and available. Sprinklers miss too many places. Hand watering saves water and you know for sure your plant got a drink.

2. When you plant, dig a big hole and partially fill it with water, preferably fertilized, before you put the plant in. This gives the roots a chance to recover from the shock of being moved. It works. Always put water in the bottom of the hole first!

3. Hoe, hoe, hoe. Buy a hoe and use it. Whatever has happened to this standby garden tool? It chops weeds, cultivates but not too deeply, and is maneuverable. You need one.

4. When you're creating a new garden, put the paths in first. Any bed 4 feet or wider needs a path. Make the path and stand on it to finish the rest of the bed.

5. Nurseries and garden centers make mistakes. Be sure you're getting the plant you want before you buy. Is it potbound? Rootbound? Last year's stock? Find out.

6. It takes a perennial plant two or three years to look its best. Trees and shrubs take up to seven years to gain stature. Don't be too dismayed and don't give up if your plantings look new for the first few years. Give them time and they will reward you.

7. You won't be a gardener until you learn to accept and appreciate weeding.

Gardening in the Midwest

T HE Sachtjen acreage, Wind 'n' View, lies eight miles northeast of Madison, Wisconsin, in a rural setting surrounded by farms, animal refuges, and preservation areas. Its six acres slope south and west from the crest of a hill overlooking the Yahara River basin and Lake Mendota. The view is spectacular; the west wind a ceaseless reminder that these gardens were once open prairie.

When my husband and I purchased this property in the early 1960s, it had been farmed to death. Not a tree stood on it; the soil was exhausted and eroding away from wind and rain. For thirty-odd years I have thought of myself as a kind of Grandma Moses of the land, transforming those bare acres into diversified gardens that now represent one of the largest private collections of plant material in the United States. Hundreds visit Wind 'n' View every year—plant societies, garden clubs, nursery owners, landscape designers, plant science classes from the university, collectors, and people who, driving by, catch sight of the gardens and can't resist coming in.

My gardens provide a continuous show from May through October. There is a country garden down by the road for motorists to enjoy; a formal herb garden with raised beds; several prairie and meadow restorations; a "people sanctuary," where I'm naturalizing bulbs in the shade of trees and shrubs; and a new miniforest as a memorial to my husband. The house itself is surrounded by other gardens: dwarf conifers, moonlight and desert gardens, an entryway garden of delicate shade lovers, a unique display of dwarf alpines with a woven tapestry effect, and more. For many years my husband and I tended an immense vegetable garden, and a perennial food garden that was both ornamental and productive. I describe those, too, and provide some of the recipes that went over best with family and friends.

I learned to garden by trial and error and by asking for advice wherever I could find it, from neighbors, more experienced gardeners, and extension classes offered by the local university. When, eventually, I was teaching some of those classes, it struck me how little written information is available to people gardening in the Midwest. In the spring and fall, our temperatures can fluctuate by sixty degrees in a matter of hours. In winter, subzero temperatures and fierce winds are killers; when these alternate with periods of springlike thaw, gardens and gardeners suffer. Outsiders have no conception of the summer sun's harsh intensity. Of all fifty states, those in the Midwest experience the most diverse weather patterns. A standing joke: if you don't like the weather now, wait thirty minutes—it will be entirely different.

Many plants that are hardy on the two coasts are delicate in the Midwest, and many that require full sun elsewhere thrive best here with afternoon shade. I envy the Northeast and Northwest their shade lovers and dwarf conifers that need cloudy, cool humidity; I covet those heavenly peaches, magnolias, and dogwoods so easily grown in the South. But we in the Midwest can console ourselves with the artemisias, salvias, butterfly plants and other prairie beauties, and even the tomatoes that gardeners elsewhere can't grow as well as we can.

We are not as besieged by insects as are other parts of the country, for the deep cold of winter kills them. Our soil is enviable, even after being worked for more than a century—not too rocky or sandy, and very rich. We experience few extended periods of 100-degree temperatures. We may plant later in the spring than other regions, but we enjoy our gardens later in the fall, often till the end of October. And there are ways to beat the zone restrictions that frustrate so many midwestern gardeners who are pining for some perennial or shrub rated too delicate for us.

The eastern exposure is a precious one in the Midwest. Where buildings or trees break the prevailing west wind and provide relief from afternoon sun, we can succeed with hybrid roses, kentucky coffee tree, rhododendron, scotch broom, and others that would soon perish in a more exposed setting. Another of my tricks, and one that you will hear much more about in the chapters that follow, is to grow from seed. A "delicate" species grown from seed sown directly where you want it has a far better chance of thriving than a potted specimen purchased from a nursery and transplanted into your garden.

New gardeners should begin with plants that are tried-and-true in their area. The Midwest is vast, and contains a vast diversity of microclimates. Good bets in the relatively temperate, once-forested areas bordering the Great Lakes may fail in more exposed settings inland—and vice versa. We can succeed with a variety of distinct garden styles, depending not only on personal taste, time, and budget but on the character of the individual site.

Remember, though, that the entire Midwest from the Gulf of Mexico into Canada and from the Mississippi Valley to the Rockies was originally a complex and balanced prairie ecosystem. Mile after mile, as far as the eye could see, the prairies stretched, encompassing countless millions of acres—seven million in Wisconsin alone. Grasses dominated all this area, from short grasses and wildflowers in the high, dry inclines near the mountains to the less arid tallgrass (or mesic) prairies thriving in the sweet black soil further east. Our soil and climate originally hosted native grasses and wildflowers (or forbs) that agriculture has attempted to eliminate in favor of the food crops that have made the Midwest rich. Restoring the native prairie—at least cultivating some of its typical plants—is one of the most rewarding projects a midwestern gardener can undertake.

Prairies are what got me going as a gardener. I remember the exact moment of my transformation. A friend had prevailed on me to join her garden club, and the first statewide meeting I attended was highlighted by a program on native prairies and restoration. I was glued to the slide presentation. This slide, that slide, the next slide all showed plants I knew I had, growing like jewels on the steep south bank of my property. I rushed home to verify: Yes, I had a patch of virgin prairie about 40 by 60 feet—the size of an ordinary home—grazed but never plowed, sporting twenty-eight species of native forbs and grasses. Its soil was completely different from the rest of what I had. It was black, slightly sandy, loamy, crumbly, rich. No wonder the settlers had been in a frenzy to cultivate it!

The die was cast. I had caught the disease. From then on, dirt was soil to me, and the land became my dependent, to husband and protect, not to own. I felt a shock of recognition when, somewhere along the line, I read the following words, attributed to Chief Seattle on the occasion of the sale in 1854 of part of his territory to the whites:

> Every part of this earth is sacred to my people. Every shining pine needle, every sandy shore, every mist in the dark woods, every clearing and each humming insect is holy in the memory and experience of my people. The sap which courses through the trees carries the memories of the red man.

We are all tied to the land with profound and powerful bonds of common necessity. The stewardship of the land, the caring and cultivation of it, is one of the most gratifying undertakings of a lifetime. I feel the same reverence for the land as Chief Seattle, and I believe we have an urgent responsibility to undo much of what our forebears did to the land in the name of development and progress. To survive, we must cooperate with our environment—we must cooperate with nature, not fight it.

Conservation must become the touchstone in our gardening. Where water is scarce, lawns are a luxury we cannot afford, and traditional gardens whose plantings are suited to a cool, moist climate must give way to natives and exotics that thrive in our region of greater extremes. Chemical fertilizers must be used sparingly, replaced by "green manuring" and other organic means of enriching the soil. Conservation and naturalizing are good for the land and good for the gardener, saving time, energy, and money. You will read much more about them in the course of this book.

One more thing: botanical names. In this book we give botanical names first, common names second if they exist. Learn your botanical names! Nothing distinguishes real gardeners from lightweights more clearly. Only the botanical names are specific. What do you mean by snow-on-the-mountain? Do you want *Pachysandra*, *Cerastium tomentosum*, or *Euphorbia epithymoides*? You could get any one of them if you don't use the botanical name. If three names are given, use them all: *Perilla frutescens* var. *nankinensis*. You are giving genus, species, and named variety. Sometimes you see three names presented differently: *Iberis sempervirens* 'Compacta' or *Iberis sempervirens* cv. Compacta. The third name is the cultivar or cultivated variety, sometimes abbreviated cv. Each name provides more information and makes your reference more specific.

People often ask me: "What is your favorite garden?" I reply, "Whichever one I'm working in." This book is the story of my gardens and of my development as a gardener. It is also an attempt to sum up and convey to other midwestern gardeners the strategies, species, and plant combinations that have worked best for me. I am convinced that they will work for you, too.

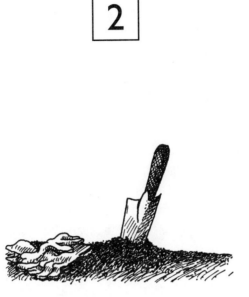

2

Care of the Soil

CARING for the land—preserving, revitalizing, and protecting it—has become a lifelong project of mine, a crusade begun thirty years ago that still challenges today. I am convinced that naturalizing is an essential part of this goal. It means less wear and tear on the land and less wear and tear on the gardener.

The latter becomes more and more important as we age.

Beginners tend to plunge ahead and plant a garden without examining their soil. Don't be foolish: Find out all you can beforehand and save yourself heartache later. Assay your piece of land and prepare the soil well. Do some research; learn what native plants formerly grew in your area. Try to integrate those plants and their needs with your gardening desires and the soil you have to work with.

Maybe your soil is sandy, with lots of small pebbles. Sandy soil drains well, but it's low in nutrients and tends to be acid. Some prairie plants, however, don't mind it.

5

Maybe your soil is heavy clay, rich but hard to work. Clay soil is dense and the very devil to wet once it dries out. But sowing and tilling in a green manure crop like alfalfa, or working in other organic matter, will transform it.

Maybe you're one of the lucky ones with a loamy soil. It's the perfect growing soil: very fertile, slow to dry out, with good drainage. Most plants grow splendidly in loams, though it can be too rich for some.

Regardless of your soil type, it will need constant care and upgrading. Fertilizers, compost, and degradable mulch must be applied yearly if soil is to remain healthy. Of course, the more land you cultivate, the more time-consuming this maintenance will be. I have six acres of land on a dry, windy hill. When my husband and I bought it, the soil had been exhausted by decades of farming. Not a single tree broke the wind or provided shade. The view was fabulous, but the property itself—its steep banks, ceaseless winds, and barrenness—sent me into a tailspin. Where to begin?

Starting with the Land: The Wonder of Green Manure

Something had to be done, and I decided to start with the land. I began years of preparing—restoring—the soil. The first step was green manuring. All soil needs organic matter. That's what makes soil alive. The simplest, least expensive, and least damaging way to get it is to plant a cover crop for the sole purpose of tilling it back into the land.

We first became aware of green manuring when we purchased a Troy-Bilt rotary tiller. A newsletter was included in the purchase, and it contained all sorts of information on green manure cropping. Now, as soon as I harvest a vegetable crop, it's pulled and tilled under. I then plant a cover crop, which is turned under when it's green and 8 to 12 inches high, either in the fall or the spring. The results have been very satisfying. My erosion problem is now minimal over the winter and through the spring thaw. I fight far fewer weeds. If we mow the cover crop, the clippings can be raked up and used in erosion-prone spots as a mulch. Turning the cover crop under in the spring provides the soil with lots of nitrogen and other nutrients so that the plants to grow there will have lots to feed on. My soil is constantly enhanced and revitalized. The results are remarkable, especially in a vegetable garden.

We've used winter oats, winter rye, alfalfa, and buckwheat as cover crops. Even annual herbs make good green manure crops. Just be sure to turn them into the soil before they go to seed. Of all these crops, I like buckwheat the best. You'd have to see the tremendous improvement in the soil to believe it. Today my soil crumbles readily, works easily, and grows things beautifully. Prepare your soil—provide it special care. Good, healthy soil is a joy to touch. Crumble it through your fingers if you haven't done so in a while, and you'll see what I mean.

Much Ado about Mulching

Our care for the land doesn't end with green manure. Many areas, including ornamental gardens and designed landscapes, can't be cropped, so you must develop another way to preserve the soil's friability. A good mulch does the job splendidly. It insulates the soil both summer and winter, holds moisture in dry stretches and cuts down on watering, keeps down weeds and helps control erosion, and, as it decomposes, adds organic matter to the soil. In a vegetable garden it keeps your produce clean and free of mud and dirt. But I've found problems with some of today's popular mulches.

If you apply standard mulches like wood chips or sawdust thickly enough to eliminate weeds, they foster insect, mildew, and fungus problems, and give you too acid soil. They might also come from diseased trees. And if the chips or sawdust haven't aged for one year, they rob nitrogen from the soil below.

Grasses, hay, straw, and other such mulches are full of weed seeds. Try my method and you won't face a sea of weeds: Buy the straw or hay in early fall and let it spend the winter in bales sitting on grass. This kills the weed seeds. About a month before planting time, wet it thoroughly and sprinkle it over your garden. Till it in when you're ready to plant. You'll face very few weeds with this technique, and your soil will blossom in fertility.

If you do plan to mulch with hay or straw, especially in a vegetable garden, be sure it has not been treated with pesticides. You do not want to mulch anything you are going to eat with material that has pesticides in it. Even if you are not growing vegetables, these treated mulches are not such a good idea. They sometimes contain enough pesticide to kill or weaken your plants.

Newspaper can be satisfactory as a mulch if you avoid colored or slick paper. Lay it out in thick pads and wet it thoroughly, even anchoring it with rocks or bricks. On our windy hill, newspapers dry out too quickly and blow away. If you garden in a more sheltered spot, you may have better luck.

You can create a great mulch from shredded and composted leaves. I like sugar maple, willow, and birch leaves, all of which break down quickly. Till them in at application to keep them put. They're good for sunny or shady gardens. Avoid heavy oak or norway maple leaves in a shady wildflower garden. They take forever to break down, and they'll smother your treasures. Never leave thick masses of leaves on early blooming bulbs or perennials.

Our local botanical garden sells cocoa bean hulls as a money-raising project. They're perfect in a shady wildflower garden, where they always look nice. And they decompose quickly. Unfortunately, they're a little expensive for a vegetable garden.

The best winter mulch is a quilt of light snow. It insulates the soil against subzero frost, and it contains minute traces of nourishing minerals that seep into the earth as the snow melts. Any topsoil the snow may have captured from winter winds will also end up on your garden.

Cleanup is simple, too—a sunny day and warmer temperatures do the job nicely. Snow is poor man's fertilizer—white manure. I'm grateful for every flake.

After snow, the next-best mulch is a living one. Ground covers are an excellent mulch, protecting and enriching the soil. I'm sure the Lord wants us to cover the ground. If we don't, He will, with obnoxious weeds.

A final mulch candidate is the aboveground growth of any of a rich variety of herbs. Yes, herbs! Many are grown in Europe exclusively for mulch. Try some mints—one in my garden grows like a weed and can be harvested several times a season. Some other good ones are the artemisias, comfrey, costmary, and sage. Even rhubarb leaves (hardly an herb) can be placed on your raised vegetable beds or between rows. (Be sure none of these are in seed when applied.)

Mulch is especially good for young trees and shrubs, but it has to be pulled away from their trunks as winter approaches. Mice and voles just love tunneling through mulch in the winter—it beats running around outside. You don't want them nibbling on your trees' tender bark! While you're at it, put guards around the trees and hardware mesh around shrubs to prevent winter damage. Even mature trees need to be checked often for damage from animals.

Forever Mulches: Some Nondegradable Options

Sometimes you want to use a mulch that doesn't break down over time—on paths, for example, or on rich soil that doesn't need the soil-building feature of degradable mulches. There are many good nondegradable mulches.

Gravel mulch has been a salvation to me. All year round, the wind dries my soil and plantings very quickly, pulling the moisture out of the soil. Gravel mulch extends the time between waterings, especially during dry spells. It lets me sprinkle without spattering the plants with mud or causing erosion. I couldn't garden without it.

I use a small, smooth gravel called Mississippi Little Joe in my area. It may be called something else in your area—these names vary tremendously from region to region. My Mississippi Little Joe is of all different shapes and earthen colors, all sized from ¼ to ¾ inch in diameter. If I could afford it, I would use no other gravel. But it's expensive. I use cheaper, "washed" gravel for dry stream beds, for patios, and for top dressing on my larger shrub-planted berms.

If you decide to try gravel mulch, arrange it around the plants carefully. Make sure you don't cover the crown, because this will lead to disease or insect problems. And don't use a larger size gravel, because bulbs and perennials won't be able to push their way up through it in the spring.

Gravel mulch is an excellent soil insulator: the ground changes temperature much more slowly under a good layer of protection. It prevents heaving in the spring. It gives a finished look to my beds. I find that it also provides a perfect germinating medium for seeds, so you'll have to dehead your spent flowers if you don't want them to naturalize and spread. Of course, that may be what you're after. I often am.

For a "killing mulch" to clear land or keep it weed-free while you decide what to do with it, any kind of old carpeting works extremely well. Contact large motels, apartment rental agencies, or carpet retail outlets in your area. Ask when they're recarpeting and whether you can pick up the old stuff.

Over time, carpet mulch can turn an unforgiving wasteland into a wonderland, revitalizing hard, compacted soil and even old driveways once the concrete has been removed. Spread 6 inches of straw or grass clippings over the area you want to reclaim. Drench it with water and then sprinkle it with rock phosphate. Then cover with carpet and anchor it well. Leave this fallow for a year.

After you remove the carpet, add an inch of compost and dig it into the bottom soil with a shovel. Plant anything and be astounded! The third year, you'll need to add a couple of additional inches of organic matter.

I rarely use black plastic as a mulch because it doesn't allow air circulation, it can't be tilled in, and it doesn't improve the soil. But it works well in tandem with the carpeting. If you place heavy-duty black plastic on the soil to be reconditioned and cover it with the carpet, you'll get very good results.

This treatment works very well in prairies, too. Use only the heavy-duty black plastic with your carpeting. It gets hot enough under there in the summer to kill weed seeds, as well as grass and grass roots. Take everything off in the spring after one year of treatment, and then till lightly and add organic matter, including a green manure crop, if possible.

Fibercloth is the miracle cloth of the nineties for gardeners. Unlike plastic, it lets moisture pass through to the soil. Yet it doesn't let seeds germinate, and that's good news. It doesn't tear and lasts a very long time. I buy it by the bolt. Besides its many applications as mulch, I also wrap it around my metal plant hoops, securing it with staples, to create an excellent protection for anything that's liable to windburn.

All of these nontillable mulches—gravel, carpeting, and fibercloth—can be used around shrubs and trees. Top-dress the cloth or carpet with gravel about an inch in diameter. This gives a tidy appearance and makes watering easier.

The Erosion Battle and Improving Your Soil

Green manuring and various mulches were crucial first steps in my battle to replenish and protect the soil at Wind 'n' View, but they didn't do enough to control the ceaseless erosion. My next step was a series of grass terraces and holding banks to prevent my soil and plants from being washed away in heavy rains. Slopes add visual interest to a garden—that's why more and more people are building elevation into their gardens today—but they demand a great deal of terracing and give the gardener one more thing to worry about.

Sod holding banks are easy to install. I'm always lifting sod to coordinate my gardens. Place the sod in crescent shapes (see illustration), first a layer with the grass side down, then a layer with the grass side up, so that the two soil sides meet. Repeat these layers until the bank is the height you want. Then fill in the edges and grade down from the top. You can top the bank with sod grass side up, or sow grass seed.

Holding banks and terraces can also be constructed with field boulders or stonework. A series of level raised-bed terraces can be "stepped down" a steep bank. I personally like boulders, especially if you have them already. They give a feeling of solidity and permanence to any garden.

In addition to holding banks, either of sod or of stone, use one of the permanent soil amendments that companies are now marketing. I add one called Turface to all my soil mixes, both for inside and outside use. It stimulates the development of root systems, keeping your soil in place, and it promotes quick drainage.

Hills aren't the only areas that suffer from erosion. Hard rains and rapid snow melts cause rivulets that create small channels, redistributing soil even on level land. To combat this, use small gravel mulch in ornamental gardens and clean grass clippings or straw mulch in vegetable gardens. Any kind of mulch will help protect against the ravages of erosion, even bales of newspapers.

Working with the Weather

Meteorological information is important to every gardener. If you're moving to a new area, check with the United States Weather Bureau for complete local weather data. Don't be misled by averages—they are the Weather Bureau's way of making ends meet. Here in Wisconsin, for example, we can have as few as 90 or as many as 170 frost-free days in a year. Our rainfall averages between 28 and 32 inches a year. Both sets of statistics depend at least partially upon exactly where in the state you are.

All gardeners must be prepared to deal with extremes; we can't trust averages, especially not in the Midwest. Temperatures here may fluctuate forty degrees in a day! In the spring, we can have beautiful sunny days of 50°F to 60°F, only to have the wind change and nighttime temperatures plummet into the low twenties and teens. Our plants and our gardeners must be able to adapt to this wide temperature variation.

Warm daytimes and below-freezing nights cause heaving, where the expansion of water in the soil pushes plants right out of it, with their roots exposed to the sun, wind, and cold. New plants are especially vulnerable to heaving. Don't let these exposed roots dry out. If you don't replant them immediately, the plant will quickly die. As long as you're in a period of severely

Soil →

Grass →

1. Sod Holding Bank

2. Holding Bank of Boulders

fluctuating temperatures, check your plants closely. A light covering of pine boughs can help. And avoid planting taprooted plants in the fall—they're more likely to heave.

Use hardiness zone maps, but realize they aren't infallible. Hardiness will doubtless continue to remain something of a mystery. How hardy is hardy? Plants hardy for the British are generally tender here in the Midwest. And the cloudy, damp British climate gives their gardeners trouble growing many native American plants.

Wind plays a lead role in the Midwest, especially on sites as exposed as mine. Young seedlings and new growth on established plants can be sun- and windburned in both winter and summer. The windchill factor is ever-present in north country wintertime. This determines whether borderline hardy plants will be around to see another spring. Winter winds burn the yews and other evergreens. Dwarf conifers suffer even more. If the winds blow without a snow cover on the ground, you can lose soil. You'll certainly lose plants. So in Zones 2 through 5, we welcome a snow cover.

The only thing worse than minus 40°F windchill factor is an ice storm. If you haven't been through one, you've missed an awe-inspiring experience. One year had a 2- to 3-foot snow cover when it began to rain. In no time, the snow was coated with a half-inch of solid ice. Then we received another snowfall. The result was that oxygen couldn't penetrate the ice layer. Many plants smothered. And the trees had little better luck—many had their branches snapped by the weight of the ice. Birches and sycamores were especially vulnerable.

And then there are the tornadoes—super winds. They threaten complete destruction, though fortunately they rarely strike.

When the Rains Refuse to Come

Drought is another weather anxiety common to the Midwest. The prairie handles this problem by going to sleep: some years, for example, there's simply no show of yellow coneflowers. But when the rains arrive, the prairie revives rapidly. Nonnative plants are not so lucky; some simply don't come back.

The very thought of drought sends tremors of apprehension up the spine of any serious gardener. Twice in my gardening years, I've come face to face with severe drought. Dry spells occur each year, but a true drought is a humbling thing. It creeps up on you. Then suddenly a mental alarm sounds and you realize it hasn't rained for weeks. When I was a less experienced gardener, I was caught unprepared. Not anymore.

Now I monitor rainfall amounts carefully. If there's no rain for a week, I start a planned regime of watering. This way I don't give the subsoil a chance to dry out. Too many people wait until the situation is desperate before taking action. That costs plants. By keeping to my schedule, I can keep a large area alive even through a sustained dry period.

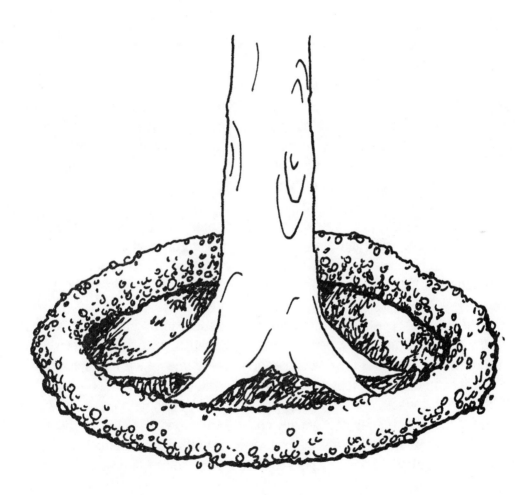

3. Irrigation Well for Trees and Shrubs

A portion of my property is irrigated with an underground system similar to the kind golf courses use. In addition, I installed a faucet near the prairies so water does not have to be hauled so far for them. In the remaining gardens, especially where I have been doing a lot of seeding or transplanting, I set extra-large, heavy-duty plastic garbage cans and keep them full of water with a sprinkling can close by.

I use water from a hose to soften dry soil, then haul water and pour from buckets for serious irrigation. I mound sand and gravel (equal parts of each) around trees and shrubs to create wells for water, and then I fill and refill these wells slowly. I can almost hear the soil and roots drink the water in. This sand and gravel mixture can be applied as a mulch on raised beds. The soil underneath stays moist for a very long time.

I've never watered my lawn. It goes into a brown dormancy after a period of drought and greens back up when the rains return.

You can take a number of waterless steps to bring your perennial plants through a drought. Removing spent blooms, called deheading or deadheading, helps. It keeps the plants from expending energy creating seeds and lets them concentrate on staying alive. Many stemmed plants can be cut back to ground level: dictamnus, delphinium, arabis, and anthemis are a few that tolerate this treatment. But don't prune off the lower branches of trees and shrubs. They help hold in moisture by shielding the soil from wind and sun.

Still, after two months of wind, no rain, and temperatures in the nineties or hundreds, your measure as a gardener and your faith will have been sorely tried. Endless watering robs time from other maintenance. The gardens look rough, uncomfortable, and inhospitable. I keep up with my large gardens because I go back to them after supper. That's sometimes hard to do when the temperature's still 93°F at 7:00 P.M. I cringe and the garden cringes. Darkness is welcome.

During these drought periods, I sometimes wonder about hauling buckets of water, dragging hoses, setting up and timing drippers—the constant repetition of all these tasks—are the garden and the land worth all this? My husband always came up with the magic words: "Be glad we have a three-hundred-foot well and you *can* water!"

I've decided this whole process builds character and develops true grit. If we persist in taking care of the land, the rains will finally come, and I won't have lost all those seeds and seedlings. The sweet rain transforms all my worries into thanks that I made the effort. How great it is to walk around, to see the plants refreshed and standing tall. God has danced in the gardens!

Winter: The Time for Rest

Seven months is enough! I need my five-month winter break from the garden. It's an essential reprieve. This vacation gives me a chance to dream again . . . and in the garden of my dreams no weeds grow. I need to steep myself as we steep a good cup of herbal tea, so I settle down with an armful of seed and nursery catalogs. They contain an enormous amount of information. Of course, they're trying to sell you, too, but they still offer lots to learn. The winter period of reflection is what motivated me to write this book. Gardeners don't dread winter. On the contrary, by the first of November we long for the magic charm of slippered quietness. We take advantage of it with contemplation and in-depth planning.

There's absolutely nothing I'd rather do than design a new garden. I always plan the paths first, because they add so much. Meandering paths create mystery and suspense. In large areas, I use strips of carpeting, reapplying as the old carpeting rots. This is 100 percent easier than trying to keep the ground clear and clean. For smaller areas a 12-inch log cut into 2- or 3-inch-thick circles is attractive. You can also use stepping stones, bricks, or gravel.

Don't be hasty: you'll repent at leisure. I often get too excited about an idea and rush into execution. Dawdle over a map; do your thinking on paper. It's easier to erase than to dig up and transplant, and you'll save time in the long run. I'm still correcting many of my early mistakes. Do your homework: Research every plant before you order it. Make sure you know its needs and decide whether you're willing to provide what it must have to flourish. Does it need shade, special soil, moisture, or a dry location? Will it live in your hardiness zone? If you doubt your supplier, check with your city's landscape designer or your county agent. They're very informed people. If you learn about a plant's special needs and decide to put yourself out to meet them, you've made a giant step toward becoming a real gardener.

When you're relaxing in the winter and planning your current or future gardens, make sure to include accessories and horticultural surprises. Paths need an objective. So do trellises and arbors. Work to create a flowing unity with a hint of secrecy and expectation. Establish an atmosphere—it can be nostalgic (an English cottage garden), trendy (ornamental grasses), or naturalized (prairies, meadows, bulbs, or herbs). Try to ensure that your garden atmosphere doesn't look crowded. A wise gardener avoids jamming.

If your garden has lost some of its magic for you, be courageous: Dig things up, throw them (or give them) away, and change the garden's look. So many gardens I visit are past their prime, full of overgrown or scrawny old shrubs. Rejuvenate your land by skillful pruning or removal. Don't hesitate to gut parts of your garden and start again. Decide what new plants you want and how many. What colors will go well together? How about the background, and paths for working and walking—if the garden is over four feet wide, you need a path! Enjoy the mapping. Revel in designing a new garden or bed. This is what a gardener's winter is for!

By all means keep a journal. I wish I'd kept one from the beginning. I wish I'd kept a list of every question I couldn't answer during the summer. Then I could research and fill in the gaps over the winter.

Winter is also the time to go over your equipment and decide what to replace. Buy good tools—rake, hoe, shovel, dandelion digger, and (most of all) a very good pruning scissor. To get ready for spring, visit the garden centers and learn what's new. Order the fertilizers you need. I like to broadcast a timed-release fertilizer on many of my areas. I often do this while there's still snow on the ground. The snow melts, carrying the fertilizer into the soil. I supplement that fertilizer during the growing season with a powder fertilizer that dissolves in water. A well-fed and watered plant resists diseases and gives you longer, more impressive performance.

While the snow lies on the ground, take a fresh look at the way you garden. Easier upkeep is a permanent goal: Keep seeking new techniques. Have the lawn abut rock walls to lessen edging and trimming chores. Today's plastic edgings are excellent; use them where you can. Spray Roundup on the edges of grass terraces. Discipline yourself to finish one project before starting another. There's no way to keep up if you don't organize and stay ahead.

The Joy Only a Gardener Knows

When summer returns, use the cool of the evening to garden reflectively. I carry my pruner and weeder all the time as I critique and plan the next day's activities. But you must develop your own techniques. Mine work for me because they're in tune with my philosophy. I hold myself accountable to the land, and I try to think of tomorrow, not just today. Always push yourself: the less you do today, the less you'll have done tomorrow. Respect and enrich your gardens with your own general philosophy.

Gardening builds your appreciation of the natural world: summer rains, winter snow cover, birdsongs, the beauty of rich black soil crumbling through your fingers, seeds exploding into life, the bounty of vegetables maturing to be stored for winter nourishment.

Gardening, as I'm sure you've noticed by now, is more than a hobby with me. It builds my pride and gives me a great sense of accomplishment and satisfaction. Let's face it, to be pleased with yourself is an essential part of life. We all get older, but gardening helps us mature wisely and accept the fact of aging. The garden's calming effect provides free therapy. The spring miracle of rebirth is like a tonic: I gain strength for another season facing the trials and tribulations nature dishes out.

3

Trees and Shrubs

WINDBREAKS or protection belts are often established to protect large fields. In the Midwest and on the Great Plains, they're a common sight. They can serve small gardens equally well. In our part of the world, we need them to deal with the fifth season, the wind. Planting a well-considered windbreak is a must for midwestern gardeners.

How to Use Windbreaks

My first experience with a windbreak was a disaster. My husband and I crammed three hundred black spruce and norway pine seedlings into a 25 by 150-foot space beside our driveway. We intended it for a snowbreak, but the trees pushed the first big snow right onto the driveway in big drifts. These trees became an eyesore as they grew, and they were the first thing my visitors saw coming or going. They're gone now, replaced by sturdy and attractive rock berms that entice everyone, including me.

When we built a new home and remodeled our gardens, we had another chance to establish a windbreak. We needed something efficient and attractive to cut the wind blowing from the west side of our property. It had to serve several purposes: to protect the garden and house from wind; to deflect deer away from the gardens; to furnish some fruit; and to provide restful shade.

Of course, homes are usually built first and landscaped after, often in rather helter-skelter fashion. We designed and planted our entire west-end windbreak before we even excavated for the house. This windbreak has been extremely successful. It provides protection against exhausting wind and weather and has great winter landscape appeal, with conspicuous silhouettes and attractive barks. Many of its trees and shrubs are heavily sprigged or twiggy to break up wind currents and snow. Large trees are carefully positioned to break wind pressure and provide relief to windburned skin and eyes. This windbreak acts as a climate conditioner, protecting my gardens and home from winter storms and shielding me from summer sun. Many of its shrubs provide flowers in the spring and berries in the fall to attract birds that control the summertime insect population. Its foliage provides brilliant fall landscapes and then, when the leaves fall to the ground, a winter mulch. Such a windbreak does not have to be reserved for a large area, either. This kind of planting on a smaller scale can create an effective buffer zone between homes on city lots.

Break the Windbreak Monotony

Windbreaks don't have to be monotonous! You can create an interesting one with thorny trees and shrubs, evergreens, and even poisonous plants. Stagger the rows; military marching rows are boring.

At its westernmost edge, my windbreak is planted with *Salix matsudana* 'Tortuosa' mixed with *Fraxinus quadrangulata*, *Quercus palustris*, *Juniperus* 'Mountbatten', and *Picea glauca*. These are underplanted with *Viburnum trilobum* and *Salix* 'Sekka'. A second staggered row repeats these plantings in a different order, replacing some corkscrews with an additional *Picea glauca* and *Rubus tridel*, and *Acer japonica*.

Closest to the house, a third staggered row contains ornamental shrubs and subtrees: *Acer ginnala*, *Aesculus pavia*, *Amelanchier laevis*, *Cornus alternifolia*, *Crataegus crusgalli*, *Euonymus alatus*, *Maclura pomifera*, *Rubus odoratus*, and *Shepherdia argentea*, with *Hemerocallis* forming a half-moon shape on each end.

As you can see, there is a wide variety of shrubs and trees for use in the Midwest besides *Forsythia ovata*. Although this is a healthy and insect-free shrub, it dismays me with its sporadic bloom and its habit of throwing up more and more stems from its base each year. I think we can do better.

Some Shrubs and Trees to Avoid, and Why

Acer negundo   box elder. Very aggressive.

Acer platanoides   norway maple. Like most maples, very aggressive. A fierce reseeder.

Ailanthus altissima   tree of heaven. There's nothing even remotely heavenly about this far-reaching, suckering tree. I've seen suckers travel 12 feet under raised beds and pop up on the other side!

Elaeagnus angustifolia   russian olive. A short-lived tree with the bad habit of partially-dying branches and trunks. When this dead growth is eliminated, you don't have much of a tree left—just a distorted, unpleasing silhouette.

Ligustrum vulgare   privet. This is definitely overused. Nurseries keep suggesting it because it's easy and dependable for them.

Lonicera tatarica   honeysuckle. An import that's trying to rule the globe.

Morus albus   mulberry. This Chinese import is another horrendous reseeder, distributed far and wide by birds. Seedlings have birchlike leaves and grow rapidly.

Philadelphus coronarius   mock orange. A very popular fragrant shrub with the disquieting vice of developing a suckering root system.

Populus deltoides   eastern poplar or cottonwood. The puffy cottonlike seeds are like a snowstorm when they fall. Many communities classify it as obnoxious. The tree also windburns easily.

Prunus virginiana   chokecherry. The birds love the fruit, so you know what that means. Many *Prunus* also sucker to develop into thickets. They're generally considered weed plants.

Rhamnus cathartica   buckthorn. If you let this get established, you'll regret it. Buckthorn is another Eurasian escapee that's made a second home in this country.

Rhus glabra   smooth sumac. This subtree reaches thicket stage quickly. It also reseeds terribly.

Robinia pseudoacacia   black locust. There's nothing lovelier or more fragrant than a hillside of black locust. But woe to those who try to grow them in a garden; they'll have a forest in no time.

Rosa   rose. So many of these are mildew prone, and almost all need demanding care.

Salix discolor and *S. caprea*   willow. Both of these share the suckering growth style of the forsythia and mock orange. Willows should not be planted near sewer lines; their root systems will penetrate the pipes.

Syringa vulgaris   lilac. Lilacs have such a pleasing fragrance—if only they weren't so susceptible to mildew.

Taxus canadensis   yew. Yews tend to be burned by winter wind and snow glare. You're always replacing them.

Tilia americana   american linden or basswood. An insect-prone reseeder.

All these trees are exercises in futility that will cause you problems in the future if you plant them now. Your protection belt will remain for a lifetime, and it won't be cheap, either. So make your selections carefully. The right plantings will keep you warm and protected, and the fruit-bearing ones will feed you as well.

Avoiding Tree Problems

Very little is written about what disappointing progress trees can make, especially those grown in containers. Nurseries only tell us the good things about what they sell, and some of them aren't true. When a nursery makes a basic error in growing a plant, we may harvest the dire results when we get our purchase home. Trees, shrubs, and perennials are sometimes left in their containers until completely root-bound. Trees and shrubs seldom recover from this strangulation. You'll have to give them a fighting chance by severe root and branch pruning. Try to straighten the roots out and anchor them in the soil. Bare-root plants from local nurseries stand a much better chance of thriving. Plants shipped long distances without careful packing may also die. Make sure your bare-root purchases will be well protected during shipment. Don't be afraid to ask.

Nurseries don't tell us how many years will pass before we'll enjoy a colorful autumn. Trees rarely live up to our expectations until they're five to seven years old. Then they take hold, and we begin to have an inkling of their future glory and comeliness. So don't be overly alarmed by a bare winter skeleton or a slowly developing tree.

The Best Trees to Beat the Wind

Here are some splendid choices for your protection belt. Each is planted at Wind 'n' View.

Abies sibirica   siberian fir. A desirable columnar tree that will eventually grow quite tall, featuring very soft silver-tipped needles.

Acer japonica   full-moon maple. When you grow these from seed, you find a wide choice of unique forms. All will provide you with blazing fall color. This is an exquisite choice for a small country lot.

Acer pseudoplatanus   sycamore maple. This is a tree of royal beauty. Give the sycamore's wide-spreading branches ample growing room, and you'll be blessed with a magnificent specimen.

Betula nigra   river birch. This species tolerates, even flourishes in, difficult, dry conditions. It's resistant to the birch borer, grows quickly, and submits to judicious pruning.

Carpinus caroliniana   hornbeam. This tree is often difficult to locate and transplant. I am fortunate enough to have two doing very well. Hornbeams have a very dense habit and need a lot of careful pruning when young to open them up. With patience and attention, you can grow a stately specimen. During its youth, the brown leaves hang on the tree all winter. A mature hornbeam has a spectacular structure and stunning fall color.

Cercidiphyllum japonicum   japanese katsura-tree. This tree has many outstanding characteristics but will need protection from the wind. Its form and bark are distinctive. The leaves rustle musically in a gentle breeze. Tree foliage has a profound language all its own, as water does. Let sound play its role in your garden. Even if you can't afford the luxury of trickling water, let your plants and trees talk to you in their unique language. Walk your gardens often with the sole purpose of listening to the rich and subtle sounds.

Cercis canadensis   redbud. The heart-shaped leaves and colorful folklore make this subtree very appealing. And it's very easy to grow from seed, as long as the seed is fresh.

Cladrastis lutea   american yellowwood. This is hardy for me, but it's a slow grower that doesn't set its clusters of yellow flowers until it's six or seven years old. The flowers turn into blue fruits that the birds enjoy.

Cornus alternifolia   pagoda dogwood. The branches develop in layers, like a pagoda roof. It's a scene-stealing center-stage performer, even though it's a subtree. It will not tolerate dry, compacted soil.

Crataegus crusgalli and *C. phaenopyrum*   hawthorn. Both varieties have sterling qualities. They're prunable and keep their bright fruit most of the winter.

Fraxinus quadrangulata   blue ash. This is a fast-growing endangered species that doesn't reseed. Nurseries are just now beginning to propagate it.

Ginkgo biloba   ginkgo. Be sure to buy a male tree. Mine came from a cutting from a male, so I'm sure of its gender. The females have unsightly seed pods that smell terrible when ripe and reseed drastically.

Gleditsia tricanthos var. *Inermis* 'Sunburst'   honey locust. This slow starter grows into a showstopper with its striking yellow foliage.

Gymnocladus dioicus kentucky coffee tree. This will make a praiseworthy addition to a landscape with its oriental winter outline. Dry the beans well, roast them, and make yourself a cup of tasty decaffeinated coffee!

Juniperus chinensis 'Iowa' juniper. This conifer maintains good color all winter.

Juniperus chinensis 'Mountbatten' juniper. Another pleasing cultivar with a lacy green foliage that doesn't windburn.

Juniperus scopulorum 'Skyrocket' juniper. This blue cultivar has an interesting columnar shape that I find intriguing. It does best in a protected, dry, sunny spot.

Larix leptolepis japanese larch. This deciduous conifer has a striking winter silhouette. Keep it a manageable size with pruning.

Liriodendron tulipfera tulip tree. This beauty is fast growing, with lovely white summer flowers. Mulch it and make sure the soil stays moist.

Maclura pomifera osage orange. This subtree grows easily from seed. It features a spreading, ebony black winter skeleton, with long thorns to keep the deer at bay.

Magnolia stellata star magnolia. A shrublike subtree, this blooms in late April and is hardy to Zone 4. It's much more dependable for me than the other magnolias because it blooms later.

Oxydendrum arboreum sourwood. This slow grower likes protection and full sun. The graceful pyramidal shape contributes to its many-faceted all-season beauty. Don't prune off the lower branches.

Phellodendron amurense amur corktree. Sumaclike leaves grow into huge branches. With age, branches and trunk develop a corklike bark.

Picea glauca white spruce. Easy from seed, this fast-growing spruce keeps its lower branches well.

Pinus mugo mugo pine. This is supposed to stay dwarf, but to keep it that way, you have to pinch out the candles (new growth) periodically.

Pinus strobus 'Pendula' weeping white pine. All the weeping conifers hold a great fascination for me. I like the idea of controlling the height and then, when you're satisfied, letting the growth cascade.

Prunus maackii amur chokecherry. With a copper-colored trunk and branches, this makes a beautiful contrasting impact against the snow. It doesn't reseed as prolifically as other prunus do.

Pyrus communis aristocrat pear. This is questionably hardy in Zone 4, but it's worth a try because of its outstanding burgundy color in the fall. Both the aristocrat and bradford varieties have lived three winters at Wind 'n' View. They have another endearing quality: their crowns grow into a perfect teardrop shape.

Quercus palustris   pin oak. This long-lived oak is the fastest growing of its race. It needs frequent pruning during its first five years. With the right pruning, you'll have cool, filtered shade as the tree ages, rather than impenetrable darkness.

Rhus typhina 'Laciniata'   fernleaf sumac. This subtree is extremely drought resistant. Its beautiful winter form can be handsomely underplanted.

Salix matsudana 'Tortuosa' and *S. sachalinensis* 'Sekka'   corkscrew and fantail willow. The corkscrew's green trunk and twisted branches form a dramatic image in the winter landscape, growing up to 30 feet. The fantail's wide-reaching branches ending in fantail shapes are a flower arranger's delight. This subtree grows to about 6 feet. Both these willows slow down their growth habit at about fifteen years of age, so they're good for small lots.

Sorbus alnifolia   korean mountain ash. This praiseworthy ornamental has small but distinctive flowers, silvery bark, and red fall berries you can dry for use in the kitchen. Pruning will bring about delightful dappled shading.

Thuja occidentalis 'Emerald'   arborvitae. This stalwart holds a good green color all winter. You'll have to hoop this with a 6-foot wire cage, since the deer love arborvitae. Deer got to mine, but they have started filling in again from the bottom. Arborvitae is one of the very few evergreens to recover from serious cropping.

I trust this selection will dispel any notion that windbreaks have to be boring. Try always to plant trees with double and triple purpose.

The Underground Tree

Let's talk briefly about the root systems of trees, as they provide tremendous competition for perennials, bulbs, and shrubs you might want to grow as an understory.

Birch, maple, elm, and most conifers shouldn't be underplanted. In particular, don't waste your time trying to plant bulbs under big trees. They *need* all their roots; don't damage roots just to put in a few bulbs. You'll find you wasted your money on the bulbs in any case. They'll disappear quickly because they can't compete for food and moisture with a large tree.

I like to plant trees and shrubs with single taproots or that are tough enough to take some digging near their roots. Some tough ones are willow, bradford or aristocrat pear, kentucky coffee tree, fernleaf sumac, sunburst locust, purple and seedless marshall green ash, red buckeye, pagoda dogwood, oak, hickory, and ginkgo.

Try to avoid planting trees that have been grafted. The desirable stock is too often grafted onto trees that have suckering root systems, like crabapples, cherries, and plums. Of course, all these will sucker and develop into unattractive thickets. Moreover, grafted trees tend to be less hardy than nongrafted ones—an important issue for those of us in the Midwest.

Whatever you do, *don't* top trees or shrubs. Pruning is especially effective at the five- to seven-year stage; go easy after that. Topping looks terrible and injures trees by affecting their food supply. Trees feed through their leaves. The remaining bark and trunk will face sunburn because of lost protection. Large branch scars don't heal: they invite disease. Any new growth that develops will be weak and suckering. You'll never again have a specimen tree.

Growing a Healthy Tree

It's just as important to understand the aboveground structure of a tree as its root structure. Most species don't have the special gift of developing specimen quality on their own, like *Cornus alternifolia* or *Pyrus*. Most need our help in their early, formative years. Pruning, thinning, and structuring your new stock is a pleasant winter task you'll look forward to. Deciduous trees have lost their leaves, so it's easy to decide what to remove. Prune all small twigs and branches from the inside of the tree and as far out on the branch as 3 feet. This will open it up and give you a view of the rest of the garden.

I've learned that the east side of a tree produces more rapid growth than the west side, which has to face more wind. That's especially true in my windswept garden. Concentrate on giving your trees a balanced look, or they're liable to mature lopsided. White paper birch trees have a further requirement: they need to be planted on the north or east, as they can't tolerate afternoon sun.

After ten years, most trees reach a size where they'll benefit from a professional arborist. But if you do your pruning homework, you can put off this expense indefinitely.

The Finest Shrubs and Subtrees

Trees furnish the skeleton for your landscape; shrubs are the musculature. They need each other to be effective.

*Don't ignore the old-fashioned beauties that are starred in the list below. They've proven themselves over the years in our parents' and grandparents' gardens; many have lost their popularity because of their habit of self-seeding, but they are ideal for home gardeners because they are long-lived, able to survive neglect, easily controlled with pruning, and responsive with a minimum of care. I've purposely grown many of them from seed to ensure their hardiness. (Most serious gardeners can't avoid growing things from seed. Besides being enjoyable, it's a way to get some treasures you'll never obtain otherwise.)

Abeliophyllum distichum   Often mislabeled white forsythia by nurseries, this shrub is only a relative of the forsythia. Despite recent glowing accolades, true forsythias (which are all yellow) aren't dependable early bloomers. Sometimes they bloom erratically, sparsely, or not at all. You'll get guaranteed blooms with *Abeliophyllum*. It flowers earlier than forsythia and lasts longer. My shrubs are grown from seed that germinated quite quickly. Grow this plant and see for yourself what a beauty it is. It layers easily and dependably, so once you get it going, you'll be able to propagate it constantly.

Aesculus pavia   red buckeye.* A southern native that nonetheless does well in a protected, Zone 5-like location. Easily grown from seed. Be careful of its poisonous leaves. It grows beautifully under trees.

Amelanchier laevis   juneberry.* This berry is better than any blueberry you've ever eaten. I fight the birds for them. I welcome juneberry as one of the earliest bloomers, and I appreciate its striking fall colors.

   The so-versatile *Amelanchier laevis* seemingly grows anyplace it is planted but is at its best near the edge of a woodland, combined with azaleas, *Epimedium rubrum*, ferns, hostas, species tulips, and primulas. The juneberry's early spring billowy white airiness is followed with delicious red berries. Its striking fall color and conspicuous silver grey silhouette during the winter make it an all-seasons botanical.

Azalea 'Northern Lights'   At last, a dependable bloomer for us northerners and midwest-erners. The buds are hardy to 45°F below. I find this shrub likes afternoon shade and moisture. Although this plant is a recent introduction, I'm sure our grandmothers would have loved it. Be sure to prune off spent blooms or it won't bloom next spring.

Berberis thunbergii var. *atropupurea*   dwarf red barberry. This offers outstanding color, and the branches don't die out as they do on some other barberries. A new cultivar, 'Rose Glow', has made a hit in our gardens and is appreciated because it is deer-proof.

Buddleia alternifolia 'Argentea'   butterfly bush. This is a cascading silvery fountain of leaves drenched with small lavender flowers. Propagates easily by self-seeding or layering.

Callicarpa japonica   beautyberry. This is an aggressive reseeder, to be contended with because the purple berries in the fall are lovely. I originally gathered these seeds in Kansas, but I share them with everyone. Beautyberry has another bad habit, shared with *Cotinus coggygria* and *Caryopteris incana*, of dying back under the soil in winter and coming up from the roots in the spring like a herbaceous perennial. After several years, a large, unsightly clump of dead stems develops. But the beauty of the berries makes it all worthwhile.

Calluna vulgaris   heather. An evergreen shrub that grows in poor acid soil with lots of moisture and sunshine. Be sure to mulch this with pine needles or conifer boughs.

Calycanthus floridus   carolina allspice.* So fragrant and trouble-free, it adapts easily and tolerates our fierce west winds.

Caryopteris incana   blue mist. Looking for fall color? Here it is: bright blue flowers in September and October. Here in the Midwest, this dies back completely in the winter, so it blooms a little later than some nursery catalogs indicate. It has attractive seed pods and looks gorgeous in front of *Rosa rubrifolia*.

Ceanothus americanus   new jersey tea. This all-around wonderful shrub blooms in July. Even the little capsule seed pods of this native are an unusual prize. The seeds are hard to germinate unless you soak the seed in hot, pure water at 135°F. Let them sit overnight and then plant them right away. Floating seeds won't germinate.

Chaenomeles lagenaria (C. speciosa)   flowering quince.* Plant this in a protected place. It forces well for early spring bouquets. The branches layer easily for propagating. It will even climb brick walls.

Chionanthus virginicus   fringe tree or old man's beard.* This imposing native has an impeccable reputation. You'll need two for flowers, planted 15 feet apart.

Cornus mas   cornelian cherry. Not a traditional favorite, but it certainly has all the qualities of one. The fruit's edible, the branches force easily for spring bouquet, and the fall color is stunning. When the cornelian cherry needs water, it lets you know by curling its leaves.

Cotinus coggygria   smoke tree. Enjoy the handsome mahogany foliage and puffy 6- to 8-inch flowers that come in July and last for months. The smoke bush will grow in any soil and doesn't need pampering, though you will see occasional dieback. Grow this and expect every visitor to ask its name. I like *Alchemilla vulgaris* underneath.

Cotoneaster divaricata   This features red fall color and red berries. Some of these plants die back, but reseeding will keep the species going for you.

Daphne x burkwoodii 'Carol Mackie'   garland flower. A tremendous asset when grown with dwarf conifers. Its early spring blossoms are deliciously fragrant, and it often reblooms in late summer.

Deutzia gracilis   This choice, May-blooming, heavy-flowering shrub has a graceful look in light shade. I grow it with a beautiful complement, the tree peony.

Euonymus fortunei 'Sparkle 'n Gold'   A delightful addition to your winter garden, pleasant all the year round.

Euonymus fortunei 'Kewensis'   winter creeper. A creeper easily propagated by cuttings.

Exochorda racemosa   pearlbush.* Displays the most pristine white flowers I've ever seen. It can get a little ragged, so keep the shape pruned. My seed came from Kansas.

Fothergilla major   dwarf alder. No plant has more dramatic fall foliage! It likes rich soil and will need some winter protection.

Hamamelis virginiana   witch hazel. The more protection you can give this shrub, the more flowering you'll see in October and November.

Hydrangea anomala subsp. *petiolaris*   climbing hydrangea. This plant won't bloom until it begins to climb, after five years of growth. It propagates easily by layering.

Kalmia angustifolia   bog laurel. This is hardy even into Minnesota. You must provide an acid soil.

Kerria japonica   This will do well in poor soil, as long as it's well drained. Prune out a few older canes during the winter for a bright green bouquet, but keep in mind it blooms from old growth.

Kolkwitzia amabilis   beautybush.* Give this lots of room and prune the old stems regularly. It blooms with forsythia. It has always transplanted easily for me.

Lonicera diervilla   honeysuckle. A native plant that's stunning and nonaggressive. It doesn't set berries.

Mahonia aquifolium   oregon holly grape. A semivining shrub with prized winter color. Every now and then it sends off a sucker that's easy to transplant—which is a good thing, because you'll want a lot of this plant. Give it afternoon shade.

Myrica pensylvanica   northern bayberry. Here in the north, it's deciduous; parts of the plant may even die back. This is a bit of a problem, but the plant soon rebounds. The clusters of ice blue berries make it special.

Paeonia suffruticosa   tree peony. This subtree doesn't die back and blooms on old growth, so don't prune it. Truly a royal member of the plant world. Astilbe looks great under this plant.

Potentilla alba 'Abbotswood'   cinquefoil. Not as aggressive and more shapely than other cinquefoils.

Rosa rubrifolia   red-leafed rose. This rose has no faults: startling foliage, pink flowers, and huge clusters of hips. It's not susceptible to disease or insect trouble. It even reseeds in moderation. A most valuable asset.

Sambucus racemosa 'Plumosa Aurea'   golden elder. You won't miss your forsythia at all if you grow this beautiful plant. Although it sometimes dies back, it reappears reliably from the root.

Shepherdia argentea   buffaloberry. Small, silky grey leaves are smothered in small, deep-golden flowers in the spring, followed by fruitlike currents and thorns. Don't rototill around this shrub: you'll sever its many surface roots and kill it. You'll need three or four plants to insure fruit. The fruits make a great vinegar.

Spiraea japonica 'Goldflame' A new variety with stunning red growth in the spring. It's very effective planted next to golden elders.

Spiraea prunifolia 'Grefsheim' bridal wreath. A new introduction that's so unbelievably smothered in blossoms you can't see *any* foliage or branches.

Tamarix ramosissima A border or background of this is like a wall of lace. Plant it in front of conifers for a truly smashing effect. If your tamarix gets straggly and blooms sparsely, cut it back to below ground level. This will force it to throw up new growth from beneath, and you'll enjoy a rejuvenated plant.

Viburnum carlesii korean spice.* A valuable, compact addition anyplace in the garden. It has an exceptionally sweet fragrance.

Viburnum rhytidophyllum leatherleaf. White flowers yield to black fruits. Don't place it near another white-flowering shrub. Propagates easily by layering or cuttings. Interplant with *Cotinus coggygria*, *Euonymus alatus*, and *Myrica pensylvanica* for a nice effect.

Here at Wind 'n' View, I've tried to make the most of the idea of trees as the skeleton of my gardens and shrubs and subtrees as the musculature that fill that skeleton out. These trees and shrubs will be here far longer than I will. Scattered here and there across my property, they frame up my gardens very nicely, creating traffic patterns and pathways that guide both the feet and the eyes. They lead one forward, around a corner, to a place where one is dazzled by some hidden wonder. And they can be focal points in and of themselves as well. They combine practicality and beauty, a glorious duo giving four seasons of service.

A Side Benefit to Trees: Shade Gardening

I've always believed that the 30 feet of a garden around the house should be extensively landscaped. We designed our house accordingly. No overhangs on the north or east side. Here grow some of my favorites: the "tender-hardies," exotics, and shade lovers. They have a cool haven when the thermometer climbs into the nineties.

Many of the shade-loving perennials (anemone, bloodroot, spring beauty, dutchman's-breeches, trout lily, and bluebell) bloom in early spring and then die back. To create an all-summer-long display of color around the front entry, I put in annuals while I can still tell where the perennials are: caladiums, impatiens, begonias, achimenes, forget-me-nots, and other prized shade lovers. One of my little-known favorites is *Alternanthera*, either 'Snowball' or 'Versicolor'. Both have stunning foliage. 'Snowball' has pink stems with green and white leaves. It's great with *Athyrium* and white *Nicotiana*. *Alternanthera* adds an unforgettable finishing touch to a garden.

With some help, I built a raised area the length of the garage, 10 by 24 feet. Part is enclosed with white fencing. Two raised levels drop down into a sunken courtyard filled with a soil mix of equal parts of compost, aged manure, Turface, sand, and topsoil, along with some aluminum sulfate. The two raised levels on the other side of the fence contain the same soil mix. I then added a half-inch topdressing of shredded, then moistened leaves, roughly forked into the soil mix.

As I emphasized in chapter 2, soil composition is all-important. This one will deliver guaranteed results. You could also include aged medium-size bark chunks and moist peat.

The Best of the Shade Lovers

My years of longing for a real shade garden have been worth the wait. I've taken pains to provide the proper habitat for my beauties, for some thrive in dappled sunlight and others bloom in full sun before the trees leaf out, dying back as tree foliage develops. Here's what I've planted.

Actaea rubra   red baneberry. Beautiful but aggressive. Use this only if you have a large area. If you get too many plants, keep them from going to seed by pinching off the seed pods.

Adiantum pedatum   maidenhair fern. My favorite fern does better if you scratch a little lime around it each spring. It's not aggressive.

Alchemilla mollis   lady's mantle. It seems to grow anyplace you plant it.

Anemonella thalictroides   rue anemone. Mark it well, because it dies back after flowering.

Arisaema triphyllum   jack-in-the-pulpit. Another reseeder.

Asarum europeum   ginger. Not as dominating as our American ginger. The leaves are more decorative, too.

Astilbe   Blooms later (in pink, white, or red) than other shade lovers.

Bergenia cordifolia   heartleaf. Its attractive large, leathery foliage provides a nice accent even after the blooms are gone.

Caulophyllum thalictroides   blue cohosh. A lovely native bush with clusters of dark blue berries for fall.

Chelone glabra   turtlehead. A sought-after native that's not hard to grow.

Claytonia virginica   spring beauty. Another ephemeral, a plant that dies back totally after blooming. Make sure you mark it.

Corydalis lutea   With icy green leaves and yellow flowers, this plant blooms all summer long and reseeds only too well.

Cypripedium hirsutum   showy lady's slipper. This is, frankly, a difficult plant to grow. On top of that, I have the distressing feeling that it, along with many other rare plants, is being harvested in a native location (perhaps Canada) by helicopter and won't have much of a chance of survival in our gardens. Always deal with a reputable nursery to avoid the desecration of these lovely plants. Never dig them from the wild yourself. Needs an acid soil.

Cypripedium calceolus var. *pubescens*   yellow lady's slipper. The same cautions apply to this as to the showy lady's slipper. In 1989, for the first time, mine set three teaspoons of seeds. I've planted them in an ideal spot with a special soil mix. Lady's slippers need a rich composted soil with mycorrhizal fungi found naturally in deep woodsy places around rotted tree stumps. It's white, and many wildflowers need it; I wish we could buy it. I took some soil from my mother plant to mix in with the seeds. These plants can stand an almost neutral soil. (They are very slow germinators.)

Dicentra cucullaria   dutchman's-breeches. Another ephemeral that disappears after blooming, so be sure to mark its position. There are others in this family that are also desirable: *D. canadensis* (squirrel corn) and *D. spectabilis* (bleeding heart). (My bleeding heart is not very hardy, but it reseeds nicely for me.)

Epimedium spp.   I have many varieties and each one is outstanding.

Erythronium americanum   trout lily or dogtooth violet. An ephemeral that's also a spasmodic bloomer. The roots grow very deep. Friends are now planting these in children's sunken wading pools. If the roots can't grow deep they will bloom!

Gentiana andrewsii   bottle gentian. A tallish blue gentian that needs morning sun and good moisture. Don't mulch this plant with anything but red granite gravel.

Helleborus niger   christmas rose. It certainly does bloom in the snow, even here in Zone 4. Mine reseed well.

Hepatica americana   liverwort. This blooms with the christmas rose and looks nice next to it. (Unlike other shade lovers, *Hepatica* will tolerate dryness.)

Hosta sieboldiana 'Elegance'   This plant tolerates neglect, competition, and dryness. It has always done well at Wind 'n' View, even in full sun.

Houstonia caerulea   bluet. A darling plant, blooming throughout the spring. It also likes gravel mulch. I've cut off the tiny seeds and patted them into the ground near the mother plant to produce many clumps. This is beautiful under tree peonies.

Hydrastis canadensis   goldenseal. Hard to find. Has deep red seed pods in clusters.

Jeffersonia diphylla   twinleaf. Truly fascinating leaves, but a very slow propagator.

Lilium philadelphicum   wood lily. Another woodland plant that's not easy to find. I've grown mine from seed.

Mertensia virginica   virginia bluebells. A little aggressive in reseeding, so once you get enough of them, clip off the seed pods.

Mitella diphylla   showy orchis. Mine was dug from an old oak forest being destroyed for development and unfortunately didn't like its new home!

Osmunda claytoniana   interrupted fern. A very special plant that isn't intrusive like *Matteuccia pensylvanica* (ostrich fern), one of those gifts I wish I'd never received, and *Osmunda regalis* (royal fern), a treasure.

Phlox divaricata   woodland phlox. If you cut this down to the ground after it blooms, the plant will get much more moundy and stop sprawling.

Polystichum acrostichoides   christmas fern. Not at all aggressive and perfect for harvest at Christmas. I like it planted near *Helleborus.*

Primula   primrose. Lots of species and hybrids. They're all nice and like the gravel mulch, where they reseed like crazy.

Sanguinaria canadensis   bloodroot. You'd better not let this one go to seed after the second year. *S. canadensis* 'Multiplex' is a double-flowered form that is much more desirable.

Smilacina racemosa   false solomon's seal. This features striking clusters of white flowers and, in the fall, large, deep red seed pods.

Tiarella cordifolia   allegheny foamflower. This is protected in our area, so don't dig it in the wild.

Trillium cernuum   wake robin. This and *T. grandiflorum* both die back after blooming.

Uvularia grandiflora   merry bells or bellwort. This divides easily and is especially good with *Fritillaria meleagris* (guinea hen bulbs), which also tolerates moist shade.

This north-facing shade garden also contains a few shrubs: azalea, *Chionanthus virginicus* (fringe tree), *Hamamelis virginiana* (witch hazel), and *Kalmia angustifolia* (bog laurel). All need afternoon shade.

If you don't have the dappled light necessary for this shady garden, you'll need to bring in a professional tree pruner to open up some of your deciduous trees. Nothing desirable grows in complete, profound shade. Don't try to plant this type of garden under evergreens, either. A certain level of light is essential, and the dense shadows cast by evergreens don't allow it through.

You will need to fertilize this shady garden with Miracid. Apply it while the plants are in bloom, following the directions on the box. Wood lily, birdsfoot and bifidia violets, *Cypripedium calceolus* var. *pubescens, Ilex verticillata* (winterberry), *Orostachys iwarenge, Clethra alnifolia, Calluna vulgaris,* and *Vaccinium* spp. must be treated. *Cypripedium calceolus* var. *pubescens* is watered with Schultz's fertilizer. Schultz's is recommended by the National Federation of Garden Clubs, and I use it all summer long on delicate plants.

I'm lucky that my shade garden gets enough light to keep the plantings happy. It's perfect for many of these plants. Many of them travel by root stolons, many reseed nicely, and many stay put. All are long-lived occupants that need little care. All they want is moist humusy soil and afternoon shade.

4

Prairies and Meadows

Prairies have a natural beauty all their own: a soft, gentle, belonging look. Their unique landscape of tall grasses and brilliant blooms is the Midwest's Garden of Eden. Sadly, our once-vast native prairies were virtually destroyed by the land-hungry farmers of the nineteenth century. But in the last couple of decades an increasing number of gardeners and horticulturists have begun to push back the green of Eurasian origin to reclaim our native American heritage. Now thousands of midwesterners have fallen in love with the beauty of restored prairies. Corporations are transforming their grounds into wildflower-strewn grasslands, and several states have planted prairie flowers and grasses on roadside banks and interstate medians. Prairie enthusiasts are drawing on centuries-old species and nature's techniques to remedy erosion and the effects of drought and overcultivation in today's stressed ecosystems. The prairies are being reborn. I hope they're here to stay.

Prairies and Burning

Prairie plants have a tough, inbred resistance. They survive neglect, drought, and pests, and are distinctly suited to the Midwest's dramatically changeable weather. They represent an appealing union of ecology, aesthetics, and practicality. They have only two requirements: undisturbed soil and regular burning. Without burning, nonnative species like queen anne's lace, bouncing bet, chicory, and dandelion overrun our native beauties to reign supreme. I grant you that a field of any of these is lovely, but all are rampant reproducers, quickly obliterating our precious native heritage.

Burning cleans up the prairie, destroys seedling trees, and removes the dead grasses that would bury the early show of pasqueflower, prairie smoke, pussytoes, buttercups, and violets. The ash that remains warms the soil, prompting a germination reaction in many prairie seeds. Rain and melting snow wash the mineral-rich ash deep into the soil. Lightning, which in ancient times often touched off the annual prairie fires, is also an effective fertilizer. Each bolt infuses a small amount of organic nitrogen into the earth. Experts estimate that midwestern soil receives six pounds of organic food per acre per year from lightning. Accompanying rain washes it evenly into the earth.

When lightning did not set prairie fires, the Indians did, to keep the prairies open and hospitable to the great herds of buffalo that provided the basis of their way of life. Firing and the prairie are inseparable. My township still permits it, as do many others in and near rural areas. If you cannot burn, true prairie restoration is probably beyond your reach. However, you can approximate by mowing annually with a sickle-bar mower. But all the dead material will have to be raked up, removed, and composted.

When I burn, usually in late February or early March, I wait for a north or east wind, so that the flames will blow toward empty lawn and fields. Some people use a propane hand torch to set the fire, but I just strike a match and set it to a clump of prairie grasses. In seconds, my three 100 by 150-foot prairies are burned.

Restoring a Prairie

Prairie restoration is quite a project. I climbed joyously on that bandwagon in the early seventies, when I discovered that the westernmost summit of my hill consisted of untouched prairie containing twenty-eight native species. My brainstorm was to start at the top of the hill with an area that had been planted in bromegrass for years, get rid of the grass, and connect with the native prairie 100 feet away. I would have liked to plow the area several times, but its sharp slope prevented that. So I made my first mistake: I went in with Roundup and killed everything. When the ground was clear, I broadcast all the seeds I had collected from surviving prairie fragments within driving distance, and from the generous teachers of the classes I was taking. Of course, the following summer was the driest we've had since the 1930s. Nothing germinated—nothing but noxious weeds, that is. They claimed the area in one season. I'm still recovering from that experience.

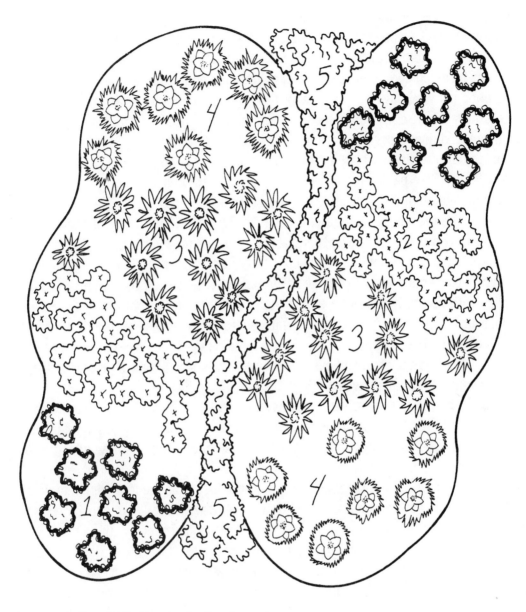

4. Plan for a Prairie Drift *(drawing by Cari Strauss)*

Plants for a Prairie Drift

1. *Aquilegia canadensis*
2. *Coreopsis palmata*
3. *Liatris pycnostachya*

4. *Anemone vulgaris*
5. *Artemisia ludoviciana*

Clearly I needed a change of strategy. The next spring I introduced oxeye daisies, thoroughwort, daylilies, flax, and even aggressive herbs to battle the weed situation. After three years, I was able to introduce natives (as plants, not seeds) in large, 12-foot, free-form drifts. They included coreopsis, gayfeather, columbine, and European pasqueflower. This last plant is not a native. I have been trying for thirty years to grow the native *Anemone patens*, unsuccessfully because my soil is too rich and loamy for it. When the European *Anemone pulsatilla* moved in and began to thrive, I accepted it; it's lovely.

I connected my drifts with silver king artemisia, yellow coneflower, and native grasses. These drifts look like paisley-patterned fabric. They keep their individuality to this day, and they help me maintain diversity and curb invasiveness.

After eight years, the prairie grasses began to dominate, and some of the exotics I had brought in to control weeds began disappearing. Still, after more than a decade, I have to dehead bromegrass, cut off white and yellow clover, and dig up mullein. I'm glad I stuck with it, though. I have ended up with a large naturalized prairie garden combining a good number of exotics with the natives. I often take groups of visitors to the bottom of the hill, and we look up at this tallgrass prairie to the summit, where the only vestiges of humankind are the conifers I put in before I knew there was a native prairie up there. We sense how the pioneers must have felt when they first laid eyes on the millions and millions of acres of virgin prairie. What a spectacle that must have been!

When we burn this prairie early each spring, the effect is awesome. With an indrawn swoosh the flames leap to the heavens in seconds; in less than a minute, the entire area is burned. I can understand how terrifying this sight must have been to settlers; I know why they dreaded prairie wildfires.

My second attempt at prairie restoration, like my first, was made completely with seeds, but you can be sure I sowed them on absolutely clean, raw soil. I was able to harvest the seeds from plants in the native prairie and my first restoration area. I then stratified them by putting them into paper bags and hanging them up in the garage for the winter. To me, stratification means many temperature changes, and I knew I'd get them in the garage. I bought some seeds, too, and in February I put down forty flats. I had good germination, and by May 15, I was transplanting into an area 150 by 100 feet. I had a water faucet nearby, so I could sprinkle my seedlings whenever they needed it. We didn't have a drought, but rain was scanty, so I had to haul hundreds of buckets of water. I refused to let things die after all the effort to plant and grow them. Of course, I didn't want to waste my seed money, either.

Finally it rained . . . a destructive blockbuster, of course. I walked the area with tears streaming down my face. My husband helped me haul rocks to fill gullies a foot wide, 18 inches deep, and more than 10 feet long. I spent all summer on my knees, filling in and replanting with purchased grasses, and both I and the prairie survived—just barely. The second year was easier, but there was additional planting and repair work, along with incessant weeding. I spent two summers hunching along with a dandelion digger.

By the third year, things looked much better. We even burned that spring. I was happy.

The Nursery That Became a Prairie

Prairies really do get in your blood. While I was tackling that last south hill prairie, my husband Bill decided that part of the west slope was just too steep for his vegetables. Suddenly, I had a third patch of land to work with. Many visitors who had seen the stunning natives I was growing had suggested that I start a prairie nursery. I thought it was a great idea; I'd specialize in rare and endangered species. The gift from my husband went right into production.

I didn't have to face the problem of clearing the land of brambles, european honeysuckle, japanese bittersweet, brome, poison ivy, buckthorn, box elder, and so on. This 40 by 70-foot area was clean, and that's such an incentive. Using wide rows 3 feet apart and mulching with marsh hay between the rows, I put in the following seeds, mixed first with three parts of sand:

Asclepias sullivantii   Another prairie milkweed with a larger white flower than the common one. Pioneers used the white sap from milkweeds to soothe burns and cuts.

Echinacea pallida   pale coneflower

Gentiana flavida   cream gentian

Koeleria cristata   junegrass

Liatris punctata   dotted dwarf blazing star

Parthenium integrifolium   wild quinine

Phlox pilosa   prairie phlox

Ruellia humilis   wild petunia. I also planted this in the rock garden with the buttercup and phlox. All three made many offspring, showing they enjoyed the gravel mulch.

Stipa spartea   needlegrass. These "needles" stick into anything and everything.

Veronicastrum virginicum   culver's root. Worthy of any garden.

Zizia aptera   heart-leafed golden alexander. Dies back after flowering.

Zizia aurea   golden alexander. This is very aggressive. I don't understand why it's so rare.

Some of these plants are endangered species; others are simply rare. I have other endangered species that need moisture and afternoon shade:

Arisaema dracontium   green dragon

Camassia scilloides   hyacinth

Fraxinus quadrangulata blue ash

Bringing plants into cultivation is the first step in saving them from extinction. The second step is to insure their survival in cultivation. Don't dig them yourself in the wild. And don't buy them unless you know they weren't dug in the wild!

In my new "production wildflower garden" were also *Asclepias tuberosa*, *Amorpha canescens*, *Ceanothus americanus*, *Eryngium yuccifolium*, three *Liatris*, and *Penstemon grandiflorus*—all favorites.

To get right to the point (and to put it mildly), the project wasn't a success. I quickly found out that business was not for me. My nursery soon became a prairie. I can look over it easily from my deck. After lifting the marsh hay mulch I'd put down between the rows, I found I'd inherited lots of weed seedlings. After I cleared them out I introduced drifts of prairie lupine from fresh seed. Now there's a blanket of blue in June. You can see it from the highway a mile away. It's really a majestic sight.

Making a Mat and Keeping the Diversity

Your two initial goals in prairie restoration should be to develop a diversity of plant life (more than two hundred species have been cataloged on one acre of prairie) and to have that diversity reach the mat stage. To create a mat or carpet will take five to seven years; to create a full-blown prairie, seven to ten years. You'll need to know your plants. And it's necessary to weed. If you can, irrigate; if you can't, be prepared to carry some water. Don't expect results for two or three years. Set your mower blades high to mow the plot each year until you have enough vegetation to burn. Getting started is definitely labor intensive. But after all the hard work, once your prairie establishes itself, it will need little care; and you'll enjoy its beauty and the satisfaction that ancient, native gene pools are being maintained.

The Right Way to Make a Prairie

When I was getting started, I made every mistake in the book. Now, let me tell you the right way to restore a prairie or make a prairie garden. First, don't bite off more than you can chew. Pick an area about 12 feet square in full sun. Banks are great if you can control erosion. Then put your design on paper, and be sure you have established pathways through it. It's no fun to tour a prairie if you can't walk comfortably in it.

Be sure you are starting with the cleanest soil possible. You can accomplish this easily by covering the entire area with black plastic. Put some old carpeting on top to hold the plastic down. Let your prairie lie fallow for two summers and a winter. Lift the carpet and plastic in the second fall. If you can, rototill or plow a couple of times, but not too deeply. Then decide whether you're going to build your prairie with seeds or with plants.

Seeds versus Plants

Prairie seeds are so mysterious. Some need stratifying (winter cold), some have a very short viability period and must be planted at once, and some can lie on the soil's surface for years before suddenly, inexplicably, germinating. But they have one major thing going for them: if they germinate, your seedlings will be tough; they will survive.

Plants are more delicate and more expensive. If you use them, they'll have to be watered. I suggest using both seeds and plants. Pat your seeds (you'll need about 15 pounds per acre) around a plant of the same variety in the fall. Viable seeds will rattle in the pod, or the pod will have started to split open, with the seed shattering or blowing from it. The more promptly viable seeds are planted, the greater the germination rate.

By planting seeds in the fall, you save valuable time in the spring because you eliminate the transplanting and watering process. When the seeds germinate around the mother plant, you'll know immediately what they are. Identifying seedlings can otherwise be quite difficult.

If at all possible, keep the areas surrounding your prairie free from dandelions, crabgrass, and sweet clover. This will save you lots of weeding. The seeds of these left by the birds will be bad enough; you don't need more blown in by your mower! Many of my headaches were caused by inadvertently blowing lawn cuttings onto my prairies. And please don't make the mistake of thinking that you can produce a prairie simply by letting your lawn go. Your lawn is mostly immigrant stock, fescues from other lands. I assure you there's nothing native there.

Be discriminating in your choices. Make good use of the lists I've supplied, and if a plant is not on my lists, don't use it. Don't plant large areas of *Ratibida pinnata* (yellow coneflower), *Tragopogon pratensis* (goatsbeard), or sunflowers. There are a few that shouldn't be planted anyplace, such as canadian thistle or curly dock. Try to aim for about 70 percent forbs (flowering plants) and 30 percent grasses. This ratio should postpone the seemingly inevitable triumph of the grasses.

Every grower, beginning or advanced, should try to avoid plants with a stoloniferous habit unless they're highly desirable and you're willing to curb them. Do without heavy seed producers. Deheading is an easy way to control seed propagating. Cut off all those fading blooms before they go to seed.

As for grasses, today I know canadian rye is a short-lived perennial and very aggressive. I would not plant any switchgrass (*Panicum*). This whole family becomes a nightmare with its unbridled reproduction. All the prairie grasses are eager to reclaim their heritage.

The Prairie Dilemma

In what now seems to have been no time, but in what has really been close to fifteen years of sweat, tears, and trial and error, my restored prairies have become tallgrass prairies, crowding out the beautiful forbs. Many people have come to tour and think this is the way it should be. But I want my prairies to have lots of flowers.

My twofold goal of establishing a mat with a diverse variety of plants has proven self-contradictory. The instant the mat starts to become a reality, the diversity begins to disappear! Forbs especially affected include *Allium cernuum, Anemone patens, Aquilegia canadensis, Asclepias tuberosa, Aster, Baptisia, Ceanothus ovatus, Dodecatheon meadia, Echinacea pallida*, and *Eryngium yuccifolium*.

Most of these aren't very long-lived. They need bare soil to reseed in . . . and where is the bare soil when you have a mat? I'm gradually losing many of those listed above, in addition to *Phlox pilosa, Liatris, Gentiana* and even the *Rudbeckia hirta*. Within a few years, I think most of these forbs will be gone. I've tried reintroducing some of them, unsuccessfully so far. I've tried to scratch out areas and dehead seedpods; I've even gone in with Roundup. But the grass root system is just too powerful.

Beyond cutting down on the initial ratio of grass to forbs and being more discriminate in my selections, I'm frankly at a loss. How will I meet my other goal—diversity? These are the issues that keep me awake at night. I've made a tremendous effort to create this prairie beauty, and I want my descendants to enjoy it as well.

When to Collect Seed

The following list will be helpful if you plan to collect seeds. I've listed them under the date when the seed will be ripe in the northern Great Lakes region. If you live further south, these seeds will be ripe earlier. If you live in Minnesota, they may ripen later. (Thanks to Marian Mooney for providing this information.)

May 15–31
Anemone patens   pasqueflower
Geum triflorum   prairie smoke

June 16–30
Aquilegia canadensis   wild columbine

July 1–15
Tradescantia ohiensis   spiderwort

July 15–31
Euphorbia corollata   flowering spurge
(hard to collect because the seed heads explode)

August 1–15

Amorpha canescens   leadplant

Anemone canadensis   canadian anemone

Ratibida pinnata   yellow coneflower

Rudbeckia hirta   black-eyed susan

August 16–31

Anemone virginiana   thimbleweed

Monarda fistulosa   wild bergamot

September 1–15

Echinacea purpurea   purple coneflower

Liatris pycnostachya   gayfeather

September 16–30

Anemone cylindrica   longheaded thimbleweed

Asclepias tuberosa   butterfly weed

Coreopsis palmata   tickseed

Eupatorium rugosum   white snakeroot

Lilium superbum   turk's-cap lily

The Best Prairie Flowers

This list of forbs (flowering plants) includes those growing on my prairies:

Allium cernuum   nodding pink onion. Much too strong for our tastebuds. You won't enjoy using it in cooking.

Amorpha canescens   leadplant. Features a silvery lavender shading on the foliage that's almost mystical.

Anemone canadensis   canadian anemone. Appreciates afternoon shade.

Anemone cylindrica   longheaded thimbleweed. Used in dried bouquets before the seedpods puff up.

Anemone patens   pasqueflower. Don't be alarmed if it dies back. This plant has been troublesome in my prairies, no matter how much I've tried to get it to stay. The soil is evidently too heavy for it. The seeds germinate easily, but when they're planted out they struggle even when I give them the best of conditions and position. A few make it through the summer, but then they heave during the early spring of the following year.

Plants for an Ornamental Prairie

1. *Sporobolus heterolepis* dropseed
2. *Anemone canadensis* canadian anemone
3. *Echinacea pallida* pale coneflower
4. *Stipa spartea* needlegrass
5. *Veronicastrum virginicum* culver's root
6. *Thalictrum polyganum* tall meadow rue
7. *Asclepias tuberosa* butterfly weed
8. *Eryngium yuccifolium* rattlesnake master
9. *Aquilegia canadensis* columbine
10. *Amorpha canescens* leadplant
11. *Liatris aspera, L. scariosa, L. pycnostachya* blazing star and gayfeather
12. *Allium cernuum* nodding pink onion
13. *Monarda fistulosa* wild bergamot
14. *Dodecatheon meadia* shooting star
15. *Geum triflorum* prairie smoke

5.   Plan for an Ornamental Prairie

Of course, I'm not about to give up. I've started a "room" of them in my new sanctuary. I've planted them along with *Geum triflorum* (prairie smoke), *Bouteloua hirsuta* (moustache grass), *Baptisia leucophaea*, *Viola pedata* and *V. pedata* 'Bicolor' (birdsfoot violet). If the *Anemone patens* fails again, at least there will be other plantings to fill in.

I finally resorted to peppering all the prairie restorations with *Anemone pulsatilla*. Like the dandelions, this pasqueflower has adapted to its new country with great vigor. But it's truly beautiful, and the prairie would be less striking without it.

Antennaria   pussytoes. Bank this around the leadplant.

Artemisia ludoviciana alba   silver king. Equally at home with the leadplant.

Aster ericoides, *A. laevis*, *A. sericeus*   heath, smooth, and silky asters. Just a few of the many prairie asters.

Baptisia leucantha and *B. leucophaea*   Both of these are outstanding. The first is 5 or 6 feet tall; the second about 18 inches. The black seedpods are delightful for dried material.

Cacalia atriplicifolia and *C. suaveolens*   indian plantain. Large leaved and tall, these both need a moist situation.

Callirhoe triangulata   poppy mallow. Very sprawly, with nice magenta flowers. Grow this in sand and peaty locations.

Campanula rotundifolia   harebell. Plant this near a path or edge.

Celastrus scandens   bittersweet vine

Coreopsis palmata   tickseed. Blooms in June. Aggressive in open soil.

Dodecatheon meadia   shooting star. Traditionally claimed to need moist shade, but I've found that not true. It grows, competes, and survives in hot, crowded situations.

Eupatorium maculatum   joe-pye weed. Aggressive. Doesn't require the excessive moisture everyone says it does.

Euphorbia corollata   flowering spurge. Scatter this about everywhere. It takes a while to grow into a stand, but it's worth the wait.

Filipendula rubra   queen of the prairie. Survives in ordinary garden soil, but needs afternoon shade.

Gentiana andrewsii   bottle or closed gentian. One of the few plants nature goofed on. Blooming late, it's overshadowed by all the tall end-of-season plants. Very, very intense blue.

Geranium maculatum   wild geranium. It, too, needs afternoon shade.

Geum triflorum   prairie smoke. Doesn't like to be burned. Can be difficult to grow.

Helenium autumnale   Spectacular fall color. Nice in fresh bouquets.

Helianthus   sunflower. There are many species. All are aggressive, so beware. They do have edible seeds and the birds love them.

Liatris aspera   blazing star or gayfeather. These are very rewarding. They have a tendency to heave out of the ground in the spring, so keep an eye on them and replant those that need help. Rodents feast on them!

Lilium michiganense and *L. philadelphicum*   turk's-cap lily and wood lily. These are beauties and easy to grow from seed. Native Americans used the bulbs as food.

Lobelia syphilitica   great lobelia. The books say it needs lots of moisture, but that's not what I've found. It does quite well with normal rainfall. (Our normal rainfall is 32 inches yearly.)

Lupinus perennis   lupine. Another spring heaver the first year of life, so be watchful. The seed spreads by exploding; it's there one day and gone the next, making harvesting difficult.

Monarda fistulosa   wild bergamot. Appreciates moisture. The root system lies very close to the surface, so it's difficult to weed.

Oxalis violacea   violet wood sorrel. A troublesome plant that doesn't propagate well; I've lost most of mine. The leaves have a sour taste and can be added to salads.

Penstemon grandiflorus   beard's tongue. This native has eucalyptuslike leaves.

Petalostemum candidum and *P. purpureum*   white and purple prairie clover. The seeds of both can be roasted and eaten. The white is aggressive.

Physostegia virginiana   dragonhead or obedient plant. Too aggressive in perennial beds but the prairie will control its vigorous root system.

Polemonium reptans   jacob's ladder. Doesn't like competition or overcrowding. Try a woodland situation.

Polygonatum biflorum   solomon's seal. Pick the arching stems laden with blue berries. They're nice in a large arrangement. The tender young shoots can be cut and cooked like asparagus.

Potentilla arguta   tall cinquefoil. Another plant for dried arranging material in the fall.

Ranunculus fascicularis   buttercup. A herald of spring.

Rosa setigera   prairie rose. Not too tall, but very thorny.

Rudbeckia hirta and *R. laciniata*   black-eyed susan and tall coneflower. The former will die out with competition.

Silphium integrifolium and *S. laciniatum*   rosinweed and compass plant.

Sisyrinchium campestre blue-eyed grass. Not really a grass but an iris. Grows very clumpy in a garden situation. This plant needs burning to survive. New plants tend to heave in the spring.

Smilacina racemosa false solomon's seal. Large clusters of red berries in the fall.

Solidago goldenrod. A large genus that can dominate an area in a hurry. These plants do *not* cause hayfever. Try *S. rigida*.

Tradescantia ohiensis spiderwort. Walk the prairie in the morning to enjoy this, because it closes up tight in the afternoon. Eat the flowers in salads or candy them for decoration on sweets.

Veronica fasciculata ironweed. Blooming in late summer, the almost-purple flowers are a showpiece. Grows well with ordinary rainfall.

Veronicastrum virginicum culver's root. Plant this near the butterfly weed. They look very good together.

Viola pedata and *V. tricolor* birdsfoot violet. Two difficult plants that don't propagate easily.

Zizia aurea and *Z. aptera* golden alexander and heartleaf alexander. The first is a little invasive. The second is a treasure that dies back in the summer.

The Best Prairie Grasses

Andropogon gerardi big bluestem

Andropogon scoparius little bluestem

Eragrostis spectabilis purple lovegrass

Koeleria cristata junegrass

Sisyrinchium campestre blue-eyed grass. Really a member of the iris family and not a grass.

Sporobolus heterolepis dropseed. Graceful arching stems. At home as an ornamental in our gardens. The seeds can be roasted and eaten.

Stipa spartea needlegrass. The seed stem is extremely sharp and will pierce or cut skin, so be careful. Used to brush hair and to hold clothes together by our Native Americans.

Use the following with caution. They will dominate in seven years:

Bouteloua curtipendula sideoats grama

Elymus canadensis wild canadian rye

Sorghastrum nutans indiangrass

Most of these grasses can be used as dried material in bouquets.

The Best Prairie Shrubs

Here are some first-class prairie shrubs:

Actaea rubra   red baneberry. Shiny, deep red clusters of berries. Needs afternoon shade.

Amelanchier canadensis   juneberry or serviceberry. Brilliant fall coloring.

Caulophyllum thalictroides   blue cohosh. Bunches of indigo blue berries in the fall. Needs afternoon shade.

Ceanothus americanus   new jersey tea. Flowers in July.

Cercis canadensis   redbud. The pink-purple flowers are another herald of spring.

Corylus americana   hazelnut. Easy to crack and nice to eat.

Hamamelis virginiana   witch hazel. A late fall bloomer.

Shepherdia argentea   buffaloberry. The silver leaves are a perfect autumn foil for the *Amelanchier.*

Spiraea alba   meadowsweet. Does well with normal rainfall. Likes afternoon shade. Doesn't die back in the winter.

Symphoricarpos albus   white snowberry. Needs competition or it will sucker and take over.

Viburnum trilobum   american highbush cranberry. Bunches of bright red berries that last through the winter. Cedar waxwings love them!

Don't plant the following unless you have acres and acres of land:

Cornus sericea   red osier dogwood. Suckers terribly. It prefers swampy places, but it will live anywhere.

Prunus americana   american plum. The birds distribute the seeds, and it also suckers like crazy. Many prunus were used for dyeing fabrics.

Prunus virginiana   chokecherry. The birds are very busy with this weedy tree. Still, there's nothing so lovely as the golden yellow fall foliage against the black trunk and branches.

Rhus typhina   staghorn sumac. A hardy native that's very attractive in the fall. You can make pink lemonade from the fruit.

Salix discolor   pussy willow. Native and very hardy.

Salix tristis   dwarf grey willow. Native and very hardy.

All of these listed above sucker and become thickets.

How to Make a Meadow

Prairies and meadows have two things in common: they don't like disturbance, and they're not put in by simply throwing a can of seeds at the ground. The Old World meadow brought over by the New England settlers is dominated by European flora and weedy American natives. Both of these thrive on disturbed soil. As in my prairies, I've tried to control the obnoxious flora to achieve year-round beauty.

Meadow fever is a pleasant disease. If you catch it, you'll reap ample returns. You'll quickly learn that meadows are as varied as the people that plant them. Mine was concocted long before they became the rage. Today, there are cans of meadow mix for sale everywhere. That wasn't the case when I made my plans.

A word of caution about these mixes. Don't be misled. Study the list of ingredients carefully to make sure you're not planting future headaches. Many of the seeds in these mixes are aggressive, reseeding quickly and crowding out the more desirable species. When I see cans that include catchfly, switchgrass, indian grass, sunflower, clover, oxeye daisy, fleabane, rocket, butter-and-eggs, california poppy, white yarrow, and "many others," I shudder.

My meadow adjoins the last prairie I restored, with a 5-foot grass buffer between. It was my husband's favorite garden and the first place he took visitors. Its location on the south bank is perfect; it can be seen from everywhere on my land. It's a large area acting as a transition from the formal gardens to the prairie and then to the farmland beyond.

Of course, my meadow isn't completely natural, even though it may appear to be. Like all the other gardens, it is a composition fabricated to please the eye. Because a meadow's purpose is not to highlight individual plants or species but to create an overall effect, it's important to keep everything in it about the same height. My goal was to create an effect of large-scale color combinations by mingling everything: annuals, perennials, and grasses; exotics and natives. I laid out the meadow in large blocks, installed some paths, and then stood on them to broadcast the seed.

In the back of my mind was an ulterior motive that I never told the plants. I studded the meadow with all-native trees and shrubs. When they start producing shade, I'll convert the meadow to a native, shady, wildflower haven. A temple of tranquility to escape to!

Developing the proper seed mix was easy, since I dehead my gardens and save the seed all year long. And I encourage my classes to make up their own mixes. It's so simple, much cheaper than purchasing a mix, and you wind up with a quality selection of seeds. I harvested about four bushels of seeds from my herb, perennial, and prairie areas. Then I mixed that seed with five parts sand before sowing it in the meadow area.

All seeds need firm contact with the soil to germinate, and many northern species need winter cold as well. I like to broadcast in the fall with seeds that live over the winter; then I pray for snow to firm them down.

Many of the trees and shrubs were also grown from seed, though I did purchase some: *Aesculus glabra, Celtis occidentalis, Betula nigra, Fraxinus pensylvanica,* several different *Prunus, Crataegus,* and *Malus* for trees; and *Hamamelis virginiana, Corylus americana,* and *Viburnum* spp. for the shrubs. These are all native, and I planted them immediately. When you plan your meadow, be sure to avoid trees or shrubs with suckering roots or you'll have a thicket in no time. Little interesting will grow in a thicket.

A novice grower might panic, watching broadcast seeds germinate. It's hard to identify things, or to separate the weed seedlings from desirable ones. Some common weeds a novice might recognize include *Taraxacum officinale* (dandelion), *Cerastium arvense* (field chickweed), plantain, *Plantago lanceolata* (white man's footprint), and *Portulaca oleracea* (purslane). Can you recognize *Conyza canadensis* (horseweed), *Ambrosia artemisifolia* (ragweed), *Brassica* (mustard), and *Capsella bursa-pastoris* (shepherd's purse)? They have all plagued me. Save yourself endless anguish and get rid of them before they go to seed.

If you haven't mastered the art of identifying weeds when they're youngsters, the alternative is to go with plants. Weeding will be much easier and less stressful, and not everybody enjoys it the way I do. I have the reputation of being a compulsive weeder. Like many garden people, when I get tired, I find a weedy mess, sit down, and attack.

For your meadow, I'd suggest these perennials: blue flax, lupine, feverfew, *Gaillardia, Liatris, Monarda,* anise hyssop, gloriosa daisy, and black-eyed susan. I'd also put in a few daylily plants. For annuals: bachelor buttons, cosmos (several kinds), larkspur (several kinds), and poppy (several kinds). For grasses: maidengrass, blue oats, beargrass, bottlebrush, blue-eyed grass, dwarf blue fescue, little bluestem, lovegrass, and dropseed. Plant the fescue and blue-eyed grass near the paths. Along the edges, include some annual grasses like harestail, quaking grass, and job's tears. They're decorative, and you may want to use them in bouquets.

A naturalized meadow, small or large, brings many returns. If the meadow replaces your lawn, you save both time and money; you won't have to worry about mowing or mowing equipment. You'll also be improving the environment by not pouring lawn chemicals into the water supply. You can even be your own florist—the whole meadow is a cutting garden for fresh and dried bouquets.

One possibility, if you don't have clean soil and your lawn is small enough, is simply to lift the sod. Another, particularly if your backyard lawn is a large one, is to consider just letting it go. This won't work for a prairie restoration, since prairies need natives, and lawns are anything but that. But meadows aren't quite so restricted. They and your lawn can be natural companions, and the combination will not unite your neighbors against you! If you want annuals, you'll have to reintroduce them frequently. Just turn over a couple of feet of sod here and there, work the soil up, pat in the seeds or seedlings, and let nature do the rest.

Large trees can become islands of beauty. If you don't have trees or groupings of shrubs to transform into islands, plant a few, lifting the sod around them to give them the best start.

These scenic islands can be used to dot an open area, screen off an unpleasant view, or border a woodland, depending on the size and lay of your land.

Of course, there is no limit to the degree of ambition you can invest in creating a meadow. If your property is level, like most city lots, you may want to do some regrading. Ideally you will establish several levels, the highest one the farthest from your home. Unless you have a large area, don't put a mound in the center. Instead build up your terrain on the sides and the rear. Now's the time to get rid of old and undesirable trees and shrubs. Cut them off at ground level and cover the spot with a berm or mound. If you have some useful trees that you want to preserve, leave the existing lawn around them for a free-form design. Sketch this on paper along with your paths. Then lay out your different levels, keeping higher areas behind lower ones.

You can leave strips of your present lawn in place to form paths. They'll be the only thing you need to mow. Or you can remove them and put in a "mowerless" path with a fiber barrier topped with gravel, strips of carpeting, or shredded bark. Stagger your shrubs with ornamental grasses as you proceed up the slopes. Save the crest for small trees and additional grasses. If you're on a steep slope, you may want to use your sod to help control erosion, removing two rows of sod, then leaving the next in place. This is called strip planting.

Turn the level ground areas into "courtyards." Create several of these and decorate them with native and exotic perennials or groupings of potted plants for color and effect. The plants that you put in your courtyards should be large—the larger the better. This meadow will face much competition from the residue of the lawn, so only large clumps of plants will survive. By the way, be careful not to scalp these with your mower when you're doing late spring or early summer mowing. You'll have to mow your meadow in the fall, as well, so it will be ready to produce its spring show for you. You'll probably also need to prune some of the woody-stemmed perennials in the fall.

You can also plant perennials along the paths, where they'll be easier to admire. Try to arrange for each path to lead to an unexpected treat, perhaps a birdbath or sundial, a pool, an ornamental pot, or a piece of garden furniture.

Letting Your Lawn Go

This is a plan for a meadow garden containing several raised beds created by lifting sod from an existing lawn.

Outline your design by spraying the lawn with a can of white spray paint. You can buy nontoxic spray paint for this purpose at many garden stores. If you change your mind, you can just mow the sprayed grass off and try again.

Then decide if you want to mow the paths or eliminate the grass and opt for an easier method. Old carpeting would work well. (It could be covered with shredded bark for a finished look.)

Form the raised beds with the sod you are lifting, thinking of it as pieces of stone. You'll need three or more layers of sod to create beds of the proper height—at least 2 feet. (Sod can also be lifted from the courtyard areas and from under the trees.)

When the raised beds have been created, use plastic edging ("shoes") to create ground-level beds around the trees. The size and shape of these beds will be determined by the spread of the tree branches, or canopy. The remaining lawn forms up the paths. Use the paths to haul in your soil mix for filling up the raised beds.

Using the diagram that follows, plant the raised beds first. Place potted plants or accessories in the tree beds, perennials along the paths or in a courtyard. All the plants I suggest have been chosen for a southern exposure. If you do not have this exposure, you will need to substitute.

If you don't already have trees growing in your yard, you might plant *Gleditsia triacanthos* 'Sunburst' in the center bed. This has a lacy open structure; it can be underplanted and the branches will cast elegant winter traceries. Two different varieties of *Malus* 'Radiant' and *M.* 'Red Jade' are tempting choices for the corners. Both will provide red fruit to brighten those corners in the winter.

Fill up all the empty spaces in the raised beds with species bulbs. This backyard garden will be easy to care for and all the plants except *Caryopteris* will survive dry spells. The perennials will need deheading as soon as they are finished blooming. Otherwise they will reseed in your raised beds.

One of the subtler pleasures of having a meadow is the joy you'll feel when artists and photographers appear. The camera captures vistas that are enlightening as well as flattering. Many times a look at a photograph will lead to improvements, so be sure to take pictures yourself if no one else has done it: they're a permanent and easy way to record what you've done. Too often gardeners consider themselves a fixture in the garden rather than an observer of it. The camera, paintings, and video provide an unprejudiced opinion. Such permanent images should be a welcome ally in your gardening endeavors.

Container Gardening

One way to add interest to a meadow courtyard is to put out delicates or annuals in pots. They can be moved indoors in winter, where they provide color through the bleak months. After all these years, I still prefer clay pots to those of wood, plastic, or stone. Believe me, I know they're heavy to move when they're full. But they are handsome, and the clay breathes. This is essential for container growing.

Your soil mix is also important. Mix equal parts of an organic compost or potting soil, Turface, and a soilless medium like perlite. You'll need 10 quarts of mix for a 12-inch pot. Add 3 tablespoons of time-release fertilizer to each pot. Mix everything together well.

Grasses and Shrubs for a Backyard Meadow

1. *Sporobolus heterolepis*   dropseed
2. *Arrhenatherum elatius* 'Nanum'   tuber oatgrass
3. *Festuca caesia*   blue fescue
4. *Miscanthus sinensis* 'Gracillimus'   maidengrass
5. *Andropogon scoparius*   little bluestem
6. *Avena sempervirens*   blue oatgrass
7. *Cydonia oblonga*   flowering quince
8. *Euonymus alatus* 'Compacta'   burning bush
9. *Myrica pensylvanica*   northern bayberry
10. *Viburnum carlesii*   korean spice
11. *Cercis canadensis*   redbud

Potted Plants for a Backyard Meadow

Appealing combinations of plants suitable for container growth:

12. Lavender and eucalyptus
13. *Allium scorodoprasum* (rocambole) and *Coleus amboinicus*
14. *Tagetes lucida* and *Tagetes signata* 'Pumila'
15. *Avena sempervirens*

These potted combinations can be brought into the house for a breath of winter freshness. The *Allium scorodoprasum* and *Tagetes lucida* can be used as substitutes for garlic and tarragon.

Perennial Flowers for a Backyard Meadow

16. *Rudbeckia hirta*   black-eyed susan
17. *Coreopsis palmata*   tickseed
18. *Liatris* spp.   gayfeather
19. *Anemone pulsatilla*   pasqueflower
20. *Aquilegia* spp.   columbine
21. *Caryopteris incana*   blue mist
22. *Asclepias tuberosa*   butterfly weed
23. *Echinacea* spp.   coneflower
24. *Malus* 'Radiant'   crabapple
25. *Malus* 'Red Jade'   crabapple
26. *Gleditsia* 'Sunburst'   honey locust

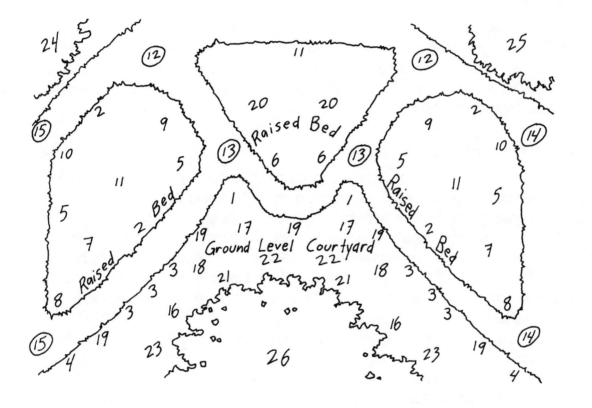

6.   Plan for a Backyard Meadow

Make sure your pots are clean. Cut up some household sponges, stuff a piece of sponge in the bottom hole, and fill in about 2 inches at the bottom with more cut-up sponge pieces. Fill the pot halfway with your soil mix. Then put in the plant and water it. Now fill the pot to within an inch and a half of the top. Place a half-inch of gravel on the top as a mulch and water again. If you follow these directions, your container-grown plants will be legendary. Place saucers underneath to prevent the courtyard earth from soaking all the water right out of the pots.

Everlasting Bouquets

Fresh-cut flowers are one of the pleasures of a meadow garden. If you want your bouquets to last for weeks, you can glycerize them as follows. Crush any woody stems. Combine 3 pints of water with 1 pint of glycerine. Place the plant material in a container with the glycerine mix. You'll need to add water occasionally. Leave the plant material in the solution until it becomes completely rubberized.

How to Showcase Grasses

I always use grasses as integral partners with the perennials and annuals in my gardens. They *do* flower: this is called inflorescence. Grasses have great ornamental value. As a nation, we've become enamored with manicured, monotypic lawns. The greener and more velvetlike, the better. Remember that lawns and hedges are like white carpeting in a barnyard; they require a lot of upkeep. Their price in time and dollars is astronomical. And they may be tidy, but they have little beauty. We think of the beauty of floral bloom, but we neglect the charm of ornamental grasses. If your gardens have become static, let them spring to life with some dazzling grasses.

Grasses have a conspicuous winter form that gives gardens a new seasonal look. Arranged with outdoor lights and some driftwood or rocks, ornamental grasses can take your breath away. They're very undemanding, too. They're easy to clean up with a hedge trimmer . . . or with a match. You'll be charmed by their striking textures and rhythmic sway. A slight breeze sets them in motion. Some have graceful arching stems; others have stiff tubular stalks. Many are tall, while others are short and clumpy. And they all flower.

Grasses add a new range of texture to your garden. They blend well with Japanese iris along with rocks and water, creating a quiet, contemplative setting.

Ornamental grasses need particular emphasis. They're very effective when contrasting habits are combined. Thin, spiky leaves get tedious if they're unrelieved. Intersperse grasses with grey-leaved artemisias, *Phlomis fruticosa, Centaurea, Ligularia*, and other perennials. All set off grasses to perfection. Ornamental grasses also mix well with evergreens. Mix columnar juniper and arborvitae with your grass plantings, and your winter garden will be spectacular.

Avena grasses are stunning with *Stachys lanata* (lamb's ears) in full sun. Blue fescue is great for borders in semishade, and sedges blend perfectly with *Asarum* in full shade. Summer gardens can take on a new kind of excitement if you give grasses a chance.

Horticulturally, we tend to associate relatives of other families with the true grasses. Irises, typhas, and rushes are often called the "grudges." These will take some shade. True grasses need sunlight.

The Best of the Ornamental Grasses

Agrostis alba redtop. I used this as the major grass in my meadow. It's lovely through all growth stages.

Andropogon scoparius little bluestem. This has little puffs of cotton all the way up its 2- to 3-foot stem. It's the last native grass to "bloom" in the fall.

Avena sempervirens blue oatgrass. Blue blades about 14 inches tall. I've never had this flower for me.

Bouteloua gracilis blue grama. A very desirable native grass that matures quickly and holds its inflorescence all winter long.

Elymus glaucus blue oats. This is aggressive in the east, but friendlier to us here in the Midwest. (4 feet)

Festuca caesia blue fescue. Plant this near the edges and walks, since it doesn't like competition. (10 inches)

Hypoxis hirsuta yellow-eyed grass. Hard and slow. Once it gets established, however, it's a delight and blooms all summer. As it ages, it becomes bulbous. Dig down at least 8 inches when you transplant or you'll cut the bulb in half. (1 foot)

Hystrix patula bottlebrush. Supposedly a shady woodland grass, but you see it in the sunny meadow. Don't let it go to seed unless you plan to propagate it. Pick it while green for nice bouquets. (3 to 4 feet)

Imperata cylindrica rubra japanese bloodgrass. Plant this near a walk or edge. (This survives the winter if planted near foundation walls.) (14 inches)

Miscanthus sinensis 'Gracillimus' or *M. eulalia* maidengrass. Doesn't dominate. In fact, you'll probably want more of it. (5 feet) (Do not burn this grass.)

Sporobolus heterolepis dropseed. One of the loveliest. (2 feet)

Sisyrinchium campestre blue-eyed grass. A member of the iris family. Burn this or clean the center out yearly or it will die. (10 inches)

Stipa spartea needlegrass. An early June bloomer. (4 to 5 feet)

Xerophyllum tenax beargrass. Even more lovely than dropseed, but so difficult to establish. This needs regular watering. (4 feet)

All these grasses are perennial and need little maintenance. They're also durable, pest-free, and definitely underrated. You can easily become enamored of ornamental grasses by retraining your eyes and thoughts to see their beauty.

You can do a lot more with grasses than simply naturalizing with them. Place them in staggered sunken plantings around a swimming pool. Highlight them with outdoor lighting, so they'll cast dark, mysterious shadows. You can sink large clay pots around stepping stones, fill them with grasses, and weave a grassy path from home to pool.

At Wind 'n' View, grasses ease the transition from the formal new sanctuary to the informal, pastoral meadow.

Whether you decide on a prairie, on a meadow, or on a lawn replacement, remember you can't lose. They're all inexpensive to maintain, they add a luscious ambience, and they're unique.

Their uniqueness makes them admirable companions. They are truly diplomats, uniting easily with other botanicals. Try: *Miscanthus sinensis* 'Zebrinus' with *Coreopsis verticillata* and *Achillea tagetes* 'Moonshine'. Take the boredom out of rug junipers by mixing them with lavender, *Festuca caesia*, and *Stachys olympica*, and prepare to be astounded with *Macleaya cordata* and *Avena sempervirens* or *Elymus glaucus* and large pines.

5

The Perennial Flower Garden

THERE must be as many kinds of perennial gardens on earth as there are plants to put in them or gardeners to dream them up. Shady woodland gardens, desert gardens featuring cacti and succulents, formal arrangements of foliage and bloom versus the riot of color, blossom, and fragrance in an old-fashioned country garden; single-species gardens, as of hosta or roses; even gardens for winter and moonlight enjoyment are well within reach of the amateur gardener, and most of them can be found in one form or another at Wind 'n' View.

Perennials are easy. They make stunning borders and charming islands or beds. They propagate via roots, bulbs, stolons, rhizomes, cuttings, and seeds. They are easily divided and can be transplanted in early spring, after blooming, or in late summer and fall before the ground has frozen. If you transplant late in the season, water well but do not fertilize, and mulch with pine boughs if possible. If you see that your transplants are heaving out of the earth as the ground freezes and thaws, simply replant at once.

Perennials are all heavy feeders and need an early spring application of all-purpose timed-release granular fertilizer, plus a second application as they come into bloom. When wellfed and properly situated, they flourish so exuberantly that they need to be watched for overcrowding. Resist the temptation to pack them in too closely to start with, and always be ready to revamp an overgrown bed. Crowded situations quickly lose their magic as plants begin to bloom less profusely and to fall prey to disease.

Know Your Exposure

The best way to guarantee success with a perennial flower garden is to be sure that the plants you want are suited to the exposure you can provide. The eastern exposure is the favored one in most midwestern settings, mine included; on the east my gardens are protected from west winds that can be ferocious. Many gardeners have the notion that full sun means sunshine from dawn to dark—not true! The years have proved to me that many plants like some protection from the midwestern sun. I rarely see ill effects with shade from 1:30 P.M. on. So save that favored east side for delicates and tender-hardy species.

On the north there's room for shade appreciators, wildflowers and shrubs especially. These generally like moisture and therefore do not combine happily with bulbs. The shrubs I suggest all like roughly the same kind of soil and will have a lengthy bloom time. You'll notice I've not selected any lilacs. These give me great trouble because of their suckering habit and their susceptibility to mildew. All those sick-looking leaves during the summer are very unappealing. I prefer viburnum, but be sure you choose the varieties I suggest, as some viburnums sucker, too.

The southern and southwestern exposures, in virtually full sun, invite the traditional country garden bursting with bloom from April to October and featuring all our old favorites. My first garden at Wind 'n' View was of this kind. It's still here, too, on the crest of the hill leading to the native prairie, with a black walnut at one end and a black spruce at the other, and sporting old-time fragrant irises, oriental poppies, blue flax, coreopsis, tiger lilies, liatris, and much more. A beautiful sight in May and June, it quietens later in the season.

Small and with a relatively short period of bloom, it is a bed I have often considered abandoning. But I am sentimental about all the gardens. When it comes right down to the nitty-gritty, I just cannot do away with Number One. It's a miniature; a small picture inside a larger one.

My Country Garden

Of course, it didn't take me long to want to improve on my first effort. My husband and I used to take drives occasionally on Sunday afternoons, over on County Trunk S and then on to Highway 12, to look at two hillside gardens I was smitten with. It seemed so generous of those owners to put gardens along the road where we all could enjoy them; soon I was planning a roadside garden of my own.

In the beginning my Country Garden was 10 by 20 feet. It quickly became 20 by 80 feet and then 50 by 100 feet, running east to west on sloping land along River Road. I spend more time in this garden than in all the others put together, its beauty always minimizing the work and problems involved.

When I began it, I was still an amateur, but oh, how I was trying! Erosion was a crisis with each storm. My initial design included rambling brick paths, for which I paid dearly. The soil eroded over them and they were impossible to weed. Would you believe that after three years, we lifted them all? My next thought: estimates on railroad tie terraces. The cost was exorbitant. In fact, this proved to be a blessing in disguise. No matter how well constructed, raised tie beds heave, sag, and are pushed out of alignment by the roots of the plant material. So we went with grass terraces. A lot of regrading was done and then we laid sod, ending up with five terraces. The plants in the way had to be lifted, covered, and after the terraces were completed, replanted. These terraces controlled the erosion problem, only to create another; the grass spread into all the beds, and when Bill mowed, their seeds blew onto the soil, making maintenance perpetual. A few years ago, these grass terraces were removed and Iowa stone walls installed. They look grand as you come up the road and also tie in with the Wind 'n' View welcome sign. The cracks in the stones make great homes for sempervivums, dianthus, euphorbias, and herb robert; even the pasques are seeding in.

Favorites of mine in the country garden terraces are hemerocallis, *Phlox divaricata*, *Echinacea purpurea*, asclepias, echinops, gloriosas, and lupines (lupines can be short-lived if you don't keep the seed pods cut off). I also enjoy *Dictamnus albus*, so stiff and judgelike; achilleas, happy-go-lucky; flax, like a ballerina dancing; iris, a straitlaced spinster; dahlia, so pompous; and poppy, a porcelain doll.

This is a garden of bygone days and old-fashioned beauty that every passerby can enjoy. I have many regular visitors who tell me they drive miles out of their way to see it and how comforting a sight it is after a bad day. Some even leave me notes in the mailbox.

A traditional flower garden is not your only alternative if you have a good southern or southwestern exposure, however. You could also consider one of these three possibilities: a desert garden; perennial herb beds; or a biennial garden.

A Desert Garden

You will need special soil conditions for this. The basic mix: ⅓ gritty sand, ⅓ small gravel, ⅓ compost or peat moss combined. Put a 4-inch layer of mix in the bed, sprinkle 1 inch of Turface on it, mix up well with a three-pronged hoe. Repeat till bed is full.

My cacti and desert perennials live happily in exposed, Zone 3 conditions, surviving whatever the winter dishes out. Not only are they trusty survivors, but many have exquisite fragrances. I have noticed that plants from the desert tend to be intensely fragrant, no doubt to attract pollinators that might be scattered few and far between. Try *Opuntia compressa*, the native prickly pear cactus, *Opuntia* 'Desert Splendor', *Opuntia* 'Smithwick', *Opuntia* 'Carno', and *Callirhoe involucrata*. Two other possibilities are *Bouteloua gracilis* and *Imperata cylindrica rubra*.

There are cultivars of cacti and succulents that do not survive our severe winters. Potted varieties can be sunken for the hot season, then lifted in the fall. If the pot is a fancy one, make sure it doesn't get buried. Many connoisseurs deliberately grow shrubs, bonsai, dwarfs, bulbs, and rare plants in collectible containers. These add charm and intrigue if located properly in the garden's design.

Rosularias and sempervivums do well in a desert situation; so will any alpine that's listed for "scree gardens." Just remember, all the cacti are very prickly, so they will be hard to work around. Once established, though, this bed will need very little maintenance.

A Perennial Herb Garden

Perennial herb beds are ideal for a southern exposure. One of their most desirable features is how they attract birds. Pineapple sage with its electric red fall flowers is irresistible to hummingbirds, as are butterfly bush, columbines, *Nicotiana*, and even *Aesculus pavia*. Provide a birdbath for even more feathered visitors. Damask roses, dwarf fruit trees with sweet woodruff below, and all the southernwoods could be grouped in the fence corners. Plant the single june pinks, the most fragrant and compact of all the dianthus, and creeping thymes, Corsican mint, and chamomile near the paths. Then sit and inhale the fragrances!

To be sure your gardens will be fragrant, avoid hybrids. Dianthus, roses, and many flowering shrubs have lost their beloved perfumes due to hybridization for larger, showier blooms. Don't be misled by the tempting photos and descriptions of hybrids in gardening catalogs. Try to find out what local gardeners or botanical societies think of them before you invest. Very few hybrids will meet your expectations. In addition to lacking fragrance, many are more susceptible to disease than the original strain.

My Formal Herb Garden

I have always loved my country garden, but it is a real conglomeration: a kaleidoscope containing every color in the rainbow. I began to yearn for a quieter-toned garden that would have a more formal aspect. Oh, how I craved a level garden with a curving granite-chip path!

The opportunity arrived when we purchased another 600 by 100-foot strip to the west of our existing property, and regraded to accommodate new barns and a root cellar. On the west, against the cellar's back rock wall, I alternated delphiniums, queen of the prairie, and gas plant. These give way eastward to pink and white coneflowers, biennial larkspur, and ironweed, which in turn yield to bottle gentians and liatris nearer the path. The path is bordered with pink and white arabis, *Campanula*, and iberis. Scattered everyplace: baby's breath, flax, and pasques.

This garden forms a lovely background for eight rectangular raised herb beds planted with every variety of annual and perennial herb, among them chamomile, salad burnet, horseradish, prunella, rosemary, parsley, dill, sweet woodruff, oregano, sage, comfrey, tarragon, borage, and lavender. I have found several unexpected plants living over the winter in these beds. My germander, sweet marjoram, sweet woodruff, and santolina have survived ten years. In summer, the herbs often exceed their predicted height in my sunny garden. To prevent overwhelming surprises, remove all seed heads.

At the eastern edge of this formal herb garden is a unique shrub border; every shrub in it was raised from a seed or cutting. It is not allowed to overgrow, so it does not produce shade till late in the day. Among its plantings are *Rosa rubriflora*, *Dictamnus*, *Euonymus europaeus*, *Exochorda racemosa*, *Campanula callicarpa*, *Viburnum rhyliodophyllum*, *Calycanthus floridus*, *Rosa pomifera*, *Clethra alnifolia*, *Prunus triloba*, and *Ceanothus americanus*. Many of these are winter hardy only because they were grown from seed. This shrub border is underplanted with *Asperula odorata*.

Your garden design can help you maintain control of your plantings. My Iowa stone terraces contain root systems and prevent overgrowing. I have very few of the truly aggressive herbs, but if you want to grow them, their expansion can be curbed by sinking a big chimney flue into the ground, filling it with soil, and then planting within this barrier.

Originally I used untreated railroad ties to build the raised herb beds (treated ones can poison you). They were only eight years old when they rotted out and were replaced with Iowa stone. Iowa stone is 8 inches thick, rectangular, all different lengths. I can lift many pieces, so it is easy to fool with, but still substantial enough not to wobble when you walk or sit on it. And I do sit!

I save the herb gardens to work in till last. The fragrance invigorates me and I can recuperate. If I sit near the shrubs, I even have shade. These Iowa stone terraces are permanent, saving money and labor. They tie the country and formal gardens together. This is my continued long-range goal, beckoning ever on: to unite without a superimposed look, to create a look of belonging, yet to electrify with the unexpected at rounding the turn of a crooked path.

A Biennial Garden

A third alternative for a southern exposure: on stage with biennials! Bogged down or annoyed with annuals that have to be deheaded if you want them to keep producing a show? Biennials give top performances, yet guarantee the option of a facelift for your garden every two years.

Biennials have the unique distinction of only living two years (unless you refuse to let them bloom). They have a leafy mound shape the first year, throw up a bloom head or stalk the second year, then die. If biennials are left to go to seed, they will repeat this cycle. Don't let this happen; after two years, any biennial will have exhausted the soil where it's grown. Collect the seeds instead and start a bed in a new location. By constantly changing your site or your choice of plants, your garden will be refreshingly new every season and you will reap many fringe benefits as well.

The following biennials not only tease our senses in the garden but brighten our homes all year round in bouquets and wreaths, and some have medicinal qualities. Most are real survivors, tolerating poor conditions and thriving on the sun that a southern exposure provides. Many are tall, so I would suggest the side of a building or in front of evergreens. Try any of these:

Althaea rosea   hollyhock

Angelica archangelica   angelica

Artemisia spp.

Bellis perennis   english daisy

Campanula medium   canterbury bell

Coreopsis tinctoria   plains coreopsis

Delphinium ajacis   larkspur

Dianthus barbatus   pinks

Digitalis   foxglove

Erysimum cheiranthus 'Allionii'   siberian wallflower

Ipomopsis or *Gilia aggregata*

Lunaria annua   honesty or silver dollar

Myosotis sylvatica   forget-me-not

Papaver nudicaule   iceland poppy

Salvia sclarea   clary sage

Verbascum bombyceferum and *V. phoeniceum*

Violas   violets

These plants are easy to grow from seed. You can start patting your seeds around where you want them as early as July. Most will germinate by fall, live the winter, and get off to a blazing start in early spring, astounding you with their display of growth by summer.

A Sunken Island Garden

The Iowa stone walls in my country and formal gardens were so successful that I couldn't resist coming up with a new garden design (my favorite winter pastime). I created an oval

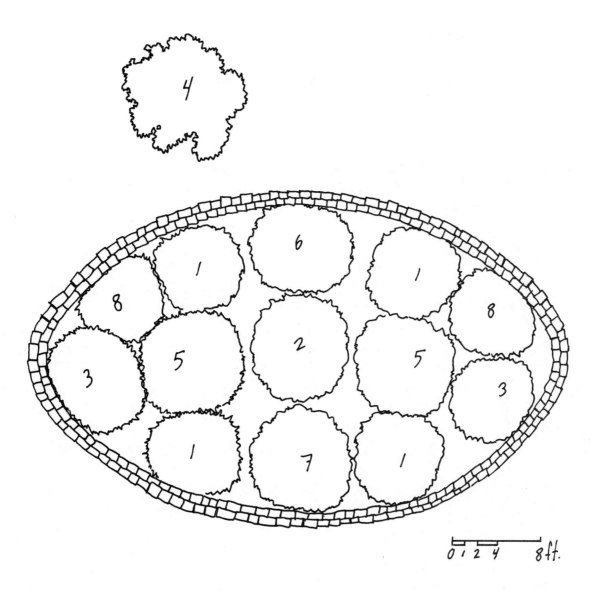

7. Plan for a Sunken Island Garden

Plants for a Sunken Island Garden

1. *Juniperus chinensis* 'Iowa'
2. *Picea omorika* serbian spruce
3. *Pyrus calleryana* 'Bradford' pear
4. *Salix* x *blanda* wisconsin weeping willow

5. bulbs
6. *Pinus mugo*
7. *Juniperus procumbens*
8. *Picea glauca* 'Albertiana Conica'

islandlike bed, 30 by 60 feet, raised about a foot above ground level inside an Iowa stone border west of the driveway, at my property's lowest point. The sheltering hillside rising to the east and the road embankment to the north give this bed the feel of a sunken garden. A columnar serbian spruce is the focal point, with bradford pears and iowa junipers at the corners. The whole area is packed with bulbs. Spring is now a glorious spectacle.

Your Outdoor Home

Each side of our home is landscaped in gardens, and each garden is unique, with a distinction of its own. Yet altogether our gardens share an appealing continuity—land and home united by careful planning and design.

I can't understand why we allow builders and nurseries today to determine what we plant around our houses. Most of us are mired in a pit of landscaping mediocrity: an arborvitae on the corners with yew or juniper by the front door and deciduous shrubs on the sides. Even worse, many of these deciduous shrubs are invasive foreigners. European honeysuckle (*Lonicera tatarica*) as well as japanese bittersweet (*Celastrus orbiculatus*) and *Lythrum salicaria*, or loosestrife, have greeted America with open arms. They are aggressive reseeders and have become naturalized in many parts of the country, forcing our native wildflowers to disappear. These invaders wake up early in the spring, shading the soil before our native treasures have a chance to get started. The birds carry their seeds everyplace; whole forests are filled with their progeny. *Lythrum* escapes to our watersheds and swamps, destroying wildfowl habitat. The National Federation of Garden Clubs is pleading with us not to buy these plants, and to get rid of them if we are growing them. Please cooperate. Even the ones sold as sterile will cross with the ones that aren't, making more and more.

If you are building a new home, don't let your builder backfill around the whole house with all the crud he dug out for the foundation. Your best soil mix should be allocated around the house. Then try to think of your home not as one, but two: an inner one for living, an outer one for growing. Give hedges careful attention and thought. They are your living outdoor walls, providing background, privacy, and accents, reducing noise, and creating snow- and windbreaks. Our desire for privacy makes these outdoor walls a necessity. The space they enclose thus becomes useful and comfortable.

Planning Your Outdoor Home

Your outdoor home can be as large as you like, up to the size of your entire lot or property. Its "walls" can be living plants, decorative fencing, railroad ties, or rocks. I like a combination of all four. Ideally your outer walls will lie at least 30 feet from your house on all sides, excluding the driveway. Whatever its size, map it on paper with great care. Once established, this outer wall will be permanent.

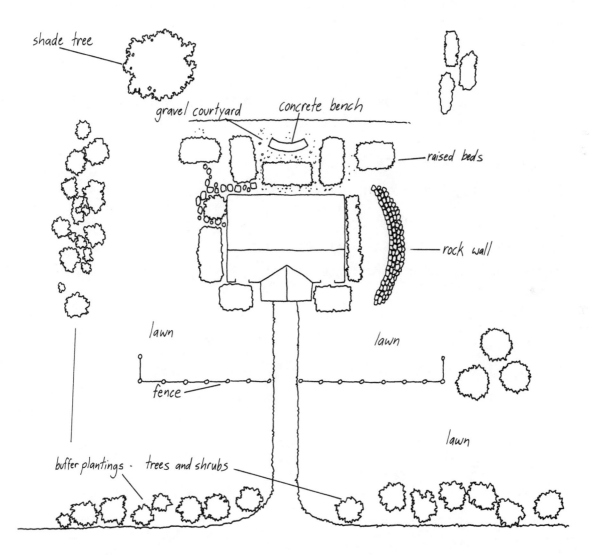

shade tree

gravel courtyard

concrete bench

raised beds

rock wall

lawn

lawn

fence

lawn

buffer plantings - trees and shrubs

8. Plan for Your Outdoor Home

Inside the outer wall place your lawn, and closer to the street plant your favorite trees, in small groves or drifts rather than in a row if you can. Statues, birdbaths, sundials, rock groupings, and sculptures can be charming, too. Think of them as accessories, as if they were paintings inside your home. A seat will add ornamental significance whether it is an odd-shaped stone, a metal or wooden bench, or an elaborate bench built around a tree. Be sure to have a dry medium underneath the seat; gravel, 3-inch-thick log circles, or concrete tiles are best. Let a winding path entice you there. Figures of birds, small animals, frogs, even shells, can create an accent tucked into a flowerbed.

At Wind 'n' View I planned fencing 30 feet from the house on each side of the driveway, leaving ample space between the fence and the small groves of trees near the walks. Because this area is in full sun, it is an ideal place to grow vines. *Apios tuberosa*, clematis, *Vitis* spp., *Hydrangea anomala* subsp. *petiolaris*, passiflora, and wisteria are all good possibilities.

Shrubs for Your Living Walls

The following shrubs will do beautifully as your living walls.

Acer palmatum   japanese maple. More fall color. (Gurney)

Aesculus parviflora   bottlebrush buckeye. Chosen for its July blooming. (Wayside)

Amelanchier laevis   juneberry, serviceberry. Very early spring bloomer. Mine were grown from seed. (Wayside)

Cercis canadensis   redbud. Be sure to get the Columbus strain. Mine were grown from seed.

Deutzia gracilis   May blooming with aristocratic foliage. (Wayside)

Euonymus alatus   burning bush. Can't be beat for fall color.

Forsythia   Make sure you buy the variety 'Northern'—it still blooms with minus 30F temperatures.

Hydrangea   For fall bouquets and wreaths, it's a treat. I put it with evergreen boughs.

Juniperus chinesis 'Mountbatten'   Very hardy.

Myrica pensylvanica   northern bayberry. Has bluish waxy fall berries. (Wayside)

Philadelphus x *virginalis* 'Minnesota snowflake'   mock orange. Very hardy—heavy bloom and scented, too. (Wayside)

Sorbus alnifolia   korean mountain ash. Striking fall color and berries. (Wayside)

Thuja occidentalis   pyramidal arborvitae. Doesn't winter-burn. (Local nursery)

Viburnum carlesii   korean spice. Sweet, sweet fragrance and fall black berries. Mine were grown from seed. (Wayside)

At Wind 'n' View I always leave room for bulbs everyplace. Have you ever wondered why tulips, daffodils, and other bulbs do so well on the south side next to the house? It's because the house overhang doesn't allow moisture to reach there. Most bulbs like it dry and well drained.

In all your planning, remember to highlight pleasing house features, and think about how the color combinations in your garden will go with the paint color of the house.

Maintenance and care include fertilizing each year, and for low maintenance practice, I encourage you to cover the soil in the outdoor living room under the trees, shrubs, and vines with fibercloth, then mulch with 1½ inches of gravel (½ inch in diameter) or medium-aged chunk bark.

Perennials to Avoid

Almost every plant has a place somewhere—but not necessarily in your garden! Certain perennials have aggressive, suckering root systems that allow them to spread like wildfire. All the mint family is invasive. *Physostegia*, goldenacre sedum, *Thymus serpyllum* (thyme), *Yucca*, *Campanula glomerata*, *Ajuga genevensis*, *Matteuccia pensylvanica*, and *Lysimachia* will not let go once they get started. You will quickly become disenchanted with all of them. *Yucca*, *Euphorbia myrsinites*, *Euphorbia epithymoides*, and *Campanula glomerata* have another disadvantage; their foliage causes rashes. *Ruta graveolens* produces a rash that leaves scars. Heed this warning and go without them.

Ah, yes, *Yucca*. I've tried everything to get rid of it. I've dug practically to China to remove its tubers, then covered what remained with black plastic and 6 inches of gravel. Three years later I removed the plastic and gravel—there were still *very* healthy tubers as big around as my legs. Now what do I try?

The following are aggressive reseeders, even though they are desirable when they can be controlled: *Platycodon* (balloon flower), *Aquilegia* (columbine), the *Lychnis* genus, *Muscari* (grape hyacinth), most of the sage family, especially clary sage, *Tanacetum vulgare* (tansy), prairie thalictrum, mother of thyme, johnny-jump-ups, *Campanula* 'Joan Elliott', *Saponaria*. All these must be watched and carefully deadheaded if they begin to spread out of bounds.

A Perennial Garden

The English think nothing of taking fifty years to create a perennial garden. This seems a bit unrealistic, given today's fast-paced style of living. The garden described below will be enjoyable in one year, sublime in three to five. Plant any of these perennials in well-drained soil with full sun. Once established, they will be breathtaking for many years. The size of your garden depends upon how many individuals of each species you plant. I like at least three of each specimen. They can be planted in a border or an island. Put the tall plants in the back of a border or in the middle of the island and graduate the remaining plants down to the edge. Don't forget an edging of some kind. This will keep your bed and your lawn contained, and it is attractive, too.

To give your plants the best possible start, dig your holes twice as big as the plant ball or pot. Put a basic mixture of wet peat and timed-release granules in the bottom of each hole. The following "recipe" will give your plants the optimum beginning and is a very long-lasting care package!

Basic Planting Mix for Perennials

Buy a small bale of peat that will fit in a large waterproof container, like a plastic garbage can. Puncture the bale of peat in many places with an icepick. Put the bale in the container that's been filled with water, leaving it there until it sinks and is thoroughly wet. Remove the bale. Empty the water. Put 4 inches of wet peat from the bale in the bottom of the container and sprinkle with 1 cup of all-around garden fertilizer. Then put in 2 inches of Turface. If you can't get Turface, use pea gravel. This is for drainage and to keep the soil from compacting. Stir, stir, stir. Repeat these layers until the container is two-thirds full. I put this in the bottom of every hole I dig.

A Moonlight Garden

A tremendous benefit of having acres of land is that something is always blooming somewhere. There's no worry about producing a continuous succession of show in just one bed. If your lot is small and you can't afford the luxury of quiet beds, please consider the feasibility of combining naturalized bulb beds with a moonlight garden. A moonlight garden should always be designed so you can see it easily from the house, preferably from an upstairs window. Mine faces east and is in full sun till early afternoon. It is a large, curved bed 12 by 40 feet in size, planted with purple heuchera, mock orange, and geraniums, among others, against a background of white spruce. Moonlight gardens are always planted with silver- or grey-leaved plants. The ones I recommend can withstand dry spells, even droughts, and will not need to be watered, making them ideal mates for the species bulbs. White-blooming plants are also used in moonlight gardens. Here in the Midwest, make sure you choose those that can stand being dry.

Each of the following has distinctive attributes. All are perennial, unless noted. Some are fragrant and can be used in potpourri; others make stunning arrangements, fresh or dried; most are striking in the moonlight set off by black shadows. Check the moon rises and sets in your area to take advantage of your garden. My exposure gives me a scenic moon for hours, so I can enjoy it at almost any time of night.

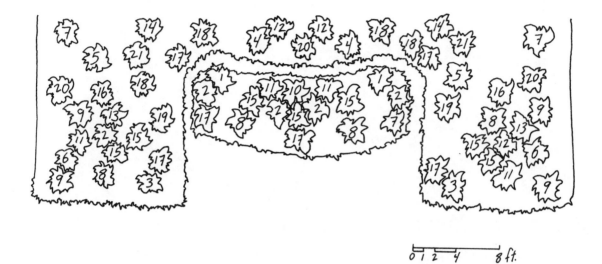

9. Plan for a Perennial Garden

Plants for a Perennial Garden

1. *Achillea filipendulina* golden yarrow
2. *Aquilegia flabellata alba* columbine or native honeysuckle
3. *Asclepias tuberosa* butterfly weed
4. *Boltonia asteroides*
5. *Callicarpa japonica* beautyberry
6. *Ceanothus americanus* new jersey tea
7. *Cercis canadensis* redbud
8. *Coreopsis verticillata* threadleaf tickseed
9. *Dictamnus albus* gas plant
10. *Echinacea purpurea* purple coneflower
11. *Eupatorium coelestinum* mistflower
12. *Exochorda gerardii* 'Wilsonii' pearlbush
13. *Gypsophila paniculata* baby's breath
14. *Iris sibirica*
15. *Liatris 'Elegance'* gayfeather
16. *Linum narbonense* flax
17. *Myosotis alpestris* forget-me-not
18. *Myrica pensylvanica* northern bayberry
19. *Papaver orientale* oriental poppy
20. *Perovskia atriplicifolia* russian sage
21. *Phlox caroliniana*

Plants for a Moonlight Garden

1. *Achillea clavennae* silver yarrow
2. *Anaphalus triplinervis*
   himalayan pearly everlasting
3. *Artemisia absinthium* 'Powis Castle'
4. *Artemisia versicolor*
5. *Buddleia alternifolia* 'Argentea'
   butterfly bush
6. *Chrysanthemum haradjanii*
7. *Euryops evansii*
8. *Lavandula angustifolia* 'Munstead'
9. *Origanum pulchellum* oregano
10. *Pinus strobus* 'Pendula' pine
11. *Salvia argentea* silver sage
12. *Magnolia stellata* star magnolia
13. Moon rocks (this is what our stone
    company calls them): rough textured,
    with many dark crevices and holes.
    Truly moonlike.
14. Ornamental statues. Doves, animals, and
    people are represented in my garden.
    Each adds a touch of buoyancy.
15. **Species bulbs** Eleven drifts (20 bulbs per
    drift) of each of these small bulbs include:
    Crocus ancyrensis; dwarf daffodils ('Tête à
    Tête' and 'Hoop Petticoat'); *Tulipa
    kaufmanniana, T. batalinii, T. linifolia,
    T. urumiensis*; *Iris reticulata, Puschkinia,*
    and *Hyacinthus amethystinus* (an alpine
    dwarf hyacinth). My collection is not typical
    because it contains no white-blooming bulbs.
    After months of winter snow, early
    white-flowering bulbs are at the bottom of
    my totem pole. (These bulbs will all
    naturalize.)

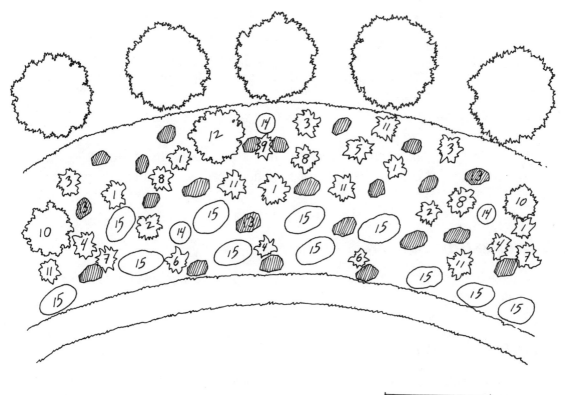

10.   Plan for a Moonlight Garden

Growing for Drought

With meteorologists predicting that dry spells, drought, and wind will persist, even worsen, as the greenhouse effect becomes a part of our future, shouldn't we consider planting for these conditions? Each of the plants listed in the Drought Garden Design will perform well despite the vagaries of the climate. Each will tolerate very dry spells and most types of soil, even poor soil, as long as it is well drained.

Just as each gardener admits to occasionally breaking every rule while seeking to grow more and more varieties, drought gardens should be as diversified as each locale will permit. In my area natives outperform exotics—this may not be true in your area. By all means bend or break the rules. Experiment, and include your favorites or plants that you hunger for. Many of these will surprise you with their adaptability.

This garden has other purposes than basic survival. Many of these plants can be dried for craft creations; others have fragrance; others are native and can be used to create a prairie garden (see chapter 4).

Drought means heartache and hard times for gardeners. Still, you can prevail if you grow any of these that are suggested.

As for trees, shrubs, and ground covers, *Gymnocladus dioicus, Cornus alternifolia, Fraxinus, Celtis, Larix, Prunus maackii,*

Berberis thunbergii, *Euonymus fortunei* varieties, and *Nepeta* are all drought-resistant at Wind 'n' View. And, of course, the desert garden described earlier in this chapter is a sure winner.

An Everlasting Garden

This garden will satisfy arrangers of both fresh and dried flowers, providing them with ample material for their skills.

A Winter Garden

Gardening is a year-round love affair for committed gardeners. Students look at me askance when I tell them, "Yes, we can enjoy our gardens even in the winter." During the winter months, we are not diverted by flowering plants. The land is in repose, awaiting the metamorphosis of spring. We are able to get an overall view of our framework: the interrelation of conifers, structures, statues, rock walls, deciduous trees, and fences. We are able to survey our holdings critically and with a fresh perspective.

Naturally we prefer a blanket of snow. This comes and goes, though, and during its absence the land is barren. If we have planted with care, the winter scene can have its own charm.

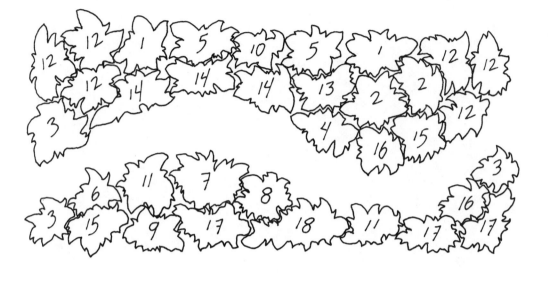

11. Plan for a Drought-Hardy Garden

Plants for a Drought-Hardy Garden

1. *Anemone cylindrica* longheaded thimbleweed
2. *Anthemis tinctoria* marguerite
3. *Artemisia schmidtiana* 'Silver Mound'
4. *Aurinia saxatilis* basket of gold
5. *Coreopsis verticillata* threadleaf coreopsis
6. *Dodecatheon meadia* shooting star
7. *Echium vulgare* viper's bugloss
8. *Euphorbia myrsinites* donkey tail
9. *Hyssopus officinalis* anise hyssop
10. *Imperata cylindrica rubra* japanese bloodgrass
11. *Juniperus* spp.
12. *Lavandula angustifolia* 'Munstead' lavender
13. *Leucanthemum balsamita* costmary
14. *Pelargonium* scented geranium
15. *Rudbeckia hirta* black-eyed susan
16. *Salvia versicolor*
17. sedums, sempervivums, and opuntias
18. *Stachys olympica* lamb's ears

Plants for an Everlasting Garden

1. *Achillea filipendulina* golden yarrow
2. *Allium caeruleum* blue globe onion
3. *Artemisia versicolor* 'Spanish Moss'
4. *Baptisia australis* or *B. tinctoria* wild indigo
5. *Belamcanda chinensis* blackberry lily
6. *Echinops exaltatus* globe thistle
7. *Elymus canadensis* wild canadian rye
8. *Eupatorium coelestinum*
9. *Fibigia clypeata* alpine grey-leaved money plant
10. *Gaillardia aristata* blanket flower
11. *Gypsophila paniculata* baby's breath
12. *Limonium* spp. statice
13. *Ratibida pinnata* prairie coneflower
14. *Sedum spectabile* 'Autumn Joy'

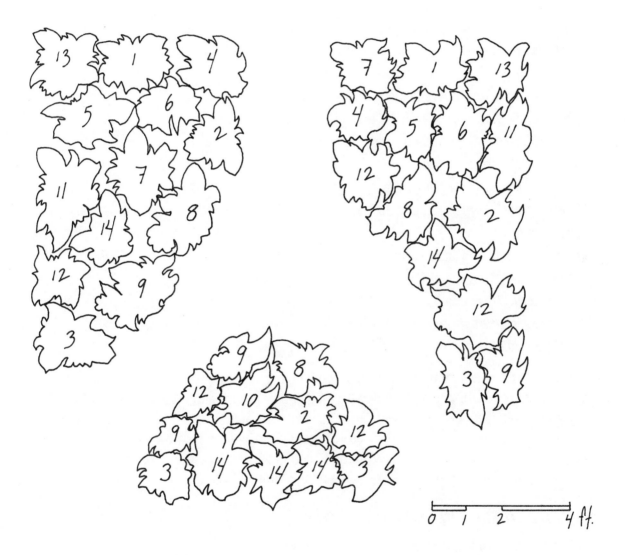

12. Plan for an Everlasting Garden

Each of the following has a distinctive winter form. Some are skeletal; others are foliated in bronze, gold, burgundies, silver, and greens. They jump out and let us know of their presence.

Allium thunbergii

Andropogon scoparius

Artemisia viridis

Berberis thunbergii var. *atropurpurea* 'Rose Glow'   barberry

Bergenia cordifolia

Delosperma nubigena   ice plant

Dianthus   pinks

Erigeron umbellatus 'Red Leaved'

Euonymus fortunei 'Kewensis'   winter creeper

Geranium dalmaticum   perennial geranium

Herniaria glabra   common rapturewort

Imperata cylindrica   bloodgrass

Lavandula angustifolia 'Munstead'

Mahonia aquifolium   oregon grape

Penstemon

Satureja montana   winter savory

Sempervivum   hen and chicks

Thuja orientalis 'Aurea Nana'   Berckman's golden arborvitae

Thymus serpyllum aureus   golden thyme

Vaccinium macrocarpon var. *Langloise form*   blueberry

There are other advantages of winter as well: no bugs to contend with; our cold kills them, whereas in the South, whitefly along with many other insects and diseases live year-round.

We can even plant perennial seeds if we have an open season—that is, no snow. Seeds can be planted outside right where they are to grow. And winter provides the opportunity of planning and organizing for the busy spring to come. What a pleasure to sit creating a garden design before a window that looks out on a gentle winter garden!

A Garden for Our Golden Years

I am gleaning from my classes, workshops, lectures, symposia, and slide programs that many people share my concern: How do we take care of our gardens as we age? Old people miss the pure enjoyment of doing, yet they cannot cope physically with the doing. I've been turning

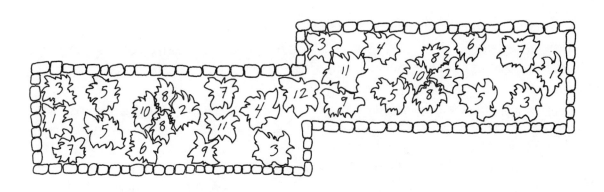

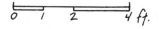

13. Plan for a Garden for Our Golden Years

Plants for a Garden for Our Golden Years

1. *Anemone sylvestris*
   (the only one that must be deheaded)
2. *Astilbe*
3. *Bergenia cordifolia*
4. *Dodecatheon meadia*
5. *Epimedium*
6. *Geum triflorum*
7. *Hosta* 'Piedmont Gold'
8. *Houstonia caerulea*
9. *Iris cristata*
10. *Paeonia suffruticosa*
11. *Spirea alba*
12. *Picea pungens* 'Glauca Globosa'

my thoughts to this problem and feel one of the solutions might be an early awareness of our coming infirmities. Start thinking ahead while you are still able to plan, cope, and instigate. Why not plan a garden now that you will be able to care for in those golden years?

Excessive deheading, pruning, and repeated planting will be targeted as no-no's in this garden. Its plants will of necessity be longer lived, less aggressive, but still rewarding. The site itself will be critical, with morning sun a requisite and shade in the afternoon. This will make work in the garden less stressful and will cut down on watering. There will have to be some kind of easy-to-install irrigation. A system or a timer-regulated switch would be ideal. If this is out of the question, at least trench plastic piping to this garden so you don't have to haul hoses around. Keep the bed narrow and freestanding so you can reach it from all sides.

Easy access and visibility are other prime requisites. My design permits even wheelchair accessibility. A working path surrounds the raised bed, and the stone wall provides sitting room, so you can sit to maintain it.

The walls should be straight, not curved, for easier maintenance. I suggest a smooth rectangular stone. Build this wall 1½ feet high and fill with a mix of Turface, sand, peat, pea gravel, and compost. The following plants are excellent choices. All need or like afternoon shade.

The *Astilbe*, *Berginia*, *Epimedium*, and *Iris cristata* should be planted to the east of the *Paeonia*, *Spirea*, and *Picea* so that they get morning sun and are not shaded too much by the larger plants.

If you can't devise this garden for afternoon shade, you could plant the following in full sun: *Achillea clavennae*, *Baptisia leucophaea*, *Coreopsis verticillata* 'Moonbeam', *Geranium dalmaticum*, *Geum triflorum*, *Helenium autumnale* 'Brilliant', *Hemerocallis* 'Stella d'Oro', *Lavandula* 'Munstead', *Philadelphus microphyllus*, *Sedum spectabile* 'Autumn Joy', and *Alchemilla mollis*, one of the few plants that will grow virtually anyplace. It, along with the lavender, should be deheaded.

A Garden for Continuous Show

Specialists and connoisseurs often tempt us into becoming biased. We are constantly being bombarded about "show." Show generally means double or many-petaled flowers, often produced by hybridization. Don't be misled. Doubles have difficulties unknown to single-petaled bloomers. Stems are often too weak to support the flowers; they are not prolific; they need extra care like pinching and frequent deheading; wind and rain cause more damage, and once fully opened, the bloom may not be distinctive.

Singles integrate more readily into an overall scheme, are easier to maintain, and will make allowances for our neglect. They are generally more appropriate for this garden of continuous show than those fancy botanicals.

What kind of plants can I grow for a progressive show in my garden? This is the question my students most frequently ask. They hasten to add: "I only have time for one garden and I want it to be lovely all season." Their idea of season is from May to September—mine, of course, is from the time the ground thaws till it refreezes.

The plants suggested here will please any audience. They are distinguished performers with aggressive tendencies. Each will help to control the others.

Plants for a Garden of Continuous Show

Chrysanthemum parthenium   feverfew. (I like my name of *summerfever* better.) If you keep deheading this, it will flesh out your bed all season. And even nicer if you can find the golden-leaved variety. These subjects and their siblings will quickly blanket your bed, transforming it into a naturalized area.

Coreopsis lanceolata and *C. verticillata*. Cut this back after the first heavy bloom and you'll get a later flush of color.

Eupatorium coelestinum   mistflower. Such a lovely fall plant, and it dries beautifully for bouquets.

Helenium autumnale   Use a hybridized form for longer bloom.

Iris   Try to find an old-timer, as they are less susceptible to the borer, and they have fragrance. Old Jake is a special one, with white flowers and a tough rhizome. With any iris, the minute I see those brown spots on the leaves that signify borer, I strip the plants to the rhizome and burn them.

Lilium tigrinum   tiger lily. This has now naturalized in the United States. It has never had a virus for me.

Papaver orientale   oriental poppy. Again, try to locate an old-timer.

Saponaria officinalis   bouncing bet. Be sure to keep her deheaded!

This plan is set up for blooming times beginning in May–June and ending in September. For a 15 by 25-foot semiborder plot, try four of each plant.

A "Renovation" Garden of Conifers and Perennials

All too often the familiar becomes invisible. This is especially true with evergreens. Did you inherit large evergreens when you purchased a home? Or perhaps those "babies" you planted years ago have grown into giants. If they are in good condition, well shaped, and you consider them an asset, they may have possibilities even though they are enormous. If they are solitary, let the spread of their branches define a large, separate island within your lawn or garden. If they establish boundaries or windbreaks, give them dramatic borders by incorporating large herbs and perennials. These often have substantial structure and will stand proud with conifers.

If you are lucky enough to have *Pinus strobus* or one of the other long-needled pines, or one of the *Picea* varieties, look at them again and start designing a new look for an old spot.

Picea (the spruces) are not as apt to die off at the bottom as pines are. Their bottom branches should not be pruned. They keep the soil underneath them cool and help retain moisture. *Perovskia atriplicifolia* is wonderfully compatible with *Picea pungens* 'Fat Albert', a very desirable slow-growing blue spruce, and planted in masses turns into a splendid fall display.

Macleaya cordata, the gorgeous plume poppy that grows 10 feet tall, is an ideal binding perennial grown beneath norway pines. Since this pine tends to lose its lower branches at an early age, the poppy, with its mauve top leaves, silvery undersides, and plumed, creamy, panicled blooms, is a great companion. Its root can be used for dyeing yarns, eggs (do not eat these eggs), and fabrics.

The annual fennel could also be included in this grouping. Its 4- to 5-foot height, early yellow seed umbels, and ferny foliage is a perfect complement to the norway pines. Both the poppy and fennel should be deheaded; do not let them go to seed. Check your exposure, as all the plants suggested here will need sun unless otherwise noted.

The Salix genus, especially *S. matsudana* 'Tortuosa' and *S. sachalinensis* 'Sekka', are too often neglected in herb gardens. These corkscrew and japanese fantail willows are highly ornamental, easily pruned so their size can be kept in context with the garden, and, of course, we know their medicinal use as the forerunner of aspirin. Flower arrangers adore their branches, and they tolerate being underplanted with *Alchemilla mollis, Chrysanthemum parthenium* 'Aureum,' and sempervivums. *Alchemilla mollis* is lady's mantle, that wonder plant that grows anywhere—in shade, sun, wet, or dry and whose blossoms dry so beautifully. The chrysanthemum is golden-leaved feverfew—grow it here, grow it there, so you always have a leaf handy to rub on bites and stings. (This must be deheaded or it will carpet the garden wall to wall.) Sempervivums are hen and chicks, charming and nearly indestructible.

Rosa rubrifolia is another excellent choice as a backdrop for an herb garden or as a transitional shrub in front of conifers. This is an umbrellalike shrub with wedgewood pink foliage, single-petaled pink flowers, and huge clusters of hips that cling all winter. This rose has no disease or insect problems, is adaptable to most situations, and reseeds nicely. It, too, can be underplanted; alliums are suggested. Another plant that is too often ignored, belonging to a large family with many uses in the world of herbs, *Allium* will keep your roses healthy. Of course, their culinary uses are legendary and even the seed pods are nice in bouquets or as accents on wreaths. (Pick them while they are still green and hang upside down to dry.)

Planting perennials with shrubs, subtrees, and conifers can transform established gardens. Herbs and grasses seem particularly adaptable to large bedfellows: the aggressive artemisias, daturas, violas, even grasses—equisetums, sedges, and others. There is a place for each of these and more.

And don't forget the fun you can have with evergreens inside your home. Evergreen needles make a great addition to potpourri blends. Cut long-needled clusters into small pieces. Place 1 cup of pieces in a plastic bag, pound with a hammer to release the fragrant essence, then add them to 2 inches of melted paraffin. (Empty coffee cans should be used.) Pour the mixture into small m.Çffin tin liners. Cool. When hardened, these little "muffins" can be added to potpourri to give a fresh scent. They will even perk up old mixtures.

Over the years, evergreens have supplied herbalists with teas and nuts. Today these trees provide holiday decorations, and the cones are used for kindling. Cones can be sliced and added to potpourri, or made into rosettes to be wired into wreaths or miniature trees. The pungent foliage of russian sage can be mixed with *Artemisia abrotanum* (southernwood) and *A.* 'Sweet Annie' and made into sachets that repel insects.

Planning a Small Garden

Gardens do not have to be large to be effective, but small gardens require very diligent planning and thought. At their best, they act as a magnetic lure; the gardener has turned every nook and cranny into an eye-captivating vignette and has found the right place for every plant, showing it off to perfection. Examine your garden if it is small, also your patio, steps, birdbath, statues, even benches and walks. Each will present a possibility. Cascading plants help to soften harsh lines and corners, disguising the spaces between buildings. There are vines that could play an important role even in a tiny space:

Apios tuberosa or *A. americana*   indian potato. A native with edible potatolike tubers.

Clematis crispa, *C. tangutica*, and *C. texensis*   clematis. All are sun-worshippers. Mine are grown from seed; purple, yellow, and deep pink. With the hybrids, you have many varieties. Clematis like cool feet. Keep the soil cool for them by placing a mound of fist-sized stones about their roots.

Hydrangea anomala subsp. *petiolaris*   Climbing hydrangea is gorgeous; you may have to tie it to the fence or trellis when it is young. It won't bloom till it starts to climb.

Passiflora spp.   passionflower vine.

Vitis spp.   grapevine. Fruit to pick right at hand. (Be prepared to do extensive pruning.)

Wisteria spp.   So fragrant. Such a nice way of greeting. (There are hardy ones: *W. floribunda*, a Japanese species.) The *W. frutescens* also grows here.

A Few Words about Annuals

Today everything I plant has low maintenance and easy methods of control as its objective, so there are very few annuals growing at Wind 'n' View. Some are a bother and do not give us much return. Their short growing season, the deheading if you want even that short season of bloom, mildew and wilt problems, the work of transplanting, and their heavy feeding schedule make them poor choices. Yet many gardeners cannot resist their beauty and their familiar appeal, so I will include a few words about growing them successfully.

Most printed instructions on seed packets tell us to put the seeds down for indoor germination in March—this is too early in the Midwest. The first week in April allows plenty of time for us.

Many annuals can be patted down where they are to grow: poppies, bells of ireland, euphorbias, and larkspur are just a few. Be sure to thin them after germination. These just listed can also be patted around after a hard frost in the fall. They are smarter than we are and will choose their own germination time. You can also pat them around after a late spring snowfall.

If you do plant annuals, be sure to clean them up after blooming. Otherwise, many of them will reseed, and if they reseed in the same place, they will be sorry-looking things the next season, having already used up the food value in their patch of soil the first year.

An effective spot for annuals that does please me: in large pots on patios, decks, porches, in the naturalized lawn grown in pots, and in hanging baskets. Remember, they will need heavy supplemental feeding and lots of watering.

Several annuals have been abused by overuse. Year after year, beds are so boring with the same old marigolds, petunias, zinnias, alyssum, ageratum, coleus, impatiens, and begonias. If you plant them, please at least make new variety selections.

And please consider the following annuals for container cultivation instead of all those ordinary choices:

Coleus amboinicus (spanish thyme), *Coleus amboinicus* 'Variegated', and *Tagetes lucida* (mexican tarragon). These three can be brought into the house for wintering over.

These are all foliage plants. Some herbs also take to pots. Chives, garlic, lavender, and parsley are perennial, but do well in pots. Annual fuchsias and verbenas would provide lots of color along with dusty miller.

The following do grow in my gardens and may make a refreshing change for you:

Clarkia. Plant where they are to grow after danger of frost has past. This plant has many color shades of rose to purple. Likes cool nights.

Coleus amboinicus   spanish thyme. So fragrant. It is light green. A good basket plant or in rocks. Slip cuttings in the fall before frost. Roots easily in wet sand. Unusual. People always ask, "What's that?" (Logee's)

Coleus amboinicus 'Variegated'   A relative of the above with white edging on a darker green leaf.

Dyssodia tenuiloba   dahlberg daisy. A little darling, only 6 inches high. Useful as a border. Has ferny leaves and deep gold tiny blossoms. Seeds live in the soil over winter and self-propagate. (Burpee's)

Echium vulgare   viper's bugloss. Could be aggressive. Pull it out when it starts to straggle.

Emilia sagittata   Red flowers are hard to come by and these are really red.

Eucalyptus cinerea   Yes, you can grow this from seed. Treat it like an annual. This looks great in rock walls. Harvest after a frost; then hang to dry. It will keep its icy blue color. The fragrance is long lasting. (Park's)

Eustoma grandiflorum   A member of the gentian family, in some catalogs called *Lisianthus russellilanus*. Starts blooming in late summer till hard frost when there is little show. I like it! About 20 inches tall with tulip or poppylike deep blue, pink, or white flowers. The leathery, icy blue foliage alone makes *Eustoma* desirable.

Gypsophila elegans   The whitest of white flowers. Great in fresh bouquets. Doesn't dry.

Iberis   candytuft. Planted once, you will have it always. Reseeds on its own.

Kochia scoparia   A shrubby foliage bush with fiery red fall color. Don't let it go to seed.

Larkspur   Such a beauty and so rewarding. Doesn't get mildew like delphiniums do. Pick and keep the seed. Resow in the fall after a hard frost. It wears the soil out if grown in the same place.

Layia elegans   tidytips. Sown where it is to grow in late spring. (Thin this.)

Papaver nudicaule   iceland poppy. A riot of blossoms even after a hard frost. All parts of this poppy are poisonous. Just remember that all poppies reseed like crazy, so all will need to be deheaded.

Pelargonium   scented geranium. Nothing bothers this large genus. Its plants provide perfect foliage accents and are fragrant to boot. (2–3 feet)

Pennisetum alopecuroides   fountain grass. Perennial in southern states, but we can grow it as an annual in our zone. Our garden centers have been selling this lately. One drawback: it has to be dug out the next spring, leaving a hole about 3 feet around that will have to be filled.

Perilla frutescens var. *nankinensis*   Such handsome foliage, use in fresh bouquets. This reseeds like crazy, so yank it out after a frost. You will still have some reseeding, which is nice. The juncos (birds) love the seeds in the winter.

Phacelia minor california bluebell. The rich blue color of this annnual certainly competes with the gentians; its leaves are similar to the herb *Chenopodium ambrosioides*. *Phacelia* reseeds the same season; the seedlings live the winter and bloom early. It is a marvelous annual for growing with bulbs, covering up their dying leaves. (Thompson & Morgan)

Salpiglossis sinuata velvet flower. Prettier than any petunia. When it starts to get leggy, cut it down to about 6 inches and it will come back again.

Salvia indigo Deep, deep blue. Strong. An outstanding background plant.

Tagetes lucida sweet-scented marigold. At frost time, slip it, root in water. (Logee's)

Tagetes signata 'Pumila', 'Ursula', or 'Lemon Yellow' A marigold with a heavenly lemon scent. Only 10 inches tall; keeps a mound shape. Very special with a long blooming time.

Complete Plant Listings

These perennials grow in the beds at Wind 'n' View.

Achillea clavennae silver yarrow. A mounded cluster of silver, ferny, leaves with lemon yellow flower heads. This keeps its shape well and dries nicely for bouquets. (2 feet)

Achillea filipendulina golden yarrow. Plant this around other herbs to increase their oils and fragrances. An early harvest will bring on a second show in the fall. (3 feet)

Acorus gramineus japanese sweet flag. This plant has a creeping root system and is a good ground cover for moist and soggy places. Grown from seed, this is another one of those plants that is not supposed to live in our zone. (8 inches)

Agastache cana mosquito plant. These leaves can be rubbed on you to dispel mosquitos. It reseeds aggressively, so be sure to dehead it. (16 inches)

Allium caeruleum blue globe onion. Easily propagated from seed. This allium dies back after blooming. The lush blue heads can be harvested for dried bouquets. (16 inches)

Allium moly lily leek or golden garlic. A perennial bulb, blooming in early June, a native of southern Europe. The umbels can be preserved for dried bouquets if hung in a dry, warm, dark place until completely dry. Unlike most of the alliums, the moly has a large starlike cluster head and a long blooming period. Don't be alarmed if this does not bloom every year. *A. pulchellum* explodes like reddish fireworks. All the alliums grow easily from seed. (12 inches)

Althaea rosea hollyhock. An old-fashioned jewel, long blooming, having many colors. Be sure to pinch the stalk when it is two feet high. This forces it to branch, making it sturdier. (3–6 feet)

Amsonia tabernaemontana willow amsonia. Most often grown in the shady garden, amsonia is just as happy in sun, in fact, requiring sun for its venerated yellow fall color to develop. (30 inches)

Anaphalis triplinervis himalayan pearly everlasting. More desirable than our native, this one does not travel all over. It, too, dries well. This plant, along with all the antennarias, is susceptible to a webbed worm, so keep checking for these and destroy them. (16 inches)

Anemone cylindrica long-headed thimbleweed. This native survives competition and still thrives. The seedpod puffs up into a ball of curly cotton, truly a curiosity. (2 feet)

Anemone x hybrida 'September charm' A friend shared three large clumps of this with me. Until then, I had no success with it. (3 feet)

Anemone pulsatilla It wakes the garden up in March. This European pasque (recently renamed *Pulsatilla vulgaris*) has adapted to the Midwest as thoroughly as dandelions. (1 foot)

Anemone sylvestris snowdrop anemone. So hardy, and it reseeds nicely; plant it with frittilarias. (18 inches)

Anthemis tinctoria marguerite. The clean-smelling foliage grown in a clump throws up 2-foot stems with many yellow daisylike flowers that last for ages despite drought. (2–3 feet)

Aquilegia flabellata 'Alba' columbine. Pure white blossoms and icy blue foliage make this a knockout. Many aquilegias do not reseed true, but this one does. (18 inches)

Arabis albida rock cress. A reliable early bloomer. Surprisingly it tolerates very dry situations, even pine forests. (8 inches)

Angelica archangelica angelica. Intersperse it with the hollyhocks; very effective with lush, almost tropical leaves. It's fragrant and used culinarywise. (Seeds must be fresh for germination, so try to buy plants.) A biennial, but if you do not let it go to seed, it will live several years. (5–7 feet)

Artemisia abrotanum southernwood. A perennial growing to heights of 6 feet. Another native of southern Europe with soft, lovely grey-green foliage that dries beautifully if wired onto wreath shapes while fresh. It is generally found in our herb gardens. Despite the general belief that most herbs have no beauty, I disagree. The lacy, fragrant southernwoods provide a perfect foil, either surrounded or as a background, and is now planted between the serbian fir and the pears. When the trees are big enough, this will be removed. (Root propagation only.) (5 feet)

Artemisia campestris, sometimes *A. caudata.* A native prairie plant. An asset if you can find the seed, holding its color whatever stage it is picked. Use it ornamentally. Another biennial, it is worth trying to locate. (3–4 feet)

Artemisia lactifolia   A creamy late-flowering plant and not intruding. Such a pleasing accent, and the stalks dry well for bouquets. It is planted in front of the pears that turn a burgundy red in the fall. (This is the best of the genus.) (4–5 feet)

Artemisia absinthium 'Powis Castle'   Most artemisias are too aggressive for any specialized garden. Not 'Powis castle', with its finely cut and divided silver foliage. (18 inches)

Artemisia schmidtiana 'Silver Mound'   Divide this useful plant in early spring. Even tiny pieces will live and turn into an appealing soft mound that everyone likes to touch. (12 inches)

Artemisia versicolor. A knockout. You will want all of this you can get. A slow grower. The foliage harkens to the hanging moss type that grows on trees down South and can be used fresh or dried. Truly a welcome curiosity. It layers easily. (10–12 inches)

Aruncus aethusifolius   dwarf goatsbeard. Dying back after blooming, this is really a dear. (Mark where you grow it.) (8–10 inches)

Asclepias tuberosa   butterfly weed. So welcome with its orange butterfly-shaped flowers. If you cut just the flower head back after it blooms, you will have a second show. (20 inches)

Aurinia saxatilis   basket of gold. No plant has such beauty as this cascading over a large rock wall. Even the leaves are attractive. Seedlings have a tendency to heave out of the ground, so check them if you have changing temperatures. (16 inches)

Baptisia leucantha   cream false indigo. An American native perennial, blooming in early summer. This stunning legume always evokes exclamations. Growing from seed to peak blooms takes five seasons, but so worth waiting for. Only seedlings will transplant in June; if you do this in the fall, they will heave during the winter. After established, though, it is long-lived. The black seed pods are perfect tucked into wreaths. If you don't pick these, they will give you a show during the somber winter months. (14–18 inches) I have a new to me *Baptisia tinctoria* (wild indigo) that is great. Supposedly limited to Zones 5 to 6, but it is very happy here, surviving for three winters. (18 inches)

Belamcanda chinensis   blackberry lily. Its bloom isn't much, but it is another nice addition in arrangements. The seed pods develop into a "blackberry." Don't pick these until the skin starts to split. (3 feet)

Bellis perennis   english daisy. Not aggressive for me. A very low edging plant, drying well—use the small flowers in potpourri mixes. (3–5 inches)

Boltonia asteroides   snowbank. Another native American perennial, blooming in late summer till frost, with a misty shower of white daisylike flowers. A low-maintenance plant that never needs staking. So distinct, planted in front of or around the russian sage. This does not reseed. It is very wind-resistant and long-blooming. (3–4 feet)

Campanula calycanthema canterbury bell. An iffy perennial of medium height and in appealing shades of white, pink, and purple, this is a favorite of hummingbirds. (18 inches)

Campanula carpatica var. *alba* A June and July white and blue flowering plant. Cut it back to the ground in July and it will bloom again in the fall. All campanulas appreciate a little lime occasionally. (12 inches)

Centranthus ruber jupiter's beard. This is a must, with pleasing deep pink rounded heads. It is perfect for fresh arrangements (dries well, too). Be sure to dehead it. (2 feet)

Ceratostigma plumbaginoides plumbago. Has stunning gentian blue flowers. It is not long-lived but worth replacing. (12 inches)

Chrysanthemum haradjanii Feathery ferny silver leaves. Plant on the west side of a high mound with good drainage so the snow will blow off it in the winter. Excessive moisture laying on this plant will kill it. Another plant worth the extra effort. (10 inches)

Chrysanthemum parthenium 'Aureum' Recently introduced with outstanding limey-colored leaves that truly glisten in the autumn. A true gem. Needs deheading.

Chrysogonum virginianum You have to see the foliage color with the flowers to believe it. (4 inches)

Coreopsis tinctoria plains coreopsis. Fine for cutting. There are short and tall varieties and both are rewarding. Sometimes this is a biennial. Another reseeder. (20 inches)

Coreopsis verticillata 'Grandiflora' threadleaf tickseed. An American native perennial, flowering all summer long. Drought-resistant. Great for edges. It's a graceful, dark-leafed, loose mound of clear yellow flowers. Free of disease and truly delightful. (12 inches)

Coreopsis verticillata 'Moonbeam' Readily propagated by root division and it blooms all season.

Crambe cordifolia It does survive our winters; the huge leaves are a designer's dream and the cloud of 10-foot-tall creamy sprays of flowers makes it gorgeous with pines.

Delphinium grandiflorum If you don't persist with nipping this plant when it is 18 inches tall, you will have to stake it. By pinching it back, you force it to branch so there is no staking required. Plant these en masse. One hovering sentinel-like stalk of bloom here and there is so inadequate. Don't shudder when I tell you to pinch the early growth. True, the blooms are not quite as tall and are a little later, but they are still effective. A much easier solution than using ineffective supports. This works with hollyhocks, too. (3–4 feet)

Dianthus barbatus sweet william, Newport variety. This is especially nice if planted by the border, sprawling with a soft look. (16 inches)

Dianthus deltoides   maiden pinks. I can't imagine why it is not being offered by our seed people and nurseries. An evergreen perennial, forming dense mats of true red flowers clinging near the ground. This "pink" has a long blooming period, and if you let it go to seed, cut off a handful and pat it around your borders. After two years, control will be necessary or it will become another wall-to-wall carpet. (10 inches)

Dianthus 'Magic Charm'   All-American winner. A hybrid of remarkable character. An annual, sometimes perennial, flowering all summer long if you keep the spent blooms picked (one of those jobs for the cool of the evening). Has fifty cent-size blooms, and it is ideal for the border instead of those boring whatsits you have been planting forever. (10 inches)

Dictamnus albus and *rubrum*   gas plant. Scatter seeds of this as soon as they are black; they do not stay viable very long. The plant is long-lived with an excellent stalk for dried bouquets. The seed rosette is a substitute for star anise. (2 feet)

Digitalis   foxglove, Little Foxy variety. It has been used medicinally for centuries. Foxy is bushy, having no problems. This, too, is a biennial that reseeds nicely. (18 inches)

Dodecatheon meadia   shooting star. Contrary to belief, this endures very dry situations. (12 inches)

Echinacea purpurea   purple coneflower. Long-lived with long-lasting flowers. Even the seedpods are attractive. There is a white one on the market now. Its children do not make white flowers, but the grandchildren do. (30 inches)

Echinops exaltatus   globe thistle. This plant must be harvested while it is steely blue before it starts to pollinate; otherwise it shatters. If you keep picking *Echinops*, it will produce globes all season. (3 feet)

Epimedium perralderanum 'Frohnleiten'   Another plant with beautiful foliage, especially in the fall. It tolerates some sun. There are many varieties of this and all are outstanding. (14 inches)

Erysimum cheiranthus 'Allionii'   siberian wallflower. Of medium height. A true gem with a pleasing aroma and delicate orange flowers. Really reseeds, but do not let it reseed in the same place. Sometimes a biennial, but will live several years if you keep it deheaded. (18 inches)

Eupatorium coelestinum   hardy ageratum. This lavender-headed late bloomer complements the boltonia aster. The flower heads dry to perfection. Hardy ageratum, or blue mistflower as it is often called, is very susceptible to early light frosts. Please cover it so you will continue to benefit from its beauty. (18 inches)

Euphorbia myrsinites   donkey tail. It is gorgeous year-round in large-rock walls. Another reseeder, so deheading is necessary. Unfortunately, it also causes rashes.

Euryops evansii   A wee tufted artemisia-like plant, it is delicate looking but tough, having great value. Locate it near the edge of your path as all will enjoy this baby. (6 inches)

Filipendula rubra   queen of the prairie. Unfortunately susceptible to mildew in the gardens but not in the prairie. She likes wet feet and afternoon shade, so try to please her. You will be rewarded. (3 feet)

Gaillardia aristata   blanket flower. Another dependable, aggressive plant, so keep the seedpods cut off. There are many varieties of this and all are desirable. (18 inches)

Gaura lindheimeri   This does indeed prosper and survive in our zones and is adorned with allover pinkish flowers and striking fall color. (3 feet)

Gentiana andrewsii and *G. septemfida*   I have tried many of this species. These two are dependable. (2 feet and 10 inches)

Glaucium flavum   horned poppy. Grow this large, silvery, icy blue-leaved plant for the outstanding foliage and the unique seedpods. They are an upbeat accent to dried arrangements. Be sure to harvest the pods before they explode. (2 feet)

Gypsophila   baby's breath. Such airiness. Try many kinds, even the annuals. (2–3 feet)

Helenium autumnale 'Brilliant'   This requires hooping in the beginning, but gains strength with age so is worth the trouble for the late season show. (30 inches)

Hemerocallis spp.   daylilies. Mix them with clumps of ornamental grasses. So many public gardens have them grouped together. This seems so mechanized and does not do them justice. You have a softening effect by including grasses and arborvitae. (3 feet)

Hemerocallis 'Stella d'Oro'   An ever-blooming dwarf daylily, it is expensive but a treasure. People are always asking me about my favorite flower and this is certainly one of them. (2 feet)

Heuchera purpurea 'Palace Purple'   I adore red-leaved anything, and this is a beauty. Mine set viable seed last year and a flat has germinated in the greenhouse, so there will be lots of it soon, planted all over. This plant keeps its burgundy leaves well into winter before going dormant. (18 inches)

Hyssopus officinalis   anise hyssop. A competitive, fragrant plant, completely at home in the meadow or in a desert. (2 feet)

Ipomopsis or *Gilia aggregata*   Everyone asks, "What's that?" The foliage is soft, feathery, and beguiling; the bloom stalk is excellent for cutting. Do not worry about it reseeding. You will be lucky if three or four live over the winter. (3 feet)

Iris   siberian and japanese varieties. Their bladelike foliage more than makes up for the short blooming time. (2 feet)

Iris sibirica 'Flight of the Butterflies'   We all seem to forget that iris, with their dramatic stiff leaves, furnish character long after their orchidlike blossoms are gone. The delicate 'Flight of the Butterflies' is unsung and needs to be seen to be appreciated. Mine are about 2 feet tall with bluish green grasslike foliage. They look great growing in front of rock walls and propagate easily by root division. (3 feet)

Kniphofia 'Little Maid'   You won't believe the bloom span; early in the season till hard frost, ten to fifteen flower stalks at a time. You will need to purchase new plants each year. It does not winterize. (18 inches)

Larkspur   The giant double 'Hyacinth Mix' is spectacular. Another must for fresh arrangements. This biennial comes in many colors. Don't let it reseed in the same place because it is a very greedy plant that wears out the soil. (3 feet)

Lavandula angustifolia 'Munstead Dwarf'   This perennial blunt-textured lavender has earned a place in my garden. I grew it originally from seed. It is very hardy, unlike many of the lavenders we try to grow in our zone. The silver, elongated stubs are another asset. Their fragrant flowers and the fact that it takes to being pruned (again, unlike the other lavenders) proves its worth, especially when planted as a base around the boltonia aster. (16 inches)

Leucanthemum balsamita   costmary. Not just an herb, it contends well with dry spells. The little round orangy buttons dry, and the leaves can be used as a fixative instead of orris root. (3 feet)

Ligularia stenocephala 'The Rocket'   Having pitch-black stems, big leaves, and startling yellow flowers that weep in hot weather, this plant requires a moist, shady situation. (2 feet)

Limonium latifolium and *L. tataricum*   sea lavender. It is pale pink and lavender until picked, then both varieties turn white. Used like baby's breath for a filler in dried bouquets. Very long lasting either picked or left in the garden. (16 inches)

Linum flavum   yellow flax. A perennial that is not supposed to live in our zone. Be skeptical and try these plants that are minimal risks. I'm so glad I do. Yellow flax is special, with lovely greenish blue oblong leaves (reminiscent of saint-john's-wort) and long-lasting bright yellow blooms. I prune it back to a mound shape after flowering and like it planted near and around the baptisia. (16 inches)

Linum perenne   Another flax. I close my eyes during the winter and visualize this treasured sky blue perennial floating on thin wiry stems. It is like an ocean wave. Unforgettable. This flax reseeds like crazy so I cut it back before it drops seeds (often it will rebloom in the fall, a great bonus). (14 inches)

Liatris aspera 'Elegance' and *L. pycnostachya*   rough and gayfeather. Both are welcome midseason bloomers. Even old bulbs will heave in the spring, so check this. They have the odd characteristic of blooming from top to bottom. (2–3 feet)

Lunaria annua   honesty or silver dollar. This has a deep magenta flower. Peel the outer layers of the seed when it is turning brown. A sound investment for show and harvest. A biennial. (20 inches)

Lycoris squamigera   magic lily. Difficult if you plant it too deep (try 5 inches if you haven't had success). Truly magic with mounds of straplike leaves dying back in late spring to be followed in July with 2-foot naked pink stalks of blossoms. (20 inches)

Lysimachia clethroides   Most of this genus is very domineering and difficult to control, much less eradicate, but not *L. clethroides*. It is exclusive and you will want more of it. (30 inches)

Macleaya cordata   plume poppy. Stunning as a background plant with large conifers. The mauve foliage sets off many other plants and the sprays of small flowers make nice fillers in a bouquet. (5–6 feet)

Malva alcea fastigiata   In the hollyhock family. It blooms all season and is useful as a background and for a long showtime. (3 feet)

Mentha requienii   Corsican mint or crème-de-menthe. Not even ½ inch high, a fully packed mound. Brush your hands over it; it smells heavenly and reseeds nicely.

Miscanthus sinensis 'Gracillimus'   maidengrass. The 'Gracillimus' variety is most important; others in this family are too aggressive. Don't burn this grass to clean it up because you will set it back and it won't fluoresce in the fall. (4 feet)

Myosotis alpestris   forget-me-not. Will need moist, shady conditions, so water it often. (6 inches)

Myosotis silvatica   forget-me-not. These are effective scattered among the *Bellis* daisies and pansies. Pick these for a fresh miniature nosegay.

Nierembergia repens   whitecup. The blue is also perennial for me, and both bloom heavily after making a very late spring appearance, so don't give up on them. (8 inches)

Origanum pulchellum   oregano. This looks like dittany of crete, with hoplike pink flowers. Grow it on rock walls. (8 inches)

Papaver orientale   oriental poppy. Such an exuberant plant with tissuelike flowers, and they can be used in fresh flower arrangements if you pick them in bud stage before there is any color showing. Immerse this bud in water up to its neck. Place in a cool dark place and when it starts to open (usually twenty-four hours) use in your arrangement. Don't be alarmed if these oriental poppies die back after blooming. The leaves can be pulled as soon as they are through blooming. (Don't worry, you won't get their roots.) This will clean up your garden. In August, new growth will appear. This is the time to transplant, water, and fertilize them. This new growth provides next year's flowers. (20 inches)

Penstemon grandiflorus beard's tongue. This 3-foot-tall native American perennial withstanding drought and all difficulties has a clumplike, leathery, blue-silver base. In the second summer, a tall stalk of lavender flowers bursts forth. This stalk, when dried naturally on the plant, is unique, has lots of winter interest and, of course, is effective in dried bouquets. Everything about *P. grandiflorus* deserves raves, and I wish it were in every garden. (I will share seeds.) (3 feet)

Perovskia atriplicifolia russian sage. No beautiful herbs? Realign your thinking! This perennial has a lavender, silvery, misty, eight-week-long fluorescence and is very strong. Never needs staking. It is very bushy and is a perfect foil amidst the boltonia and penstemon. This plant is difficult to transplant as it has a sheathing on its roots and if the sheathing is disturbed or destroyed, the plant will die. Even the seedlings have this sheathing, so dig them very carefully. (Other plants, including some conifers, also have this protective sealant.) (3 feet)

Phlox caroliniana 'Miss Lingard' This is not as susceptible to mildew as the other varieties. We read about powdery mildew being caused by damp mugginess, but mildew- susceptibles need afternoon shade in the Midwest. Keeping your plants healthy is one means of fighting this unsightly disease. Don't let them get bone dry. Water in the early morning, thin out the middle of the phlox so the air circulates, and give them shade from 1:30 P.M. on. I also have the notion that heavy soil contributes; when the soil is lightened, the mildew is, too. Sulfur dust and Karathane can be used. By the time you go through that, it is easier to get rid of the plants. This, *P. divaricata*, and alpine are the only phlox at Wind 'n' View. (2 feet)

Primula denticulata, *P. japonica*, and *P. vulgaris* These plants perform well for me. They must have afternoon shade, humusy soil, and moisture. Check young plants for heaving in spring and do not fertilize with nitrogen. (8 inches)

Chrysanthemum coccineum painted daisy. An insecticide is made from this. The clump wallows around for a couple of years, but after that, the stems get strong and tough, resisting the wind. (18 inches)

Rudbeckia hirta black-eyed susan. This native grows anyplace. An old-fashioned flower that still has appeal. (18 inches)

Rudbeckia gloriosa daisy. Weave this throughout an informal border; it will provide lavish backbones and many babies for weeks during the summer. (20 inches)

Salvia argentia   Growing well from seeds, this is not particular, liking each place I have put it. A large rosette of silver leaves the first year and mauve flowers thereafter. It is spectacular. (10 inches, then 2 feet the second year.)

Salvia azura pitcherii   Truly an azure haze when flowering, there is no other plant that compares with this hue. This should be grown en masse, in a meadow or in a naturalized setting.

Salvia sclarea   clary sage. This has a wonderful ambrosia. The clary sage can be steamed and the strained liquid used for an eyewash. (3 feet)

Salvia tricolor viridis   My goodness! Another amazing beauty from the world of herbs, a biennial or reseeding annual sage that is striking. Upright stems with the leaves provide the show in shades of purple, pink, and white. This mixture scattered throughout our garden ties it all together during midsummer and with an extra bonus, too—it's fragrant. (18 inches)

Santolina chamaecyparissus and *S. virens*   Both are hardy in my raised herb beds. (I did mulch these the first winter with pine boughs.) (16 inches)

Sedum spectabile 'Autumn Joy'   One of the most popular sedums, giving year round "joy" even in the winter. Buy the plant initially. It can be lifted and divided as the clump enlarges. (20 inches)

Stachys olympica   lamb's ears. So easy to propagate by layering, often rooting itself, taking to a rock wall with grace. Children love to touch it. (18 inches)

Teucrium chamaedrys   germander. Not as reliable as I would like it to be. (14 inches)

Thalictrum polygamum   tall meadow-rue. Like amsonia, it is associated with shade, but I have it planted in the prairies and perennial gardens in full sun with no ill effects. It even reseeds there like crazy. (6–8 feet)

Verbascum   arctic summer mullein. This rounds out any electrical garden. This is the knock-out punch! We all know the weedy, stalky mullein that grows along our roadsides, but arctic summer is snowy white with large nubby knobs that explode into many brilliant yellow flowers. This hardy biennial has a mound of enormous white leaves the first year and sometimes erupts into a 7-foot-stalk of bloom in the second year, occasionally reseeding. Grow this to believe it. Stunning in fresh arrangements or dry it for Christmas accents. (5–7 feet)

Verbascum bombyciferum and *V. phoeniceum*   mullein. One silver and stalked, the other a bushy plant of many colors that is long lasting for picking. (2 feet)

Vernonia noveboracensis   ironweed. Nothing equals this New York variety for a late fall show. Don't let it go to seed. (3 feet)

Viola spp.   Many of these become biennial after you buy them as pansies. (6 inches)

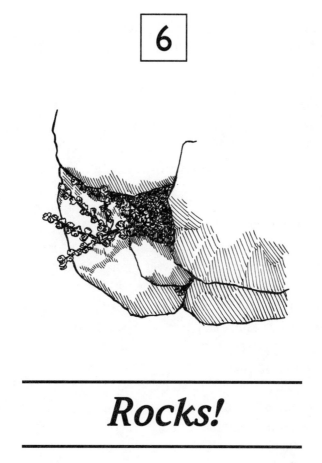

6

Rocks!

ROCKS! As you have gathered from my descriptions so far, gardening at Wind 'n' View would not be possible without them. Rocks as holding banks to control wind and water erosion; rocks as building blocks for the terraced beds that punctuate our hillside; pebbled pathways and pebble mulches for practicality and visual charm. The older I get, the more uses I find for rocks in my gardens. They have never yet let me down.

Rock Berms

Rocks were the inspiration and the solution for those three hundred miserable conifers I put along the west side of our driveway as my first attempt at a windbreak, way back when.

Despite my efforts to transplant them, give them away, and use them ourselves as Christmas trees, they were still haunting us after twenty years. I hated them. Only green on the top and exposed sides; the centers were completely browned out. We had bought our land for the view, yet we couldn't see anything to the northwest, and there's a smashing view that way. They just had to go.

First we tried to cut them down. Talk about mess—I couldn't believe it. To begin, the branches were cut off with chainsaws as high as the men could reach. Then the trees came down and were sawed up into manageable pieces. Next, all the branches were shredded into a truck and hauled away. We stopped counting how many truckloads. Later the stumps were routed out, leaving enormous piles of sawdust that we couldn't grade back into the soil. (Fresh sawdust uses up all the nitrogen in the soil, ruining it for years.) All this sawdust had to be hauled away. Finally new soil was brought in and the operation graded. All this, and we'd only gotten rid of a third of the trees. There had to be another way.

After much worry and fretting, I came up with the idea of cutting off the trees as close to the ground as possible and then building rock berms over the stumps. I could then plant in these rock berms. This strategy has been a huge success. We took out another third of the trees one winter and finished the winter following, creating three rock berms all together. Each season I planted another section; that was manageable without being overpowering. These berms are each 8 to 10 feet across and about 40 feet long.

We took all the rocks we could from our own property, but even so we had to have some bigger ones delivered. The trees in each berm area were felled 3 or 4 inches off the ground and hauled away. Then we placed 3- to 4-inch stones between the stumps, leveling off the area. A double row of large stones was put down to create a lower tier 7 feet across and following the basic contour or pattern I had established, and then 6 inches of coarse gravel was placed inside this double row, along with sand to fill in the cracks. This was topped with 1 foot of soil and aged manure. Another double row of stones was placed on top of the first tier and centered to create a second tier 2 feet across; this was filled in just like the first.

It worked out to have a sunken courtyard between two of the berms and three other ground-level courtyards by the lower curved one. A shredded bark path expedites traffic to other gardens and there are brick stepping stones throughout the courtyards. The top tiers are planted with shrubs, dwarf conifers, grasses, and miniature roses. The middle tiers hold rare perennials, bulbs, and ground covers. Poppies and primroses fill the sunken courtyard; the ground-level courtyards hold combinations of bulbs and low-growing plants. The three different heights display each form to perfection.

Berm plantings include *Allium caeruleum* and *A. pulchellum*, *Aruncus sylvester* 'Kneiffii', *Campanula carpatica*, *Fibigia clypeata*, *Gentiana lagodechiana*, *G. septemfida*, *Geranium lancastriense*, *Gypsophila petraea*, *Herniaria glabra*, *Hieracium lanatum*, and *Microbiota decussata*.

If I had these berms to do over again, I would only change two things. I would have treated my stumps with a quick-decay application before I filled in over them, and if I had had the room, I'd have made my tiers a little wider. A lower level 12 feet across and the second level 9 feet across seems ideal. And remember, if you decide to build rock berms, never use limestone for your gravel base. It will make your soil too sweet for many plants.

The "Odd Couple" Rockery

My strategy for raising the ground level with rock berms was so successful that I repeated it immediately, creating a raised Iowa stone island on the east side of the driveway near the road. In this raised island bed I paired rocks with herbs, an unusual but effective combination that led to my nickname for this particular garden: the "odd couple" rockery.

Traditionally, people have grown herbs for utility first, as medicines and flavorings, and for beauty second or not at all. Many herbs have undeservedly bad reputations as invasive spreaders or ungainly-looking stragglers that should be hidden away by the kitchen door. In fact, herbs are beautiful, and their aggressive tendencies can be controlled easily by deheading seedpods and containing root systems. Rock gardens automatically do the latter, as they are planted above ground level. And deheading seedpods is much easier in a contained, raised bed where you can get at the plants than in a wide plot or kitchen garden at ground level. Herbs generally like good drainage, and this is also easy to achieve in a raised rock bed. I have concluded that far from being an odd couple, rocks and herbs are natural soul mates.

Building an "Odd Couple" Rockery

For this garden you need plenty of Iowa stone or boulders about a foot high, and a site in full sun. The oval bed measures about 15 by 30 feet and rises from ground level to 7 feet high at its highest point. It is a stone-studded mound rather than a tiered garden, each stone worked firmly into the soil for stability. For the soil mix, use equal parts sand, humus or compost, and soil. Starting at the top of the mound, space *Asclepias tuberosa* (butterfly weed), *Dictamnus albus* (gas plant), and *Perovskia atriplicifolia* (russian sage). The two latter can be used to repel insects and for medicinal purposes; *Asclepias tuberosa* makes a good fabric dye in tones ranging from grassy green to rusty, earthy shades. Between each plant place a 12-inch stone, worked firmly into the soil.

Stepping down lower into the mound, plant *Chamaemelum nobile* 'Trenague' (chamomile; this variety doesn't flower so there are no seeds), *Mentha requienii* (corsican mint), and *Thymus serpyllum* 'Lanuginosus' (woolly thyme), *T. s.* 'Coccineus' (red thyme), and *T. s.* 'Thracicus (lavender semi-woolly thyme). Tuck one *Genista tinctoria* (dyer's greenwood; it produces a wonderful bright, clear yellow) at each end of the oval. As before, place a 12-inch stone between each plant, but also set a smaller stone (7 to 8 inches) behind and in front of each. All the second tier plantings will grow over these stones. The chamomile can be used for tea, or cosmetically or ornamentally, and the thymes for flavoring. The greenwood is a dyer's dream.

The bottom tier of our oval will contain *Achillea umbellata*, *Chrysanthemum haradjanii*, and *Artemisia schmidtiana* 'Silver Mound' interspersed with *Salvia viridis* (sage) and several annuals. *Tagetes signata* 'Pumila' (lemon-scented marigold) is an annual whose seed you can save to replant again next spring. Add *Ocimum basilicum* (annual bush basil), *Coriandrum sativum* (coriander or chinese parsley), an annual that reseeds itself, and *Satureja hortensis* and *S. montana* (summer and winter savories); these too are annuals that reseed. These are all culinary herbs that can be used as well in potpourri and sachets. As before, a 12-inch stone should be placed between each plant. Pinch the sage early in the season so it gets bushy. It blooms magnificently all summer. This is a magnificent small garden, all perennial except where noted, full of beauty as well as utility—the best of both worlds.

A Rock Wall Herbary

I disagree with the many gardening writers who maintain that rock gardens need a lot of care and attention. I find it to be just the opposite, especially with a rock wall herbary. A low rock wall studded with herbs is so convenient—you can harvest standing up, weed easily, and the herbs stay clean because they're up off the ground. A rock wall herbary will protect its plantings from winter winds, and the sun-warmed stones seem to help in protecting against early frost damage, especially if the wall is built facing south. (Late afternoon shade is ideal.) A wall garden is easy to mulch, too; just gather up discarded Christmas trees and stand them against the stones. A rock wall herbary is perfect for a small area in full sun. If your area is shady, a wall herbary can sometimes lift the plants into a patch of sunlight. This kind of garden is relatively easy to build, and maintenance is nominal if you make sure you get the weeds out when they are babies (you mustn't let the weed roots get deep into the rock crevices). Top-dressing the exposed areas with a 3-inch layer of pea gravel reduces or eliminates weeding and provides erosion control.

Several years ago, when we built our root cellar and drying barn into the side of the hill, we flanked the entrance with stone walls and stuffed them with herbs and low-growing perennials that get lost in a ground-level garden: *Veronica, Sedum, Ajuga, Waldsteinia fragarioides* (barren strawberry), *Euphorbia myrsinites* (donkey tail), and *Phlox subulata*. If you already have a rock wall in existence, you can make it into an herbary by pounding and forcing entries into or between the stones with a pry bar, then planting seeds and tamping them in with the flat end of the pipe. Plant the seeds in late August or September. If you have bare spots you can get at, insert these plants there, too.

Try to have all your plants ready so you can plant while you build. If your plants are in pots or sectioned plastic flats, soak them before planting. Sprinkle in small pea gravel as you plant; this will help to hold the soil until the roots take. Hand sprinkle very carefully until all is soaked.

The following plants will be smashing in your wall.

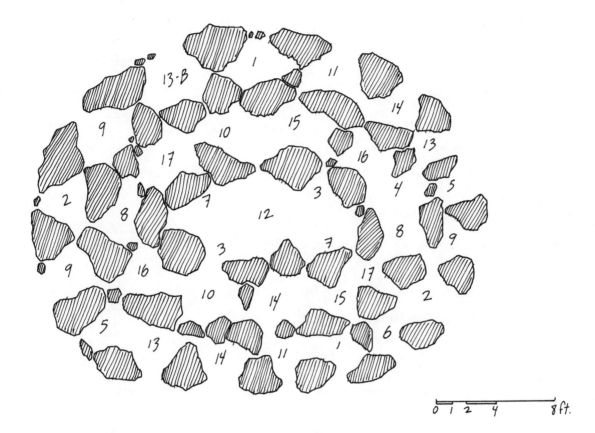

14. Plan for an "Odd Couple" Rockery

Plants for an "Odd Couple" Rockery

1. *Achillea umbellata*
2. *Artemisia schmidtiana* 'Silver Mound'
3. *Asclepias tuberosa*
4. *Chamaemelum nobile* 'Treneague'
5. *Chrysanthemum haradjanii*
6. *Coriandrum sativum*
7. *Dictamnus albus*
8. *Genista tinctoria*
9. *Lavandula angustifolia* 'Munstead'
10. *Mentha requienii*
11. *Ocimum basilicum*
12. *Perovskia atriplicifolia*
13. *Satureja hortensis*
14. *Satureja montana*
15. *Tagetes signata pumila*
16. *Thymus serpyllum* 'Lanuginosus'
17. *Thymus serpyllum* 'Coccineus'
18. *Thymus serpyllum* 'Thracicus'

Perennials

Achillea filipendulina   golden yarrow. For the top tier, where it can grow tall.

Alchemilla vulgaris   lady's mantle

Allium spp.

Anthemis tinctoria   marguerite

Artemisia abrotanum   southernwood. Place on either side of the golden yarrow. There are many varieties of this, all lovely.

Artemisia pontica   roman wormwood. (Don't use this unless you can really encircle it; it's very aggressive.)

Artemisia schmidtiana 'Silver Mound'

Asperula odorata   sweet woodruff. For a shady spot.

Leucanthemum balsamita   costmary

Chrysanthemum parthenium 'Aureum'   feverfew. (Don't let it go to seed).

Lavandula angustifolia 'Munstead'   lavender

Melissa officinalis   lemon balm

Mentha requienii   corsican mint

Oreganum vulgare 'Aureum'   marjoram

Salvia spp.   sage

Santolina chamaecyparissus   lavender cotton

Satureja hortensis   summer savory

Satureja montana   winter savory

Sempervivum tectorum   hen and chicks

Stachys lanata   lamb's ears. Another striking cascading plant.

Symphytum officinale   comfrey

Tanacetum vulgare   tansy

Thymus spp.   thyme

These last two are very aggressive. If your space is limited, I would omit them. If you do plant them, put them in some kind of a deep container so they can't travel all over. You will need to plant your patches of dill and copper fennel along the top of the wall, with the yarrow. Lay this out according to the scale you have established and work it all in. These last six are 3 to 4 feet tall.

Tapering down on the sides toward your ground-level courtyard, put a clump of *Pyrethrum* (painted daisy) on each end, along with *Artemisia ludoviciana alba* (silver king).

Annuals

Ambrosia

Borago officinalis   borage. So lovely when cascading.

chervil

coriander

scented geraniums

Most of the plantings I suggest for the courtyard are not winter hardy and will have to be lifted if you don't want to buy them new each spring. Sink your pots of *Rosmarinus officinalis* (rosemary) on all four corners. Surround the pots with *Origanum dictamnus* (dittany of crete) and *Teucrium chamaedrys* (germander). Center your pots of *Cymbopogon citratus* (lemon grass) and *Lippia citriodora* (lemon verbena) interspersed with *Tagetes* (marigold), anise-flavored *Ocimum basilicum* (basil), ornamental peppers, and clove pinks.

For the paths that encompass the courtyard and wind about the stone walls, nothing works better than the creeping varieties of *Thymus serpyllum* (thyme), such as 'Annie Hall', 'Coccineus', 'Caraway', or 'Splendens'. All are valuable for their clean, sweet smell that perfumes the air and their exquisite carpet of flowers.

Scatter clumps of *Poterium sanguisorba* (salad burnet), *Chamaemelum nobile* 'Treneague' (chamomile), and *Mentha pulegium* (pennyroyal) among the thymes and tuck *Mentha requienii* (Corsican mint) into the stones at ground level. We can't walk on this often, but if it's out of the main thoroughfare, it should be all right. Your new garden is completed.

Pot herbs—those green, leafy plants we grow for vegetable greens or as flavorings for salads, soups, stews, egg dishes, and drinks—prefer good, rich, well-drained soil in full sun. Yes, they will survive in terrible conditions, but why put them through that? Their taste becomes bitter more quickly and they loose their potency rapidly if they are grown under stress. Well-drained soil is essential, and so is pinching off flower buds as they develop. When herbs bloom, the leafage deteriorates and the fragrant oils disappear.

Nonculinary herbs that we grow for potpourri, sachets, decorations, and fragrances can tolerate stress and poor soils. In fact, stress develops a strong essence and helps maintain a long-lasting aroma.

Don't be misled by promises about permanent fragrance. There is no such thing. All your potpourris will have to be touched up occasionally with essential oils and new spices. Or make new mixtures. Lavender and scented geranium leaves ('Mabel Grey' and 'Little Gem', from Logee's) do have a longer-lasting perfume than most herbs.

New House; New Opportunities

In 1989 my husband and I yielded to a temptation that had been tugging at us for several years. We sold our original home, along with half an acre of our property (including the rock berms I had raised along that first driveway), and built a new home down the hill and to the west of the first. This had several advantages, among them the opportunity to design a home from scratch and to plan some new gardens that would reflect all I had learned in twenty years of making and rectifying gardening mistakes. We tackled and solved many landscaping problems before we ever broke ground for the house itself, and we incorporated many changes in grade or ground level into our basic outdoor design. My love affair with rock gardens needed more scope, and our new landscape plan has provided this.

Against the west wall of the new house we put in a double rock wall with two level terraces. Perennial culinary herbs are planted among the rocks, and annuals grow on the terraces. Herbs that we use daily grow just outside the back door, where they can be picked easily.

Perennials

Allium schoenoprasum   chives. Grown inside or out, chives have showy lavender flowers that make pleasing vinegars. The chopped bladelets are added to dips, salads, and egg dishes.

Artemisia dracunculus   french tarragon. If you've grown this from seed, you have the wrong one. Root propagation only. French tarragon needs to be lifted, divided, and reset every three years. One of few herbs that holds its flavor when dried.

Levisticum officinale   lovage. Another herb that dries well. Mix equal parts of dried lovage, tarragon, and parsley to make fines herbes. Add this flavoring to anything but desserts as a substitute for salt. Lovage is very tall and should be planted near the door instead of in the rocks. Don't let it go to seed!

Mentha spp.   The entire mint family is too persistent. I plant it in pots and sink them in the ground. When winter approaches, I cut slips and plant them in pots indoors, throwing out the older plant. Then I set the slips out in their pots in spring.

Poterium sanguisorba   salad burnet. If you have a snow cover, this herb can be picked and eaten all winter in green salads.

Rumex acetosa   sorrel. Buy the French variety. The young tender leaves are delicious in a garden salad, or put them in a pot of soup for extra zip. I plant this at my kitchen door. This must be kept deheaded.

Salvia officinalis   garden sage. Can be harvested all winter; much better than trying to dry it.

Satureja montana   winter savory. Also winter harvestable. Rub the leaves on bee stings, and season beans, cream sauces, and salads with it.

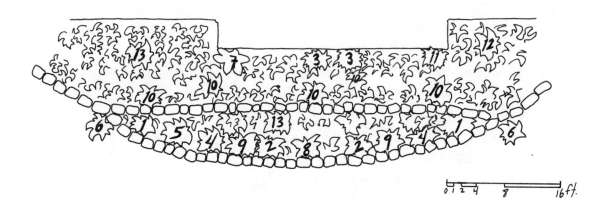

15. Plan for a Rock Wall Herbary with Two Terraces

Perennial Plants for a Rock Wall Herbary

1. *Allium schoenoprasum* chives
2. *Artemisia dracunculus* french tarragon
3. *Levisticum officinalis* lovage
4. *Mentha* spp. mint
5. *Poterium sanguisorba* salad burnet

6. *Rosmarinus officinalis* rosemary
7. *Rumex acetosa* french sorrel
8. *Salvia officinalis* garden sage
9. *Satureja montana* winter savory
10. *Thymus* spp. thyme

Annual Plants for a Rock Wall Herbary

11. *Anethum graveolens* dill
12. *Anthriscus cerefolium* chervil

13. *Ocimum basilicum* basil

Thymus spp.   thyme. So ornamental. At home in the herb garden, in rock walls, between stones in paths, or in a rock garden. Garner and use for seasoning all winter.

Dried herbs deteriorate very quickly. Do harvest any of the suggested ones during the winter. They will be better than anything you buy in a jar.

Annuals

Anethum graveolens   dill. Of course, the seed head is for pickles. I use the ferny leaves for seasoning cucumbers, coleslaw, and dips. These leaves freeze well; stuff chopped into ice cube trays, fill with water, freeze, remove from trays, place in labeled plastic bag, and use all winter.

Anthriscus cerefolium   chervil. Once you plant it, you will always have it. Reseeding, but who could object to this delicate herb? Before it flowers, chop up the leaves and add to salad dressings, or use as a parsley substitute.

Ocimum basilicum   basil. So many are ornamental now, use them for borders or mix them into a flower bed to keep your flowers healthy. Basil is the pesto herb. Make a lot of pesto, freeze, use all winter in any tomato dish.

Rosmarinus officinalis   rosemary. Has a lovely blue flower around Christmas. Sprinkle the leaves on a beef roast or stuff them into slits on a potato and bake.

The rest of the ornamental herbs will remain in the formal garden.

The taller herbs are in the back (lovage, french sorrel, and dill). The shorter herbs are scattered throughout the stone wall, between stones, and in the level terraces.

Another Driveway

The driveway at our new house has presented a challenge, just as our old one did. The new one is 200 feet long, designed with a double rock wall terrace (this one professionally built) on the west. As I sit in my studio today, I look up repeatedly, watching each boulder put in place. Trees will grow on the ground level; shrubs and tall perennials on the middle level, against the huge boulders; the shredded bark upper terrace will be home to dwarf conifers and alpine shrubs. Color-coordinated combinations of perennials that enjoy a rocky locale complete the plan.

My greenhouse is full of shrub seedlings that will be transplanted to the middle level in June, and others will be purchased. Included are the following:

Acer ginnala   amur maple

Caryopteris   blue mist

Clethra alnifolia   summersweet

Cotoneaster horizontalis   rock spray

Euonymus alatus   winged euonymus

Euonymus europaeus   spindle tree

Forsythia 'Northern'

Diervilla lonicera   bush honeysuckle

Microbiota decussata   russian arborvitae

Prunus besseyi   sand cherry

Rhus aromatica   fragrant sumac

Stephanandra incisa 'Crispa'   cutleaf stephandra

Viburnum carlesii   korean spice

I have decided on a pattern of shrubs and perennials that repeats every 20 feet the full length of this slightly curved driveway. The repetition provides order and structure as a balance to the pleasure of variety in foliage and bloom.

Foliage for Color, Texture, and Show

Designing a color-coordinated garden is difficult; nothing ever blooms at the same time in succeeding years. New plantings will bloom very late their first season. It is best to wait until the second year to determine a more realistic schedule and transplant accordingly. Weather plays an unpredictable role in defining your bloom schedule. It is no wonder that to avoid frustration many coordinate foliage rather than bloom. And when bloom is long gone, there will still be beauty to enjoy.

Ever-goldens, ever-blues, and ever-reds can be woven among flowering perennials for a sensational effect, as in creating a tapestry or collage. Put golden foliage next to deep green or blue. Many herbs have distinctly different foliages; consider the scented geraniums and the ferniness of dill and fennel. Do not ignore the shimmering quality of silver foliage. It is harmonious with everything but chartreuse and can forge peaceful, cool oases among vibrant colors.

The texture and size of leaves should be considered in a garden design as well as the color of the foliage. Leaves can be roughly classified into five groups: grassy, ferny, large round, small round, and normal. Think about these shapes as you plan. The pleated leaves of *Alchemilla*, the oversized lavishness of *Rheum palmatum, Glaucium flavum, Brunnera macrophylla*, and *Macleaya cordata* are outstanding and will add a special depth to any perennial garden. These large-leaved plants need to be established by a corner or near steps, even stuffed into rocks, so they can be relished. Some ethereals really complement the large-leaved plants: *Perovskia, Thalictrum, Gypsophila*, and *Amsonia*.

Heuchera purpurea 'Palace Purple', combined with the gold thread *Chamaecyparis pisifera* 'Filifera Aurea Nana', is outstanding. The ivy-shaped mahogany leaves grow in a mound with airy creamy flowers in midsummer, resulting in seeds that germinate true.

Other stunning combinations: pink astilbes, *Anemone* x *hybrida* 'September Charm', and caladiums; the blood red-leafed "sport" of *Lobelia cardinalis* with *Cimicifuga racemosa* 'Atropurpurea' and *Hypericum prolificum;* yellow-leaved hostas with any of the red-foliaged plants for striking fall color. Silver foliage goes with just about anything; *Artemisia pontica* (roman wormwood) is very aggressive, but controllable in rocks. The lacy ferns are a perfect accent with *Ajuga genevensis* and *A. ocymoides,* two more aggressors that can be controlled when planted between large rocks.

You wouldn't think *Lychnis coronata* and *Coreopsis verticillata* 'Moonbeam' could team up, their colors are so intense. They do, and so does *Artemisia schmidtiana* with *Salvia nemorosa* 'East Friesland'.

The kinship of blues and yellow provides a special attraction. Combine *Achillea filipendulina* (golden yarrow) with the above 'East Friesland'. (If you cut each back after their first bloom, you will get a second flush of color in the fall.) Plant these two with a background of arborvitae.

Stephanandra incisa 'Crispa', green, but with reddish purple autumn color, tumbles over and through the rocks and prunes well for fresh bouquets. It is remarkably effective intertwined with species *Clematis.*

Other combinations for sunny spots: *Sedum* 'Autumn Joy' with *Miscanthus sinensis* 'Gracilimus' for an unexpected all-winter-long bonus; *Artemisia ludoviciana alba* (silver king) and *Rudbeckia triloba* (branched coneflower) for a stunning contrast of glistening black against silver. Try *Genista tinctoria* (dyer's greenwood) and red *Dianthus deltoides* (pinks), or *Eupatorium coelestinum* (hardy ageratum) and *Solidago* 'Laurin' (goldenrod) for an unbeatable fall matchup. The creamy yellow of *Artemisia lactiflora* and the blue whorls of *Salvia pitcherii* make another striking fall twosome. *Geum* x *borisii* (avens), with its warm orange shades, blends dramatically into a colony of *Corydalis lutea* and *Geranium* x 'Johnson's Blue'.

Assemble a curving sweep of mixed groups of *Aquilegia canadensis* (columbine), *A. flabellata* 'Nana', *A.* x *biedermeiers,* and *Semiaquilegia adoxoides.* These columbines will give you a six-week splurge of color. If you remove the spent bloom stalks and leaves, you will have a resurgence of new leaves to provide character in the fall.

Try the winning alliance of *Mertensia virginica* (virginia bluebells) and *Stylophorum diphyllum* (celandine poppy) for a spectacular spring exhibit. Contrary to belief, both do well in full sun. *Achillea tagetes* 'Moonshine' with *Salvia nemorosa* 'East Freisland' and *Papaver orientale* (oriental poppy) with dwarf creeping blue veronicas are good company for the following group, which require afternoon shade: *Cimicifuga racemosa* (bugbane and snakeroot), *Thalictrum* (meadow rue), ligularias, epimediums (bishop's hat), *Polygonatum odoratum* (japanese solomon's seal), *Geranium endressii*, and *Hosta* 'Frances Williams'. Mix that dear little creeping dwarf *Euonymus fortunei* 'Kewensis' with any of these.

Don't forget the grasses—*Avena sempervirens* with its willowy blue wands and the clumpy *Festuca ovina* 'Glauca' provide striking settings for any of your yellow flowers. The harmonious blending of deep-hued blues and golden yellows echo the beauty of sun and sky and are appealing additions to any sunny garden.

The following are shade-loving couples and trios to grow under shrubs: *Asperula odorata* (sweet woodruff) under *Malus* (crabapple) and *Philadelphus microphyllus* (dwarf mock orange); *Dryopteris erythrosora* (japanese sword fern) and *Lamium maculatum* 'Beacon Silver' under *Kalmia latifolia* (mountain laurel). *Primula* (primroses) with *Tiarella cordifolia* (foam-flower), *Phlox paniculata*, *Myosotis* (forget-me-not), or all four are stunning under *Magnolia stellata* (star magnolia); and don't overlook *Amsonia* (blue star) and *Pulmonaria officinalis* (lungwort) under any of the malus family. *Dicentra* (bleeding heart) and *Arabis* (rock cress) are splendid under amelanchiers and azaleas.

Foliage is absolutely worth its keep. Too often we neglect or do not appreciate the usefulness of a striking season-long perennial that can satisfy a twofold need, for bloom and then for the beauty of its foliage. The majority of gardens today are too small to afford the luxury of growing plants only for short-term, spectacular bloom.

Ferns, grasses, and hostas also fulfill a particular mission; they are accessories, covering for showier plants that suffer mildews and fungi seasonally, have leaves that collapse during the heat of the day, or simply are boring after their bloom is spent.

Don't overlook the following fine performers. *Helleborus* (christmas rose), the earliest of all to wake up, has leathery, aristocratic evergreen leaves, and it flowers through the snow. Both *Bergenia* and *Brunnera* have handsome, large, long-lasting leaves; so do many of the *Dicentra* (bleeding heart), *Sanguinaria* (bloodroot), and *Aquilegia* (columbine), and also *Corydalis lutea*, with its icy blue foliage (it seeds around but is easily controlled and grows anyplace.) Each of these could form a carpet with ideal growing conditions, and in a shady area, so could *Athyrium goeringianum* (japanese painted fern) and the golden-foliaged hostas, along with *Polystichum acrostichoides* (christmas fern) and *Alchemilla mollis* (lady's mantle).

Many others furnish lovely flowers followed by colorful foliage: *Paeonia* (peony), including the less familiar tree peony (this does not die back and must not be pruned). Its winter silhouette is almost bonsailike, and it has appealing fine-cut leaves. Tree peonies need protection from wind and midday sun. So do siberian iris and *Centranthus ruber* (valerian), and these make a nice foil for the tree peony.

This is not true of the following three sun lovers for hot, dry spots: *Glaucium flavum* (horned poppy), grown for its enormous icy blue leaves (often wintering over for me and if it doesn't, it will reseed nicely), planted with Iowa junipers and *Asclepias tuberosa* (butterfly weed). This is really a smashing threesome.

So make a conscientious effort to tour your garden often, listing what blooms simultaneously. During the winter, plan new and pleasing color unions. You will have the urge to try my combinations and to create a new garden emphasizing foliages—and don't forget, sometimes charming effects happen accidentally.

A Boggy Garden

A dry stone waterway to control road runoff will lie on the east side of my new driveway. Luckily, our township sands rather than salts in the winter, and 50 feet of grass will separate the road from the waterway, so pollutants from the road should not be a problem. Many m+idwestern areas use a salt and sand mixture for slippery, icy winter conditions. Check this out. You will need to grow salt-tolerant botanicals if you garden near a salted roadway.

The low area where the waterway will lie is going to be a perfect spot for a boggy garden, and I plan to take advantage of it. The waterway will be paved with smooth, round 5 to 6-inch stones, with plants placed randomly between them.

The following tolerate wet conditions, and I will choose among them:

Arisaema atrorubens   jack-in-the-pulpit. This could become aggressive, so dehead it.

Caltha palustris   marsh marigold. Do not eat the raw leaves. Cook young, tender ones in three changes of boiling water for thirty minutes for an early spring treat.

Erythronium americanum   trout lily. Grows in rich, moist soil and needs shade.

Gentiana andrewsii   bottle gentian. Blue as blue can be, easy to propagate by seed.

Gentiana crinita   fringed gentian. It's a difficult-to-propagate and short-lived biennial.

Hosta   Hostas like wet conditions, growing well on stream or pond banks.

Iris pseudocarus   yellow flag. This iris will actually survive in standing water.

Iris versicolor   blue flag. Remember, all irises are poisonous.

Lilium canadense   canada lily. Hard to locate. You will have to grow it from seed.

Lilium superbum   turk's-cap lily. Can grow 5 feet tall. This native is spectacular.

Osmunda regalis   royal fern. Needs wet feet all the time. It often dies back.

Pontederia cordata   pickerel weed. Chop the young leaves and add to salads. The seeds can be eaten raw, too.

Primula japonica and *P. deniculata*   primroses. We can grow these treasures in the Midwest if we water and fertilize them. They enjoy a moist atmosphere and rich soil and are at home along a streambed. Often I see them growing with species bulbs and can't figure out how the bulbs survive in a moist situation. They aren't supposed to.

Sagittaria   arrowhead. A water plant with potato-like tubers, very good if cooked.

Sarracenia purpurea   pitcher plant. Insects drown unappealingly in these pitchers. This plant is grown for its handsome foliage.

Scirpus   tall bullrush. For boggy places; the spring shoots, fall seeds, and root stock can all be eaten.

Plants surviving in bogs, marshes, swamps, and wet places are hard to come by. All these thrive in the wet. Many of them, though, do very well in ordinary growing conditions if you give them extra drinks during dry spells.

Alpine Rockeries

During the past five years, I have visited rock gardens in ten different states. From the very large ones created for botanical and public gardens to the ones growing in old stone watering troughs on private property, each was as distinctive as snowflakes are said to be. It is very easy to become fascinated, wooed by the fact that many plants will grow in a rock garden that won't grow in any other situation.

Don't think you have to be a professional to create a successful alpine rock garden (though it's true that after a while you may become one). The alpines discussed in this chapter do not require genuine alpine growing conditions or professional expertise. All are hardy in Zones 4 to 5 and maybe in Zone 3 as well. All will thrive in a raised, well-drained bed unless special requirements are noted.

Rock Berms for Alpines

The southern and southwestern exposures are always the most difficult for me because of erosion and wind. My good experiences with rock berms at the first house, plus the changing grade levels produced by excavating for our new home, convinced me to build several rock berms on the west—brand new ones, inspired by fresh thoughts.

For the alpine berm, the topsoil was graded into a low, irregular mound 15 feet wide and 120 feet long, tapering off at the southern end, where it connected with the grass holding banks of the hillside. By having the land slope off at that end, I was able to add more levels and hence more interest. Mounds, berms, or raised beds are especially effective for you if your lot is flat.

A second, lower mound, 15 feet wide but only 60 feet long, was constructed 30 feet east of the first. Both earth mounds were banked with rocks to hold the soil in place, thus helping to control erosion. My hope is that the many different levels will break force of the wind, too. My husband and I then arranged stones as large as we could manage in natural groupings within each mound, placing the boulders as carefully as we later placed the plants. Then the berms were top-dressed with a mixture of sand and gravel 2 to 3 inches thick. This topdressing will require only light maintenance—very few weed seeds will germinate in it, and those that do will be easy to pluck right out.

I chose to plant this berm with alpine seed from the American Rock Garden Society seed list and the Denver Botanical Gardens—an enormous project. Seed of elfin creepers, mounds, tufts, clumps, and clusters each under 8 inches high soon were blending together in an undulating flow of color. Their roots seek the moist coolness underneath the rocks; the sand and gravel mix allows their leaves and flowers to drain and dry off quickly, as alpine plants require. If you go with plants instead of seed, be sure to set each plant in at an angle. If their crowns do not dry off quickly, they will rot.

Many alpine gardeners want their rocks to look weathered and quicker than nature decrees. A mixture of half buttermilk and half water brushed onto the rocks periodically will hasten the process. This treatment is especially effective on stepping stones, causing them to blend into their surroundings swiftly.

The following alpines are growing successfully now at Wind 'n' View.

Aethionema grandiflorum var. *Warley Rose*   The steel blue elfin-sized foliage mixes well with sempervivums and succulents.

Alchemilla erythropoda   Truly a dwarf lady's mantle. An outstanding creeper.

Alyssoides graeca   Slightly larger than most alpiners desire, so grow it in a rock wall. A mustard whose seeds develop into large, round pealike pods that are excellent for dried bouquets.

Anacyclus depressus   A silver, ferny rosette whose white, daisylike flowers are red on the underside.

Andromeda grandiflora 'Compacta'   bog rosemary. A desirable low shrub with drooping clusters of flowers; requires a boggy situation.

Androsace sarmentosa   rock jasmine. Needs the perfect spot. Eventually it will find happiness and be a joy in your garden. This grey, furry rosette has pink flowers on short stems.

Aquilegia spp.   columbine. There are many desirable ones for your rocks. Most are easy and reseed in cultivation. Try *A. saxi-montana* and *A. flabellata*. *A. jonesii* is difficult and needs a high, well-drained, limey spot.

Arenaria montana   This has never seeded around for me, and how I wish it would. A June delight with long-lasting, billowy white blooms. The plant itself has been short-lived for me.

Armeria caespitosa   thrift sea pink. A grassy, compact bun with pink flowers that reseed.

Artemisia viridis   A low-growing evergreen staying green all winter long. Early in the spring it develops a fresh apple green color and scent. (Don't let it go to seed.)

Cerastium alpinum var. *lanatum* A smothering of white flowers late in the spring, standing above small whorls of woolly mounds. A chickweed that's not obnoxious.

Delosperma cooperi and *D. nubigenum* ice plant. Yes! These are hardy in Zone 4. The trick is to give them initially a long growing season. Keep them indoors the first winter. Plant them out very early in the spring after hardening them off. They will develop a good root system via this treatment and will survive future winters. *D. cooperi* dies back and comes out very late. *D. nubigenum* has wine-red, lush foliage all winter. Plant these high so the snow blows off them.

Delphinium tatsienense It is about a foot high in bloom with a deep true-blue, long-lasting flower. Cut it back and you will have a repeat show in the fall. A reseeder you will welcome.

Dianthus amurensis, *D. deltoides*, *D. haematocalyx*, *D. pavonius*, and *D. 'Tiny Rubies'* These are just a few of this genus. All are hardy; the *D. deltoides* are very aggressive. Some have icy blue foliage all winter; still others are fragrant, so they have many unique qualities. These crossbreed—the seed does not come true to the parent and the offspring are a muddy pink, so don't let them seed.

Dorycnium hirsutum Wide spreading but only about 6 inches high. The leaves are feltlike and elegant.

Draba olympica and *D. repens* Both are easy and rewarding. Gather seeds when viable and pat around immediately. They will germinate easily and quickly. *D. olympica* makes a tufted mound between rocks and *D. repens* creeps around and about.

Edraianthus graminifolius So easy to propagate. Grows in crevices, a mound of thick, grassy blades with early summer violet blue flowers.

Eriogonum umbellatum 'Red Leaved' Even if it didn't have small clusters of yellow flowers, it should be in your garden because of the stunning red foliage all winter.

Fibigia clypeata grey-leaved money plant. A ruffled cluster of silvery grey leaves the first year. The second year it throws up many stems of small yellow flowers, each developing into a small silver dollar as it dries. Not grown for its flowers but for these minute decoratives. Best of all, it is perennial!

Genista tinctoria Known to herbalists, worthy of the alpine garden. A shrub type, 12 to 14 inches high, that is clothed in brilliant yellow blooms during the month of June.

Gentiana andrewsii, *G. lagodechiana*, and *G. septemfida* Many gentians have been tried. These three are successful.

Geranium dalmaticum and *G. sanguineum* var. *prostratum* The first, a year-round beauty with its mounded shape, fragrant leaves, large pink flowers, and crimson fall foliage. The second, a long summer bloomer, semicreeping. Neither are aggressive. You'll want more of them.

Helianthemum spp. Many varieties grow in my gardens. All propagate easily from freshly sown seeds. They do not like wind, so give them protection between large rocks or with an eastern location.

Helichrysum argyrophyllum 'Moes Gold' Such a stunning addition with its small, silver-satiny leaves and stray-flowerlike yellow blossoms; it propagates easily from seed—necessary because it doesn't survive our winters.

Herniaria glabra A small, bright green beaded creeper that is evergreen all winter. Little pieces break off all the time; plant them, and they will root and grow.

Hieracium lanatum Don't let this scare you—two varieties can be welcomed. Both have silver leaves. One creeps around between stones; the other is a larger-leaved rosette. Both types have yellow flowers and are easy to control with deheading.

Hypoxis hirsuta yellow-eyed grass. It blooms all summer long and is so compatible with allium. There is more information about this in chapter 4, where I discuss grasses.

Imperata cylindrica rubra 'Red Baron' japanese bloodgrass. An exotic that is so worthy of our attention. Nonaggressive; grow in a sunny, well- drained, dry location. Especially effective in a desert garden. Doesn't winterize unless planted by the house foundation.

Iris cristata caerulea and *alba* The white is more difficult and harder to transplant, heaving in early spring, so check it often.

Linum capitatum flax. An opulent yellow long bloomer with clumpy greenish blue leaves that make the plant interesting when not in flower.

Orostachys spinosa A cactuslike alpine that grows in a mix of sand and gravel. Must be well drained. It seldom flowers in our zone but has great charisma nonetheless.

Penstemon spp. *P. aridus, P. davidsonii, P. grandiflorus, P. hirsutus, P. hirsutus* 'Pygmaleus' (a wine red clump of low curly leaves all winter), *P. pinifolius*, and *P. virens* are all desirable. Most have glorious foliage and propagate easily.

Phlox spp. Like the penstemons, another large family. Books are written solely about them. My favorites are *P.* 'Arroyo' and *P.* 'Tangelo', *P.* 'Ronsdorf Beauty', *P.* 'Schneewittchen', *P. bifida* 'Betty Blake', and *P. divaricata* 'Chattahoochee.' All have enduring characteristics and are creepers that don't die out in the middle like *Phlox subulata*. They are not long-lived but propagate easily from cuttings, and they self- seed.

Ranunculus fascicularis buttercup. Do not be misled if people tell you this is weedy. It is a dear, with porcelainlike yellow blossoms early, then dying back during the heat, returning in the fall and staying evergreen all winter.

Rosularia pallida   A velvety cushionlike rosette that forms into a large mound. Easy to grow, with fascinating traits and appearance. The rosettes do not die back after blooming.

Sempervivum spp.   A genus that is becoming very difficult to identify. They crossbreed and are not true. Buy what you like. Most accept terrible conditions as long as they are in full sun.

Solidago spathulata   A goldenrod, and this one is not obnoxious. There is another comely goldenrod: *Solidago* 'Laurin'. Just 16 inches tall, with a long, August-through-October flowering time. Neither of these has ever suckered in my gardens.

Thalaspi spp.   Some are white, others pink. Both have a burgundy foliage during the winter. The drabas and thalaspis bloom at the same time in late March and are tough little gems. Watch out for the busybody white thalaspi.

Thymus serpyllum 'Necefferi'   Everyone that sees this thyme wants it. There are other cultivars that are equally delightful, among them *T. s.* 'Aureus', 'Albus', 'Lanuginosus', 'Coccineus', and 'Minus'.

Viola pedata and *V. pedata* 'Bicolor'   birdsfoot violet. Violas you'll want more of, especially the 'Bicolor'. It's truly lovely and produces few progeny, another worthy attraction. *V. nuttallii* has a profusion of yellow flowers that delights everyone all season.

Naturally mistakes have been made. I discovered that alpines that are not aggressive in Denver, Colorado, love Wind 'n' View! The dracocephalums reseeded everywhere and I've gotten rid of them. Such a shame; their fragrance was so refreshing. Beware of *Aethionema cordifolium*, often called *Iberis jucunda*—a sprawly, weedy thing. Others that have to be watched: *Viola bertolonia* and *Limonium bellidifolium*. Still others grew too large for my under-10-inches-high limit, so *Thymus mastichina* and *Scutellaria baicalensis* have been transplanted to a shrub berm; they are both appealing additions.

Erinus alpinus has not thrived for me, but friends in the area have been successful with it. Most of the dianthus have been disappointing, especially the deltoides and pinks. They are heavy reseeders and should be propagated by cuttings, not seeds.

Nevertheless, this world of alpine plants is stimulating. I need to know more about it.

Dwarf Conifers for an Alpine Setting

Plantings in this alpine berm include many hardy dwarf conifers.

These are carefree because they are slow growing: you will not be trying to do something about them twenty or thirty years from now. Dwarf conifers create a forever landscape, lending a magical quality that is enduring. Even on a very small lot they encourage visions of space. If you make a mistake, it is easily rectified. Dwarf conifers are transplantable, and unlike their gigantic relatives, they need no pruning.

More and more nurseries know what you are talking about if you ask for dwarfs these days. Gardeners are beginning to accept the fact that very few city lots have space for the full-sized, 100-foot evergreens. Dwarfs in fifty or sixty years reach 10 to 20 feet. Some are prostrate, others weeping; many grow in narrow columns, and still others are rounded. They come in all shades of greens, gold, blue, rust, and steel; there are even variegated varieties. These dwarfs can contend with a wide range of growing conditions. Most accept drought once they're established. All like a well-drained situation, so they thrive in raised beds. You can forget about fertilizer, and best of all, you can plant them as soon as the ground thaws in the spring up until it freezes in the fall. Try to buy three-to four-year-olds; larger ones will be very expensive. There are over fifteen humdred types on the market today, but many are not hardy in the Midwest. The ones I suggest in the following list will give you great satisfaction—you can have faith in their survival.

Abies balsamea 'Nana'   balsam fir. Has startling bright green new growth in the spring. Reaches a maximum of 3 feet in ten years.

Chamaecyparis nootkanensis 'Aurea'   Similar to *C. pisifera* 'Filifera Aurea Nana' but the foliage is not as threadlike. This is especially effective draped over stone walls.

Chamaecyparis pisifera 'Filifera Aurea Nana'   A spreading semiweeper. *Aurea*, of course, means "golden," and this stays golden all winter. Perfect in a winter garden between medium-sized stones.

Juniperus communis 'Compressa'   This is a must; the foliage does turn a rusty blue in the winter, but it recovers well in the spring. It has a columnar habit that looks best in groupings.

Juniperus procumbens 'Nana'   A prostrate that doesn't grow as fast as the carpet types. Very easily pruned, with nice green color all winter.

Larix decidua 'Pendula'   A creepy crawler that should be planted so it will grow over and down a medium-sized rock. This layers fairly easily for propagation and can be pruned.

Picea abies 'Gregoryana Parsonii'   A knobby, upright slow grower that's very hardy.

Picea abies 'Nidiformis'   birdsnest spruce. This picea is a spreader, growing about an inch a year. It keeps a pleasant green color all winter. Nip the new growth to control the size after three years of age—keep nipping each year.

Picea glauca 'Conica'   dwarf alberta spruce. This needs protection from winds. It needs no pruning, maintaining its dense conical shape by itself.

Picea pungens 'Glauca globosa'   This has captivated me with its blue foilage.

Pinus aristata   bristlecone pine. Lives to be thousands of years old. A very slow grower with silvery pitch-tipped needles. Plant by steps.

Pinus cembra blue swiss stone pine. A very slow grower with a tightly clumped and bunching habit. It looks well by steps and is very effective with outdoor lighting.

Tsuga canadensis 'Coles Prostrate' So slow growing, you will need a magnifying glass to see the difference each year.

Tsuga canadensis 'Curly' Also very desirable—a more upright variety.

Tsuga canadensis 'Pendula' sargent's weeping hemlock. You will need to prune and train it to keep it from becoming too prostrate.

These dwarf conifers all provide continuity and a sense of stability in a garden. In my "woven tapestry" foliage garden, they form the foreground structure for *Crambe cordifolia* (sea kale), *Euonymus alatus* 'Compactus' (burning bush), *E. fortunei* 'Variegated', *Betula pendula* 'Trost's Dwarf' (birch), *Berberis thunbergii* 'Rose Glow' (barberry), *Calamagrostis* (a grass), *Miscanthus sinensis* 'Gracilimus', and several varieties of *Astilbe*. Interwoven among the dwarf conifers, these perennials will give a tapestry effect in the years to come.

Miniature Roses—Small Miracles

Not only dwarf conifers have found a permanent home at Wind 'n' View. Miniature roses, thorns or no thorns, are also included in the alpine garden. One in particular, 'Magic Splendor' from MB Farms, is totally captivating. It is a tiny shrub, green-touched with dark red leaves, blooming a little later than most others. The deep red, velvety clusters of flowers hold as buds for ages, and even when they begin to open they hold a tight shape and do not shatter. (Many of the other miniature blossoms start to shatter the day after the buds open.) 'Magic Splendor' more than lives up to expectations. I don't spray my miniatures, and none has developed any problems. So carefree, blooming prettily till hard frost. Their little buds can be dried in silica and added to potpourri mixes. Sorry, but they don't survive minus temperatures and must be lifted if you want them to winter over.

Early Shrubs, Late Perennials

The upper berm, constructed to the east of the alpine berm, has a distinct new format as well. Early blooming shrubs (*Azalea* 'Northern Lights', *Calluna vulgaris* (heather), *Cornus mas* (cornelian cherry), *Deutzia gracilis*, *Microbiota decussata*, and *Potentilla fruticosa* (cinquefoil) have been interplanted with late-blooming tall perennials: *Artemisia lactiflora*, *Gaura lindheimera*, *Helenium autumnale*, *Kniphofia* 'Little Maid' (poker plant), *Lysimachia clethroides* (loosestrife), and *Salvia azurea* var. *grandiflora*. These rare combinations intrigue me with their balanced early performance followed by another act in the fall.

A Protected Courtyard

Enclosed by the alpine and shrub-and-perennial berms, and set down at ground level, is a large, protected courtyard where my southern aristocrats grow. Sheltered by the berms and by windbreaks to the west, in full sun most of the day, and made extra-resilient by being grown from seed, these beauties are thriving as much as two zones below their usual range. I prize this garden for its color, fragrance, and—I admit it—novelty in the upper Midwest.

Sanctuary

With the pace of years quickening, a concern for easy maintenance is increasingly on my mind. The sanctuary, my latest garden, has been planned and planted with low maintenance as a priority. I will still have to prevent the encroachment of trees and shrubs, the smothering of spring bulbs under heavy accumulations of fallen leaves, and, of course, weeds. I do anticipate less care, especially when this garden becomes well established.

Next to low maintenance and easy control, fall color was what I was after as I planned the sanctuary. The bright leaves on trees and shrubs, the hips on roses, fruits that garnish shrubs and evergreens, late-flowering perennials and fall-blooming bulbs—all these enhance and prolong the sanctuary's season, and my pleasure in it. There are wildlife and bird sanctuaries; mine is a people-pleasing sanctuary. As the trees grow and provide shade, cool breezes will provide relief from summer heat. We can find refuge there.

Poets compose, actors and musicians perform, artists paint, and gardeners grow. Paintings, plays, and musical compositions remain unchanged across the centuries, but a garden fluctuates constantly. We are its keepers, observing and controlling its change. The painter does not achieve a masterpiece at the first sitting, nor do gardeners ever cease in their attempts to create a "perfect" garden. Our artistry cannot be timeless and we accept this fact. Nature sculpts and paints, its spectrum changing continually. Nature is ageless, a keeper, too, of civilizations.

My new sanctuary is 60 feet by 400 feet, on the westernmost portion of my property. To create it, this sloping west bank was graded into three giant steps, with scalloped rather than straight edges built from fieldstone. Once again the stonework is providing a holding bank, lessening the force of water rushing down the hillside during storms and thaw runoff.

Along the western edge, above the windbreak, trees are staggered, and they will eventually provide light shade. Each tree and shrub was planted in order to take advantage of the cast of its shadow. The chiaroscuro of light and shadow must be considered in the largest and even in the smallest of gardens; shady situations do not all have the same degree of light. Light angles are controlled and filtered by the height of the sun at a given time of day. The northern exposure may not receive any direct sunlight, yet that north light can be very bright.

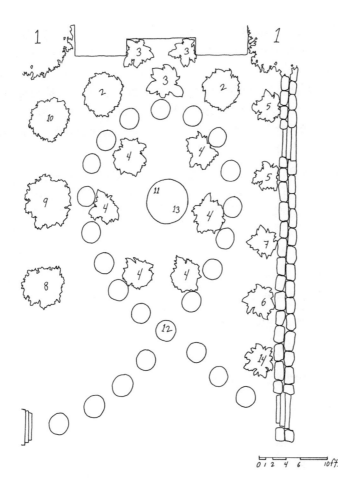

16. Plan for a Protected Courtyard

Plants for a Protected Courtyard

1. *Acer palmatum* 'Atropurpureum' red maple
2. *Paeonia suffruticosa* tree peony
3. *Juniperus scopulorum* 'Skyrocket' juniper
4. *Thymus serpyllum* 'Citriodorus'
5. *Chamaecyparis obtusa* 'Nana Gracilis' false cypress
6. *Cytisus scoparius* common broom
7. *Chaenomeles speciosa* 'Cydonia' flowering quince
8. *Cornus mas* cornelian cherry
9. *Deutzia gracilis*
10. *Larix* x *pendula* weeping larch
11. sundial and cranes
12. rounds of embossed concrete
13. *Daphne* x *burkwoodii* 'Carol Mackie'

A serpentine path weaves through from south to north, with subpaths branching off east and west to grass terraces. The central path leads to the new alpine garden, then to the house. Each side of this wandering path is divided into "rooms," twenty in all, individually color coded, and including trees, shrubs, bulbs, shady areas, desert, and prairie spots. Every growing thing that went into the sanctuary was thoroughly researched. I investigated every need and asked myself whether I wanted to meet that need in my garden. The only plants in my sanctuary are those for which I answered Yes.

The sanctuary contains exotics like *Polygonatum odoratum* (japanese solomon's seal), hostas, astilbes, and rare ferns; natives like *Stylophorum diphyllum* (celandine poppy), hepatica, and anemones. The following perennials have been planted in its scalloped rooms:

Allium   onion, garlic, etc.

Agastache cana

Anemone x *hybrida*   japanese anemone

Aruncus aethusifolius   dwarf goatsbeard

Belamcanda chinensis   blackberry lily

Ceratostigma plumbaginoides   plumbago

Chrysogonum virginianum   gold star

Hemerocallis   daylily

Heuchera purpurea 'Palace Purple'

Ligularia senecio   golden spire

Lycoris squamigera   magic lily

Mentha requienii   corsican mint

Miscanthus sinensis 'Gracilimus'   maidengrass

Oreganum pulchellum   oregano

Primula   primrose

Pyrethrum   painted daisy

Santolina chamaecyparissus   lavender cotton

Teucrium   germander

Many of these are short-lived herbs that will die out as the shade increases. Others will flourish with additional shade.

Spring Show with Species Bulbs

The sanctuary will awaken in spring with a crescendo of thousands of species bulbs cycling into bloom over a period of weeks. They will provide color and interest in the sanctuary before trees and shrubs come into leaf.

Species bulbs are the smaller, earlier-blooming, nonhybridized bulbs. Many of these are being imported. Worldwide harvesting is taking place to satisfy gardeners' longing for these little treasures from other lands. We need to learn their needs so they will reproduce for us and not be wiped out, as the prairies were in this country.

Species bulbs can reproduce themselves if we give them the proper conditions. We cannot modify the climate, so we modify the soil. These bulbs need a healthy root system, so add a lot of coarse sand and organic material (humus/leaf mold) to their soil, avoiding limestone. Many are native to the Mediterranean and will grow handsomely in the Midwest if we give them a bed of fast-draining soil. Put sand and gravel in the bottom of your holes, then mix in a bulb fertilizer and add the bulb. For years I used bone meal. Lately its value is being questioned, and a special bulb fertilizer may be preferable.

Remember to plant bulbs together or with other plants that have the same preferences. Most species bulbs require a summer dry period, so don't plant them where you're going to be doing a lot of watering or where it's sandy. Species bulbs like warmth.

For our climate, plant these bulbs in late fall, being sure to buy top grades from reliable dealers. If these bulbs have been stored improperly, you can't expect good results.

Eranthis hiemalis (winter aconite) and *Anemone blanda* (windflower) seldom produce for me. They've been stored improperly after being dug during their spring bloom; when our garden centers get them in the fall, they are just dumped into cardboard bins, drying out even more. The sooner you buy and plant them in the fall, the better chance you will have of getting them to grow.

Soak these tubers overnight in pure warm water in a thermos. Plant according to their instructions and lightly water till the ground freezes. Don't plant them underneath trees or shrubs with suckering or spreading root systems, that is, maples, plums, or cherries. The tree roots will quickly destroy your bulbs by absorbing all their nourishment. If you plant under ideal trees, make sure you are using bulbs that bloom before the trees leaf out. A general rule: plant a 2-inch-around bulb about 7 inches deep. It is better to be on the deep side than on the shallow. If you planted too shallow, the bulb will only bloom one time.

More points to remember when planting species bulbs: they need lots of sun, deeper planting in relation to other small bulbs, late planting—November is suggested—lots of elbow room, and no neighbors throwing shade. Use only the lowest of cover plants, if any. Don't be disappointed if they don't give a big performance the first spring. The second year will be worth waiting for.

You can try to coordinate blooming times of these bulbs by keeping records of what blooms when from the first season, then transplanting. However, our ambiguous weather seems to make coordinated blooming nigh onto impossible. If it doesn't rain or snow when these bulbs are growing in the spring, water. This is the time they need it. Once the blossoms die, fertilize and water well. You need healthy leaves to produce food for the bulb so it will bloom next year. Don't cut off the leaves till they yellow. (One of the attributes of the species bulbs: it doesn't take long for them to die back.) If you want these to naturalize, leave one seed pod but cut the rest off.

Don't do any raking in the early spring. You could rake the buds off.

If you have become as excited about these "wild" or species bulbs as I have, consider constructing a raised bed with a southern exposure, preferably under the house eaves where little rain will reach it so that the bed will stay dry during the summer months (no watering is required).

Bulbs need to complete their life cycle. They get smaller and smaller each year if you let them propagate. Multiplying is easier to achieve if you lift the bulb. Do this in the fall before the ground freezes. Break off the smaller ones that stud the main bulb and reset them all, giving each of them the same treatment—a well-drained soil with fertilizer mixed in. Never set a bulb right on top of fertilizer. Always combine the fertilizer with sand and gravel and put in the bottom of the hole 2 to 3 inches thick, then set in the bulb.

Once tried, the small wild species bulbs will soon win you over. The stoloniferous varieties of wild tulips include *Tulipa tarda*, *T. urumiensis*, and *T. kolpakowskiana*. These are reliable reproducers with a long life span. The hybrid *T. fosterana* tulip will also naturalize.

Liliums are very easy and quick to grow from seed. Start the seed on a wet blotter or heavy paper towel. Once germinated, transplant where you want them to grow. Keep moist until they die back. Often these will bloom the next year. Scilla, galanthus, puschkinia, chionodoxa, and *Hyacinthus amethystinus* are self-seeding reproducers.

My favorite groupings include *Crocus ancyrensis* in front of arborvitae or columnar junipers, blooms about March 19; alliums with *Arrhenatherum elatius* var. *bulbosum* 'Variegatum' (bulbous oat grass); chionodoxa, puschkinia, *Scilla hispanica*, and wood hyacinth with *Magnolia stellata*—if you are lucky, they will all bloom together, depending on that old man winter—; chionodoxa, *Tulipa kaufmanniana*, *T. pulchella* 'Violacea', and *T. praestans* planted in clusters; *Iris reticulata* and *Galanthus* with *Festuca ovina* var. *glauca* (blue fescue), along with *Tulipa pulchella* 'Violacea'.

You can scatter scilla around by the paths or under azalea and forsythia.

Forget about *Muscari* (grape hyacinth) and *Ornithogalum* (star of bethlehem). Both of these will take over. I went from twelve bulbs of star of bethlehem to a bed 4 feet square in six years. The *Muscari* seed blows all over, and soon you have little blades of it everyplace.

Be sure to plant *Tulipa batalinii* and *T. kaufmanniana* (water lily tulip) separately, in large groupings.

Fritillaria tolerates shade and is striking with *Uvularia*.

Eranthis (winter aconite) is difficult; plant it in rich composted light soil and mulch with leaves. Try to get a friend to share this with you in late spring for successful transplanting, or try the soaking suggested above.

Oxalis adenophylla has been hardy for years in my gardens. The flowers and foliage are outstanding.

Don't neglect the fall bloomers: *Crocus kotschyanus*, *C. sativus* (saffron; this is hardy), and *C. speciosus*. You will need many of these in drifts to be effective; one here and there is lost. Even *Colchicum* will grow and bloom in the fall if you find the right spot for it. *Iris pumila*, a dwarf, is doubly rewarding, blooming in both spring and fall, and the pink fall hyacinth is a must.

We can also grow hardy *Cyclamen hederifolium* in Zones 3 and 4. The trick is to find fresh tubers. The dealers are not dependable. Mine came from the American Rock Garden Society's plant sale. Do not plant these deep; the eye must be just under the soil level. Use rich, composted, viable soil.

You should know that bulbs, which are onionlike, have a compressed stem and roots (includes tulips, daffodils, and some lilies). Corms are basically thickened stems. Crocus, gladioli, and some of the irises are corms. Tubers are similar to potatoes, and include winter aconites, anemones, and cyclamens. Rhizomes are thickened underground stems. Bearded irises and caladiums are two examples.

The "ordinary" hybrid bulbs that we are most familiar with, like tulips, hyacinths, and daffodils, are planted deeper than the species bulbs, bloom later, and take longer to disappear. They need the same kind of well-drained site if you want them to live for years. Plant these in late September and October. They need six weeks before freezing and after planting to establish a root system. Don't cut the leaves off until they are yellow. Be sure to fertilize (as soon as the petals fall, cutting off the seed pods), forking or hoeing the fertilizer in.

Other genera of bulbs, most of these native to our country, are *Arisaema*, *Erythronium*, *Trillium*, and *Asarum*. These require rich, moist, shady places, under trees and shrubs in filtered high light. *Asarum* and hepaticas tolerate dry shade.

Two winters ago we lost three 23-year-old gorgeous weeping birches. Being told they had lived their natural life span wasn't any consolation. They left a bare spot roughly 25 by 35 feet that proved irresistible. We had just visited friends' gardens in Lake Mills who had a large, naturalized area of scillas. Thousands of them, truly an astonishing sight.

Our area was much smaller, but it seemed a perfect place to transplant our aggressively reseeding grape hyacinth and star of bethlehem. They could have a good time carpeting it. This naturalized bed is on the east side of the first driveway. After digging deep holes, putting in gravel, then torpedo sand, adding and mixing in fertilizer, the bulbs were planted at the proper depth. Daffodils were also included, along with alliums. This area is not watered during the summer so there should be maximum cover soon. It will never need mowing, spraying, or the care that lawns and roses require. Naturalizing saves resources; it is cheaper and certainly less work than more formal gardening.

The two bulb rooms in the sanctuary were established in roughly the same manner, using a selection of species tulips along with many types of *Lilium*, many of these from seed.

If you intend to pursue naturalizing, you must have nerves of steel to face criticism for bare places that have not yet filled in, or, if you are recreating prairie, to tolerate the wait for the first mowing, after growth is 9 to 10 inches tall. Still, this is a satisfying way of gardening. The intent is to establish a self-sufficient area that is loosely informal, appearing to be undesigned. The garden is not imposed on the land—and it is the lowest-maintenance garden possible.

The sanctuary, like almost all the gardens described in this chapter, was constructed by hand without heavy machinery. This is easier on the land and on your pocketbook. You eliminate the land being torn up and the extra expense by building your rock gardens yourself.

7

Fruit and Vegetable Gardening and Cookery

FRUIT and vegetable gardening is a way of life at Wind 'n' View. For years, my family and I have eaten what we grow, harvesting, canning, freezing, and drying our own produce.

In this, we are not alone. I imagine there are more vegetable gardens per capita in the Midwest than anywhere else in the country. But more city and suburban gardeners should try raising at least some of their own food. Eating truly fresh fruits and vegetables is healthy, cheap, and indescribably delicious. Less than a century ago our parents and grandparents ate hundreds of different plant foods. Today over 80 percent of all our food comes from fewer than a dozen plants. Fifty percent of "fresh" produce sold in our supermarkets from December to April is imported, most of it from Mexico. Mexico's pesticide spraying rates are the highest in the world. A single crop may be sprayed twenty-five to fifty times a season. Scary, isn't it?

Your own frozen food is more nutritious than grocery store "fresh." The quicker a fruit or vegetable is frozen, the more food value it retains. Often supermarket produce has been picked prematurely and has spent five days in a truck before you even buy it. Pick your own, eat or freeze at once—that's what fresh means.

My husband, Bill, used to vegetable-garden with the same intensity that I flower-garden. At one time we had two full acres in vegetables! That's a lot of vegetables for just two people. He rotated crops and companion-planted, mixing herbs and annual flowers in with the food crop. Together we trial-tested fourteen varieties of tomatoes, plus melons and miniature vegetables. As soon as a crop was through producing, it was tilled under as green manure.

We were really too successful with our vegetable gardens. The care, harvesting, canning, and freezing became overwhelming. No matter how much we gave away, there was always a surplus. We couldn't stand to see it go to waste after all our efforts. I had become keener and keener about the ornamental gardens and didn't want to devote as much time to the produce beds. It was time for a change, and we never did anything halfway.

We decided to sell our original home and build a new one where the vegetables had been. This reduced our produce beds to a realistic size and gave me the opportunity to invent some wonderful new gardens. One of these is a food garden that I will never sacrifice: an ornamental garden of perennial food-bearing plants.

An Ornamental Perennial Food Garden

As usual, this idea had been simmering in my mind, just waiting for its moment. I liked the thought of having a food garden go to bed for the winter and then waken in the spring. No waiting for the soil to dry off so we could cultivate, or having the seeds fail because it was too cold or wet. It was an idea I had to explore—and you can take advantage of it. My ornamental perennial food garden has proven itself. My trials will be your triumphs.

My everbearing garden is 40 by 70 feet, butting up against the south end of our asparagus bed. The asparagus fern, or foliage, provides a natural-looking divider between the rock garden and the ornamental food bed. If you have a permanently situated vegetable garden already, by all means plan your perpetual garden with that as an anchor. Wherever you locate your garden, be sure it will receive full sun.

We were fortunate in that the land for this garden had been cleared and only needed a minimal amount of preparation. I hope you have the same conditions. If you are starting from scratch and converting grass or a lawn, may I suggest the black plastic and carpet treatment detailed in chapter 2. Let the soil lie fallow over the winter, and then prepare your soil carefully. Take time to give it the proper treatment. Remember, this garden will not be changed for many seasons, if ever. Mix lots of spoiled hay into the soil. If you can't get that, use marsh hay, or clean, weed-free, untreated grass clippings. Spread evenly 3 to 4 inches thick, sprinkle with 10-10-10 fertilizer (10 pounds per 100 square feet), wet it down, and anchor this with chicken wire. This will decompose in a hurry. Then till it into the soil. You will be providing lots of necessary organic matter. After deciding on a size and shape and preparing the soil, plant—but don't overplant. Hold yourself in check with tight reins. Draw up a map! It is easier to move a pencil line on paper than it is to dig up a shrub or move a plant. Plan well. Nursery stock is so small when it's new, we forget how fast it's going to grow. And this garden will not be replanted. Once it is established, you will be able to harvest greens and other vegetables very early in the spring, and fruit all season.

When your design is finished and your soil prepared, the excitement really begins. What to plant? Consider your favorites first; then try some things you have never grown. Whatever you decide, when you're ready to plant, remember to dig big holes for your fruit bushes and trees, and put a scoop of fertilizing mix in the bottom of each (see chapter 5).

Plantings and Recipes for an Ornamental Perennial Food Garden

Here is a description of each plant in my Ornamental Perennial Food Garden, with a recipe or two to guide you when your crop is ready to be picked. Because people—even experts—generally refer to food plants by their common names, listings are alphabetical by common name throughout most of this chapter. None of my plantings has ever been sprayed.

Asparagus *Asparagus officinalis*

This highly prized vegetable needs a well-drained location in full sun. A member of the lily family, asparagus has been cultivated for at least two thousand years and even grows wild. Once planted, either from seeds or from roots, it will be ready to harvest in the third spring.

Creating an Asparagus Bed

If you are going to plant seed, dig a rectangular trench 4 feet wide, 12 feet long, and 1 foot deep. If you want to set roots, dig the trench 15 inches deep. Bank the soil you dig up on either side of the trench. Into the trench put 3 inches of good mulch—leaves, untreated grass clippings, or peat moss—and mix up with some soil and 1 cup of slow-release fertilizer. Or you can use 3 inches of aged compost. Then add 2 more inches of your banked, reserved soil.

Sprinkle your seeds over the surface and rake lightly into the soil. If you are using roots, bury them about 3 inches below the surface. Then tread on the soil to pack it down and water it well. Leave all the remaining banked soil, covering it well with heavy black plastic.

When your seedlings are 3 inches high, sprinkle on another inch of your reserved soil and 1 cup fertilizer. Repeat this procedure all summer, every time you see that the fern is 3 inches higher. Start again the next spring with the first 3 inches of new growth, and continue until you've used up all your reserved soil. A very good root system will develop with this method. By late spring of the second year you can go through this trench with a rototiller, blades set high. Hand-weeding an asparagus bed is agonizing; rototilling will help to keep the weeds down. By the third spring, you should have harvestable spears. After this, till the bed gently and dress with rotted manure each spring as soon as the soil is workable. Pray for warm rains in May. This bed should produce for at least fifteen years.

As for harvesting, some people like the smaller stems, but it's bad for the roots to keep picking these. Ideally the stalks should be the size of a woman's middle finger or bigger when they are harvested. I snap off the stalks by hand—what doesn't snap will be too woody to eat. Start at ground level and work up the stem until it snaps.

I add more asparagus rows every three years; I don't want to run out in my lifetime. We never have enough.

If you finally get enough planted to satisfy your springtime longings, you might want to try for a fall harvest. Divide your bed in half. Cut from one half until mid-June. Let the other half grow to ferns. Cut off the ferns in August and rake in 1 cup of bone meal. Wet well. If it gets dry, you'll have to keep watering. Stalks will soon appear and you can cut these until cold weather sets in.

You might hear that an application of salt will keep the weeds down. Don't fall for this; it ruins the soil. Handweeding and mulching are the only effective control and it's much easier to weed baby weeds than established ones. Keep after them!

Cooking and Serving Asparagus

We wait so impatiently for asparagus to "pop" in the late spring! The best way of all to serve it: hot, dressed with salt, freshly ground pepper, and browned butter. After a couple of meals of this, sprinkle the cooked asparagus with freshly grated parmesan cheese. In a couple of weeks, serve the hot asparagus with a thick sauce made by mashing 2 peeled, hard- boiled eggs and creaming them into 1 stick of softened butter. Add 1 tablespoon fresh lemon juice and a few dashes of freshly grated nutmeg.

Then try all my favorite recipes, below.

Do you want to impress people? Serve just the raw, 2-inch tips with a tomatillo dip or curried cream cheese. Save the stems for soup.

We usually have asparagus and spinach ready at the same time. Both are abused with poor cooking techniques. Asparagus should be cooked in a single layer with water to cover, or else steamed. I cut my stalks in two and cook the lower parts 2 minutes before adding the uppers. The asparagus should be tender-crisp. Test it. (I do not add salt to any vegetable until after it's cooked.)

I blanch spinach in a large pot in lots of boiling water for one minute—uncovered. Add cold water to stop the cooking. Drain and squeeze gently. Prepare any way you like. I like to brown 2 tablespoons of butter, add the spinach and 1/8 teaspoon grated fresh nutmeg, and reheat gently.

Asparagus and Spinach Soup

Serves 4

1 cup onion, minced

4 tablespoons butter

½ cup fresh spinach, cooked as above and chopped

2 cups fresh asparagus, cut into 2-inch pieces and cooked as above

3 cups chicken or turkey stock

⅛ teaspoon grated nutmeg

½ teaspoon dijon mustard

1 tablespoon lemon verbena leaves, minced, *or*

1 tablespoon lemon juice

½ cup heavy cream

Salt and pepper to taste

In a heavy-bottomed Dutch oven, sauté minced onion in butter until golden. Add spinach, asparagus, and stock and cook 10 minutes. Cool. Process roughly in a food processor and return to pan. Add seasonings and heavy cream. Reheat—don't let it boil!

Scalloped Asparagus

Serves 6

1 cup white sauce

2 cups fresh asparagus, cooked as above, cooking water reserved

½ teaspoon worcestershire sauce

½ cup mild cheddar cheese, grated

3 hard-boiled eggs, sliced

1 cup salmon, flaked, skinned, and boned (canned is fine)

Thin white sauce with ½ cup cooking water from asparagus and the worcestershire sauce. Stir in the grated cheese. Spoon a little sauce into a buttered baking dish, and arrange in alternate layers the eggs, asparagus, and salmon. Top with the rest of the sauce. Bake 20 to 30 minutes at 350°F, until very bubbly.

Fake Hollandaise

Makes about 1 1/2 cups. Surefire easy, this keeps in the refrigerator 2 to 3 weeks.

> 1 cup mayonnaise
>
> 2 eggs
>
> 3 tablespoons fresh lemon or orange juice
>
> 1 teaspoon lemon or orange rind, grated
>
> 1/2 teaspoon salt
>
> 1 teaspoon dijon mustard
>
> optional: 1/2 cup dairy sour cream
>
> 1/2 teaspoon paprika

In a small saucepan on medium heat, whisk all ingredients until smooth. Do not boil. Serve hot or cold with fresh asparagus, or prepare the following variations:

1. Roll each spear of cooked asparagus in a thin slice of ham. Place in buttered baking dish and pour 1/2 cup white wine over. Heat in oven at 350°F; then spread with Fake Hollandaise and reheat just until hot. Serve as is or on a toasted English muffin for brunch.

2. Lay cooked asparagus in a buttered baking dish, spoon sauce over, and top with cooked bacon and peeled fresh tomato slices. Lay American cheese slices over all. Bake at 350°F until cheese is melted and vegetables are hot. Serve over cooked rice.

3. Add cut-up cooked asparagus to hot salsa and serve over an omelette.

4. Chop a couple of peeled hard-boiled eggs into the hot sauce and pour over freshly cooked asparagus spears.

Asparagus Mainlines

Serves 6

> 12 spears asparagus, cooked as above
>
> 12 thin slices ham
>
> 2 1/2 cups fresh or frozen tomato pulp (from peeled, crushed fresh tomatoes)
>
> 2 cups swiss cheese, grated
>
> 2 tablespoons flour
>
> 1/2 cup fresh coriander, minced
>
> 1 cup heavy cream
>
> 6 slices french bread, cut 1/2 inch thick

Roll each asparagus spear in a slice of ham and lay in a buttered 9 by 13-inch Pyrex dish. Pour the tomato pulp over. Mix the flour with the grated cheese and sprinkle over the tomatoes. Then sprinkle on the coriander and pour the heavy cream gently over all. Bake till bubbly at 400°F. Toast the sliced bread and lay one slice in each of six shallow bowls. Ladle the hot sauce over the toast and pass the asparagus roll-ups separately.

Asparagus Vinaigrette

Serves 4

½ cup tarragon pesto (substitute tarragon for basil in any pesto recipe)

½ teaspoon dijon mustard

2 hard-boiled eggs, chopped

¼ cup dry white wine

20 stalks fresh asparagus, cooked as above and chilled

Fresh salad greens

Blend mustard, eggs, and white wine with tarragon pesto. Arrange the asparagus on a bed of fresh greens and pour the dressing over.

Asparagus Remoulade

Serves 6

1 cup mayonnaise

2 tablespoons dill pickles, chopped

1 tablespoon capers, chopped

1 tablespoon garden cress, minced

1 teaspoon dijon mustard

1 teaspoon tarragon vinegar

10 stalks fresh asparagus, cooked as above,
cut into 1-inch pieces, and chilled

In a small bowl combine all ingredients except asparagus and mix well. Gently fold in the asparagus. Serve on a bed of fresh lettuce or use to stuff fresh avocados or tomatoes.

Asparaguacamole

If you happen to overcook some asparagus (heaven forbid), make this delicious and low-calorie dip. It's great with fresh veggies or as a salad dressing.

3 cups asparagus, cooked and chopped

2 tablespoons onion, coarsely chopped

1 tablespoon spicy mustard

½ teaspoon chili powder

1 tablespoon garlic chives, coarsely chopped

Salt and cayenne pepper to taste

Whirl in food processor until it's a texture you like. Taste; if it isn't hot enough, add a little more cayenne.

Layered Asparagus Salad

Serves 6

2 cups asparagus, cooked as above, cut into 2-inch pieces, and chilled

4 fresh radishes, very thinly sliced

1 cup carrot, peeled and grated

Fresh salad greens

2 tablespoons rice vinegar or other mild vinegar

2 tablespoons horseradish mustard

6 tablespoons safflower oil

Salt and pepper to taste

In a deep glass bowl layer salad greens torn into bite-size pieces, then the asparagus, then the radishes, and last the carrot. Whisk the remaining ingredients together and drizzle over the vegetables. Toss just before serving.

Bayberry *Myrica pensylvanica*

Deciduous in the North, the waxy berries were once prized as the makings for fragrant, long-burning candles.

Beebalm *Monarda didyma*

Another native from the prairies. Its lemon scent enhances potpourri; the dried leaves make a fragrant tea. The leaves and flowers of the red variety can be chopped into salads. (2 feet)

Burdock *Arctium minus*

Burdock is a native of Eurasia, cultivated there for its root and tender stalk. If you grow it, don't let it go to seed. The seeds are encased in burrs. Since it is biennial, burdock needs to grow for one year before it is harvested. You'll need about six clumps of it. When two or three new leaves appear early in the second spring, dig up the root.

Burdock Strips

I burdock root, well scrubbed
Milk and water in equal parts
Cracker crumbs and parmesan cheese in equal parts
Butter
Salt and pepper

I use a vegetable peeler on the root, first peeling it and then paring it into long, thin strips. The root will darken if exposed to air, so I drop the strips into cold salted water as I peel. Combine the milk and water and simmer the strips in this until just tender. Drain and plunge into cold water to stop cooking. Drain again, and shake the strips in a paper or plastic bag containing the crumbs and cheese. Melt the butter in a heavy skillet and fry the strips on both sides. Serve hot with salt and pepper. This is good!

Bush cherry or sand cherry *Prunus besseyi*

This is a hardy shrub with silvery green foliage, growing to around 4 feet high, with white flowers in May. It suckers and reseeds aggressively and needs vigorous control. It sets purple-black, marble-sized fruit in great quantity. These make excellent pies and preserves, and the fruit freezes well. Cherry chutney is good too—substitute pitted cherries for the ground cherries in the chutney recipe later in this chapter.

Black Cherry Brandy

Makes 1 quart

2 pounds black cherries, pitted, pits reserved
I quart good brandy

Combine cherries with brandy. Nest several clear plastic bags inside each other and put the cherry pits in the innermost one. Twist-tie shut and crush the pits with a hammer. Add the crushed pits to the brandy mixture. Cover and let stand 4 to 6 weeks. Strain and pour the brandy into pretty bottles. Good over custard, ice cream, or as an after-dinner drink.

Frozen Pie Filling

I quart black cherries, pitted
2½ tablespoons flour
¼ teaspoon salt
½ cup sugar

Mix well together, pour into resealable plastic bags, and freeze. Of course, this can be used for jams and jellies as well as pie filling. Sliced apples can be frozen like this, too. These frozen cherries can be added with their juice to cooked rice for an easy dessert.

Cherry Cranberry Relish

Makes about 4 cups

1½ cups fresh or frozen cranberries
I orange
I lemon
2 cups dark brown sugar, packed
1½ cups raisins
I cup fresh or frozen black cherries, pitted
½ cup distilled white vinegar
½ teaspoon each of ground cinnamon, coriander, and nutmeg
½ cinnamon stick

Rinse cranberries. Quarter the orange and lemon, remove seeds, and cut into small pieces. Do not remove peels. In a large saucepan mix these fruits with the remaining ingredients.

Bring to a boil and simmer about 15 minutes. Remove the cinnamon stick. Cool and refrigerate. Will keep a month in refrigerator, or freeze in small containers. A welcome respite from cranberry sauce. A large tablespoonful can be placed in a canned or poached peach half and served hot or cold.

Cherries in Vinegar

Makes 3 quarts

2 cups red wine vinegar

2 cups sugar

4 cups pure warm water

4 pounds black cherries, washed and pitted

Have sterilized pint jars ready and sterilized lids and rings waiting in a boiling water bath. Heat the vinegar and sugar together in a large, heavy kettle (not aluminum) until sugar is dissolved. Continue to heat to a full, rolling boil and keep boiling until sugar begins to caramelize. Averting your face, very carefully add the warm water. Stir. Add the cherries and boil 30 seconds more. Pour into sterilized jars, seal, and process for 10 minutes.

Melon-Cherry Salad Bowl

Serves 4

Fresh garden greens

1 cup melon balls (any variety)

1 cup fresh black cherries, pitted

1/3 cup small-curd cottage cheese

1 cup mayonnaise

Line a large, shallow bowl with fresh garden greens. Arrange melon balls and cherries attractively over the greens. Blend or process the cottage cheese with the mayonnaise and serve on the side.

Molded Cherry Salad

Serves 4

1 small package cherry-flavored gelatin

1 cup boiling water

1 cup ice cubes

1 cup fresh apple, peeled and grated

1 cup fresh black cherries, pitted

Fresh salad greens

Dissolve the gelatin in the boiling water and add the ice cubes. Stir. Chill until barely thickened and add the apple and cherries. Pour into an oiled mold and chill until firm. Unmold on fresh salad greens. This salad needs no dressing.

Don't forget to eat all the cherries you can when they're ripe on the trees, and remember they are great stirred into muffin and pancake batter.

Currant *Ribes sativum*

My ornamental food garden wouldn't be complete without the currant. Maybe you have never thought about this old-fashioned fruit; it is time you did. If for no other reason, grow currants because they make a superb vinegar. This fruit can be mixed with blueberries, cherries, or raspberries for preserves and can take the place of cranberries in sauce. Fresh whole currants can be added to pancake and muffin batters and even to your favorite drop cookie recipe. To freeze whole currants, simply rinse, remove stems, place in plastic bags or containers and set in your freezer. Currants can also be dried. Follow the instructions for drying juneberries (*Amelanchier*), above.

Buffaloberries (the fruit of *Shepherdia argentea*) can be substituted for currants in all these recipes.

Currant Vinegar

Makes 5 pints

4 cups fresh currants, rinsed and drained
10½ cups distilled white vinegar
Honey to taste

Put the currants in a glass bowl with the vinegar. Cover and let stand overnight. Sterilize your bottles. Pour the berry mixture into a large, heavy kettle (not aluminum) and bring to a boil. Boil uncovered 3 minutes. Let the vinegar cool, and taste it. If it really bites, you might want to add some honey, tasting until the flavor pleases. Strain into your bottles; cap and label. Age two to four weeks in a cool, dark place. It will keep indefinitely if stored in a cool place away from light.

Currant Apple Jelly

Fills 24 1/2 pint jars

> 6 1/2 cups currant juice
>
> 7 cups apple juice
>
> 2 boxes fruit pectin
>
> 7 pounds sugar

Have your half-pint jars sterilized, their lids and rims standing in boiling water, and your paraffin melted before you begin.

Bring the juices to a full boil in a large, heavy kettle (not aluminum). Add the fruit pectin, stirring constantly. Add the sugar and bring back to a hard boil. Boil 2 minutes, remove from heat, skim quickly, and pour into waiting jars. Try a pork roast basted with this jelly.

If my apples start to spoil during the winter, I extract their juice and freeze it. Then when the currants are ready, I have lovely concentrated apple juice to make currant jelly with. If I'm in a time bind, I sometimes pick the currants, extract their juice, and freeze it as well. In the winter, I make the jelly when I have time for it. Having a steam-method juice extractor is a big help all year long.

When I make currant juice, I rinse the currants and put them into the extractor stems and all, taking care not to force any pulp into the juice. Pulp makes the juice bitter.

Cumberland Currant Sauce

Makes 1 pint

> 2 cups water
>
> Peel of 1 orange (no white part), minced
>
> Peel of 1 lemon (no white part), minced
>
> 1/2 cup currant jelly
>
> 1/4 cup tawny port
>
> 1/4 teaspoon each: dry mustard, ground ginger
>
> 1/8 teaspoon cayenne pepper

Bring the water to a boil and add the orange and lemon peel. Boil 3 minutes and strain through a fine strainer into a heavy kettle (not aluminum). Discard the pulp left in the strainer. Add remaining ingredients to the kettle and simmer uncovered until smooth, 3 to 5 minutes. Turn into a heat-proof jar and chill. Serve chilled with cold meats, chicken, and ham.

Currant Sherbet

Serves 4

1 ¼ cups sugar

½ cup water

4 cups fresh currants, rinsed

2 egg whites

¼ cup sugar

Combine the 1 ¼ cups sugar, water, and currants and bring to a boil. Boil until fruit is soft, press mixture through a strainer, and cool. Beat the egg whites with the ¼ cup sugar until nearly stiff. Fold in the currant puree and pour into a deep container. Cover and freeze about 4 hours, stirring at least twice.

Currant "Cranberry" Sauce

1 ½ cups sugar

2 cups water

4 cups fresh or frozen whole currants

Boil the sugar and water together for about 5 minutes. Add the currants and simmer 5 minutes longer. Cool and chill. A nice change from cranberry sauce, this relish is to be spooned rather than poured.

Fresh-Tasting Juice

I like to add ½ cup fresh or frozen currant or buffaloberry juice to a quart of apple, plum, or grape juice. These juices are often so flat tasting—the currant juice really adds piquancy. When extracting the juice, I lay a couple of sweet cicely leaves on top of the fruit.

Fresh Fruit in Brandy

Fills 4 pint jars

I cup dried currants or juneberries

I cup peach brandy

I ½ cups water

I cup sugar

I large fresh lemon

6 or 7 large fresh pears

I cup fresh tayberries or raspberries

Soak dried currants or juneberries in the brandy overnight. Strain, reserving the fruit and brandy separately.

Have 4 sterilized pint jars ready, their rims and lids waiting in a boiling water bath.

Bring sugar and water to boil in a heavy saucepan (not aluminum). Simmer 3 minutes and reserve in the same saucepan. With a vegetable peeler, remove four 2-inch strips of peel from the lemon and reserve. Squeeze the juice from the lemon into a large bowl of water. Pare the pears, cut in half, and remove the cores with the tip of a small, sharp spoon. Drop the pear halves into the lemon water as you work. When all are peeled, cut, and cored, drain them and pat them dry. Divide the pear halves, the tayberries or raspberries, and the drained currants or juneberries between 4 sterilized pint jars. Add a strip of lemon peel to each jar. Combine the reserved brandy with the sugar syrup and bring to a boil. Pour the hot syrup over the fruit, leaving ½ inch head space in each jar. Put on the lids and rims, adjust, and process in a boiling water bath for 25 minutes. This brandied fruit keeps well for a year.

Fireweed *Epilobium angustifolium*

Always flaring up after a forest fire in Zones 3 and 4, with very showy flowers. Truly an ornamental. The young spears are eaten like asparagus. The seed blows. It is a reseeder, so keep eating it and what you don't eat, dehead.

Ground-cherry *Physalis pruinosa*

This is an exquisite new plant, an improved form of the cape gooseberry. A hybrid, it is not perennial, but I find it so valuable that I grow it anyway. Its large golden yellow berries are encased in husks that must be shucked off before the fruit is eaten or cooked. Ground-cherries are delicious raw or in chutneys, pies, and jams. A close relative, *Physalis ixocarpa* (tomatillo), is great for salsas and other dips.

Ground-Cherry Preserves

Makes 3 pints

4 cups ground-cherries

2 tablespoons crystallized ginger, chopped

¼ cup fresh lemon juice

1 package fruit pectin

3 cups sugar

Have your half-pint jars sterilized and ready, your lids and rims waiting in a boiling water bath.

Crush the ground-cherries in a large saucepan (not aluminum). Add the ginger, lemon juice, and pectin; stir well. Bring to a boil and add the sugar, stirring constantly. Bring back to full boil and then remove from heat. Skim off froth, pour into waiting jars, and seal.

For a gourmet treat, baste roasting Cornish game hens with these preserves.

Ground-Cherry Chutney

Makes 8 pints

1 pound tart apples, peeled, cored, and chopped

½ cup chopped onions

2 cups ground-cherries, pitted but left whole

1 clove garlic, crushed

4 pounds vine peaches* or fresh mangoes, peeled, seeded, and chopped

⅔ cup crystallized ginger

2 tablespoons mustard seed, crushed

1 tablespoon chili powder

1 tablespoon canning salt

1 quart cider vinegar

1½ pounds brown sugar

Have your pint jars sterilized and ready, your tops and rims sterilized and waiting in a boiling water bath.

Combine all the ingredients in a large, heavy-bottomed kettle (not aluminum) and bring to a boil. Simmer about an hour, or until the chutney's thickness pleases you. Pour into hot jars and seal. No processing is necessary. This chutney will keep two to three years in a cool, dark place. (*Vine peaches are a much less expensive alternative to mangoes. They are a native American annual available as seed from Nichols garden nursery. See the section on melons later in this chapter for more information.)

Hawthorn *Crataegus*

Often used as a stock for grafting and for windbreaks. The flowers make a nice-tasting wine punch. (30 feet)

Hawthorn Punch

1 packed cup freshly picked hawthorn flowers
1 large orange, peeled
4 sprigs lemon grass, 4 inches each
½ bottle rosé wine
1 bottle rhine wine

Cut the stems from the flowers. Slice the orange into a bowl, add the flowers and lemon grass, and bruise together. Add the wines, cover with plastic wrap, and chill overnight. Strain onto ice block in punch bowl. Garnish with flowers.

Juneberry *Amelanchier canadensis*

A shrubby, small tree whose fruits taste better than blueberries—much sweeter. It's very hardy, thrives in any soil. This native has no pest problems and never needs spraying. It's beautiful, exploding into white bloom very early in the spring; you harvest the yummy berries in June. Nothing beats the foliage for fall color. All good—I can't think of a thing detrimental about it (except that the cedar waxwings and robins like the berries as much as I do).

The frozen, drained berries can be used in muffins, pancakes, and waffles and mixed with fresh fruit for fruit salads. Of course, they can also be defrosted and eaten with the syrup as a breakfast fruit.

Frozen Juneberries

Make a simple syrup of 1 cup sugar dissolved in 3 cups water and brought to a rolling boil. Let the syrup cool and pour over rinsed fruit that has been packed in 1-cup cartons. Freeze.

Juneberry "Raisins"

If you have enough harvest, the berries can be dried in a food drier and used like raisins. Spread clean berries evenly on the food drier trays and dry until they look shriveled and crisp. Store in clean, capped jars. Check every day for moisture—if you see any, put the berries back in the drier for another round. My grandchildren love these special treats.

Pickled Juneberries

Makes about 2 pints

2 cups juneberries

½ cup water

¼ cup distilled white vinegar

1 cup sugar

½ teaspoon crushed cinnamon from sticks

½ teaspoon whole allspice

½ teaspoon whole coriander or cloves

Tie spices together in a small cheesecloth bag. Combine the first four ingredients, add the spice baggie, and bring to a boil. Boil rapidly until syrupy, about 10 minutes. Remove the baggie, pour the berries into sterilized, hot jars, and seal. No processing is necessary. Serve at holiday time or any time in place of cranberries.

Molded Juneberry Salad

Serves 6

1 cup pickled juneberries, drained (reserve juice)

1 3-ounce package lemon-flavored gelatin

1 cup pineapple tidbits, chilled and drained (reserve juice)

1 cup pineapple juice (from tidbits)

Heat the juice from the pickled berries and add the package of lemon gelatin. Stir until dissolved. Add the pineapple juice and stir. Add the pineapple tidbits and then the berries and pour into a mold. Chill until set. This is a relish-type salad, good with pork, fowl, and game.

French Juneberry Dessert

Serves 8 to 10

Crust:

2 cups all-purpose flour
1/2 cup brown sugar
I cup chopped walnuts or pecans
I cup butter

Mix well with hands and press into a 9 by 13-inch Pyrex dish. Bake at 400°F for 15 minutes. Cool, then crumble crust with hands or fork and place back in dish.

Filling:

I 8-ounce package cream cheese, softened
I cup superfine sugar
I large carton Cool Whip or I pint heavy cream, whipped

Cream the cream cheese with the sugar until smooth and light. Fold in the Cool Whip or whipped cream and pour over the cool, crumbled crust.

Topping:

2 cups fresh or frozen juneberries (if using frozen, reserve juice)
1/2 cup berry juice or water
I tablespoon cornstarch

Heat berries, juice and/or water, and cornstarch to boiling. Stir and cook until thickened slightly (mixture will turn clear).

Cool. Spoon topping over individual servings.

This is delicious, but juneberries taste best of all when you get up early some June morning, go outdoors, and pick a bowlful—or just stand there and gorge on them.

Meadowsweet *Filipendula ulmaria*

This lovely, elegant perennial with white flower heads was used in frontier days to flavor applesauce, teas, and syrups. It was added to rhubarb to save on sugar, and it is perfect for fresh bouquets. (4 feet)

New jersey tea *Ceanothus americanus*

This low-growing shrub, a prairie native, has creamy, lovely flowers in July. A tea made from its dried leaves is very high in vitamin C; it helped keep our soldiers alive during the Revolutionary War. (2 feet)

Onion family *Allium* spp.

What would we do without onions in our perennial food garden—and our cuisine? The following are my favorites.

Egyptian onion *Allium cepa* var. *Viviparum*

This is a curiosity, unusual as a plant, but with all the versatility of the ordinary onion. No garden would be complete without onions, and the Egyptian is a perennial and really suits our purpose. It develops its bulbs at the top of the green shoot instead of underground. The weight of this top bulb bends the plant to the ground, where it roots. Then you have another plant established. I caution you: the Egyptian onion is aggressive. If you don't want it to take over, keep those tops cut off. These onions are great pickled—just the right size. The green stem can be used like chives. It's easy to grow, very rugged and hardy. Do not fertilize with high-nitrogen products— no manure, weed, or leaf composts.

Maple Onion Casserole

Serves 8

Butter a round, 2-inch-deep Pyrex dish. Fill half full with:

> Egyptian onions, peeled and sliced in two

Mix up the following and spread over the onions:

> ⅔ cup leftover cornbread bits
>
> 4 tablespoons melted butter
>
> ½ cup minced celery and leaves
>
> ¼ cup dark raisins
>
> ½ cup chicken stock
>
> Salt and pepper to taste

Drizzle over all:

> 10 tablespoons maple syrup

Cover with aluminum foil. Bake at 350°F for 35–45 minutes. Test to see if the onions are done. It's gourmet! (Always make a big batch of cornbread—it's great for lots of things. I freeze it in pieces and crumbs to have on hand.)

Impossible Onions

Serves 6 to 8

2 tablespoons butter

1 cup onions, chopped

½ pound fresh mushrooms, sliced

½ cup baby swiss cheese, grated

10 slices french bread, ½-inch thick

2 cups thick white sauce

½ cup milk

2 teaspoons soy sauce

Salt, pepper, and dried herbs to taste

Butter a 9 by 13-inch casserole. Sauté the onions and mushrooms in the 2 tablespoons butter until soft; arrange in buttered dish and sprinkle with the grated cheese. Lay the french bread slices over the cheese. Thin the white sauce with the milk, whisk in the soy sauce and seasonings, and pour over the bread. Let stand in refrigerator overnight. Bake at 350°F for 45 minutes.(I always keep white sauce on hand in the refrigerator—it saves so much time.)

Garlic chives *Allium tuberosum*

So easy to grow and so worthwhile! This chive has a mild garlic flavor. It will reseed itself or clumps can be lifted, separated, and replanted to start new patches. I lift two or three, pot them, and bring them indoors for winter use. The leaves are great for snipping and adding to fresh greens. I don't like them frozen or dried—why bother when you can have them fresh?

The fresh flower blossoms make a tasty flavored vinegar. Fill a clean pint jar with clean blooms. Heat white vinegar and pour over them to cover. Cap and store for a month in a cool, dark place. Strain the vinegar and pour into another clean bottle. You will like the fragrance.

The dried flower blossoms make interesting flower arrangements. The fresh flowers can be pulled apart and added to salads. This is a plant that the honeybees like.

When you harvest the stems, don't cut a handful straight across. Instead, take a few stems and snip right down to the soil. Leave a lot of the clump or it won't keep producing.

If you have trouble digesting onions, chives are a perfect solution. You will like their delicate flavor—and no backtalk.

Rocambole *Allium scorodoprasum*

Another enigma of the plant world, this reproduces like the Egyptian onion and is a must in our perennial garden. Before rocambole, I was always throwing away rotten garlic. Pick the bulbit clusters anytime before they start dropping from their stalks. Plant a few and put the rest in a paper bag in a cool, dry place. Mine last all winter—super keepers. Use in anything calling for garlic.

Rocambole Vinegar

Makes about 1 pint

> 1/2 cup rocambole buds
> 2 cups distilled white vinegar

Put the rocambole buds into a clean pint jar. Heat vinegar to boiling point and pour over the buds. Cap and place in the refrigerator. Remove buds from the vinegar after 24 hours or the vinegar will become too strong. Store this vinegar in the refrigerator to prevent spoilage.

Garlic Dressing for Salads

Makes about 1/2 cup

> 1/2 cup olive oil
> 2 tablespoons rocambole vinegar
> 2 tablespoons honey
> 1/4 teaspoon paprika
> Dash of cayenne

Put all ingredients in a pint jar and shake well.

Shallot *Allium ascalonicum*

The French have made this clovelike cluster of bulbs the king of the onion world. Eat the stems as well as the cloves; their flavor is sweet and appealing and they don't make you cry. You can easily pot them for winter use. They have a much longer storage period than most onions. Put in a paper bag and then in a plastic one, twist-tie shut, and keep them in your bottom refrigerator bin all winter. Very expensive if you buy them at the supermarket. I planted a dozen bulbs several years ago and have harvested bushels from these originals.

Plant the ones you have left over from winter, leaving one-third of each clove exposed. Don't bury them. When the stems fall over and turn yellow, start harvesting the shallots. Hang in mesh bags to dry. My friends like a pound at Christmastime, along with some dried mint and a pot of parsley—the makings for a chinese sprout salad.

Chinese Sprout Salad

Serves 6

1 15-ounce can mandarin oranges, drained

3 shallots, peeled and sliced thin

2 tablespoons fresh parsley, minced

1 teaspoon dried mint leaves or 3 teaspoons fresh leaves, minced

2 cups chinese bean sprouts, rinsed and drained

1/2 cup walnut pieces

Gently mix all ingredients. Toss with Southern French Dressing (below).

Southern French Dressing

Makes about 3/4 cup

3 tablespoons extra-fine sugar

2 tablespoons orange juice

2 tablespoons fruit vinegar (apple, raspberry, cherry, etc.)

1/2 teaspoon salt

1/4 teaspoon dry mustard

1/4 teaspoon paprika

1/2 cup light olive or canola oil

In a clean pint jar with a lid, dissolve the sugar in the orange juice. Add all the ingredients except the oil and shake well. Add the oil, shake again, and serve.

Primrose *Primula vulgaris*

I can't imagine anyone having enough of these beauties to make wine from them, crystallize them, or pickle them. In days of yore, all these things were done.

Redbud *Cercis canadensis*

These lovely little purplish-pink flowers can be picked for salads and used as a garnish. (20 feet)

Rose apple *Rosa pomifera*

To have a rosebush growing in our ornamental food garden must sound queer, but this plant produces a brilliant orange golf ball–size fruit known as rose hips, nature's richest source of vitamin C. These hips make delectable jelly, nectar, tea, and more. You can extract the juice from fresh hips and freeze it to use all winter.

All the parts of the rose are edible—foliage, petals, and hips. The hips of the meadow rose, *R. blanda*, can be boiled in water to create a soothing liquid for itches and sores. Rosewater, an ancient flavoring, is made by filling an enamel kettle with rose petals, adding water to cover, bringing to a boil, and simmering for a few minutes. Strain, pour into pretty little bottles, and give as gifts. Or you can welcome guests with a tall glass of rosewater diluted to taste and served over ice.

Rose Hip Tea

Rose hips, washed, chopped, and dried in a food drier or your oven
Boiling water
Honey

Store dried rose hips in a glass jar, never in a metal tin, and brew the tea in a china, not a metal, pot. Use 2 cups boiling water for each teaspoon of dried rose hips. Steep the tea for 5 minutes, covered, and pass honey as a sweetener. If you have any unsweetened tea left over, use it to water your houseplants or freeze it in cubes to add lift to fruit juices.

Instead of paying a fortune for oranges all winter, drink rose hip tea!

Rose Hip Jam

Makes 6 pints

To make the puree:

8 cups fresh rose hips, harvested before they are soft
Water to cover

Wash the rose hips, trim off any stems, and cut in two. Place in a heavy kettle (not aluminum) and add water to cover. Bring to a boil and simmer until hips are soft. Press the hips through a strainer into a large bowl and measure the puree. You will need 4 cups.

To make the jam:

> 4 cups rose hip puree
>
> 1 cup canned crushed pineapple, with juice
>
> 1 fresh lemon
>
> ½ cup water
>
> 5 cups sugar

Slice the lemon thinly and boil in the water 15 minutes. Strain out the pulp and add the liquid to the rose hip puree. Stir in the pineapple and the sugar. Bring mixture to a boil and simmer slowly until thick. Pour the jam into sterilized ½-pint jars and seal.

Rose Hip Conserve

This conserve is uncooked. Served over ice cream or custard or spread on buttered toast, a spoonful a day is nature's answer to vitamin C capsules.

To make the puree:

> Rose hips
>
> Honey

Spread ripe rose hips out to soften on racks or trays in a shady spot. Do not let the fruits touch each other or they will rot. When the hips are soft, whirl them briefly in your food processor or blender and then force the fruit through a sieve with a wooden spoon to remove any pips and skin. The puree should be thick, a rich red in color. Measure the puree and add 1 part honey to every 2 parts puree. Pour into sterilized half-pint jars and seal. Because honey is such a good preservative, this conserve will keep well.

The pips and skin you strained from the puree can be dried thoroughly and used for tea.

Rose Hip Soup

Serves 6

To make the juice:

> 1 pound rose hips, stalks and stems removed
>
> 2 cups water

Combine rose hips and water in a large, heavy kettle (not aluminum) and bring to a boil. Simmer until fruit is very soft. Mash fruit against side of kettle to help break it up. Set a strainer or sieve over a large bowl and pour in the fruit. Let it drain into the bowl overnight. Discard the pulp and reserve the juice. It is highly concentrated and strong flavored.

To make the soup:

2/3 cup rose hip juice (freeze any you have left over)

1 1/2 cups chicken stock

1 large onion, chopped fine

1 large carrot, peeled and grated

1 tablespoon butter

1 tablespoon flour

2 teaspoons sugar

1 teaspoon worcestershire sauce

Pinch of ground coriander

Salt and pepper to taste

In a heavy saucepan, sauté the onion and carrot in the butter until soft. Stir in the flour and cook a few minutes. Add the juice and stock and bring to a boil, stirring. Add the sugar and seasonings. Cover and simmer 20 minutes. Serve hot.

Sweet cicely *Myrrhis odorata*

Be sure the plant you buy is a native of Britain. There is an American variety that is worthless.

Sweet cicely is truly a plant for the North. Plant it in the shade. It sometimes has a two-year germination period, but its handsome foliage and beautiful blossoms in May are worth the wait. The bees love them. Often called candy plant, the leaves can be eaten from spring till hard frost. The green, anise-flavored seeds are fun to chew. Pour boiling water over crushed seeds or roots to make tea. Crushed seeds can be substituted for cloves or caraway. Mince the leaves along with tarragon and add to omelettes, or shred the leaves and add to green salads for a suggestion of anise flavor. Cooked, for some reason the leaves of this plant counteract tartness, saving on the amount of sugar required for a recipe, especially one involving rhubarb. Or tie it up in a cheesecloth bag as a bouquet garni—the anise flavor disappears when cooked.

Sweet Cicely Turnovers

Makes 6

Pastry for one 9-inch single-crust pie *or*

1 tube prepared crescent roll dough

1 cup sweet cicely leaves, stems removed, chopped

2 sorrel leaves, ribs removed, chopped

¼ cup brown sugar, packed

¼ cup cream

Extra brown sugar

Roll out your own pastry and cut into 3-inch squares, or open the tube of prepared dough and unroll each crescent into a square. Mix the chopped leaves with ¼ cup brown sugar and put one tablespoonful into the middle of each pastry square. Fold over diagonally to form triangles, and press edges to seal.

Brush with a little cream and sprinkle with more brown sugar. Bake at the temperature on the can, or at 425°F, till light brown and crisp.

Sweet cicely's ferny leaves are lovely in a floral bouquet, but they need conditioning. Pick early in the day, set in water, place in a dark room overnight, and arrange the next day.

Sweet woodruff *Galium odoratum*

Needs shade like the primulas and sweet cicely, blooming in early spring with tulips and daffodils. It is great underplanted with shrubs. Must be dried to have fragrance—use the fresh, though, to make the old-world May wine cup. (4 to 6 inches)

Swiss chard *Beta vulgaris cicla*

This is a perfect vegetable for our perennial garden. Easy and almost indestructible, it can be eaten from early spring to late frost. If the summer is hot and dry, keep the big leaves picked. The minute you have rain and cool weather, start picking the smaller leaves and stalks. Both the leaves and the stalks can be eaten. The tangy, ruffled leaves are similar to spinach; the stalks are like asparagus. This plant is a rich source of vitamins A and C and iron.

The simplest and one of the tastiest ways to prepare swiss chard is to simmer the leaves (no stalks) gently until wilted. Drain and toss with 2 tablespoons browned butter, several gratings of fresh nutmeg, and salt and pepper to taste. For a heartier variation, add 2 peeled, sliced hard-boiled eggs and 1 tablespoon fruit vinegar (preferably currant vinegar) to the browned butter mixture.

Chard-Sorrel Gratin

Serves 8

2½ pounds fresh chard leaves, washed and drained

⅓ cup plus 3 tablespoons olive oil

1 cup onions, coarsely chopped

1 tablespoon garlic chives, minced

½ cup fresh sorrel leaves

1½ cups cooked rice

¾ cup parmesan cheese, grated

½ cup fresh bread crumbs

Heat ⅓ cup olive oil in a large, heavy-bottomed pan (not aluminum) and sauté the onions and garlic together. Add the chard ½ pound at a time, stirring after each addition until slightly wilted. Add the sorrel leaves and cook about 5 minutes. Do not drain.

Stir in the cooked rice and ½ cup parmesan cheese. Season to taste and turn into a buttered casserole dish. Blend the bread crumbs with the remaining parmesan cheese and spread over the casserole. Drizzle with the remaining 3 tablespoons olive oil. Bake in a preheated 400°F oven for 30 to 40 minutes.

Elegant Side Dish

Serves 4

1 cup cashew pieces

½ cup milk

1 tablespoon garlic chives, minced

1 tablespoon soy sauce

Salt and pepper to taste

3 to 4 cups chard leaves, cooked and drained

1 tablespoon onion, grated

Whirl the cashew pieces with milk, garlic chives, soy sauce, and salt and pepper in your food processor until they are thick and creamy. Place the chard and grated onion in a large, heavy-bottomed pan and pour the cashew mixture over. Heat, stirring, until steaming hot. Transfer to a heated serving dish and serve at once, dressed with additional cashew pieces.

Chard Rolls

Serves 6

12 large, perfect chard leaves, washed, dried, and ribs removed

¼ cup hazelnuts or brazil nuts, chopped

1 cup onion, chopped

1 tablespoon garlic chives, minced

1 tablespoon each olive oil and butter

1 tablespoon fresh parsley, chopped

1 tablespoon fresh basil, minced

¼ cup celery, minced

⅛ teaspoon cayenne pepper

3 cups cooked, seasoned brown rice

1 cup ricotta cheese

1 cup chablis or other dry white wine

Sauté the nuts, onion, and chives in the olive oil and butter. When onion is transparent, remove from heat and add parsley, basil, celery, and cayenne. Stir in the brown rice and ricotta and mix well. Put ⅓ cup of this filling on each chard leaf, overlapping where stem was removed, and roll up. Fill a buttered baking dish snugly with the rolls and pour the chablis over them. Cover with aluminum foil and bake at 350°F for 35 to 40 minutes. This dish freezes well.

Special Chard Soup

Serves 6

2 pounds fresh chard, leaves and stems separated

1 pound celery hearts

1 large onion (1 cup chopped)

1 loaf italian bread (3½ inches wide)

Garlic-flavored olive oil

3 cups heavy cream

2 tablespoons fresh lemon juice

Fresh parsley for garnish

Roughly chop the chard stems, celery hearts, and onion and simmer in seasoned water to cover until barely tender. Tear the chard leaves into bite-size pieces, add to the other vegetables, and simmer until chard leaves are wilted. Cool. Process the vegetables with their liquid in two or three stages, emptying the puree into a large kettle.

Cut the italian bread into 3/8-inch slices. Brush each side with garlic-flavored olive oil and toast 15 to 20 minutes in a 350°F oven until golden brown and crisp. Set aside, keeping warm.

Heat the puree until simmering and stir in the heavy cream and lemon juice. Taste for seasonings and adjust if necessary. Reheat but do not boil. Ladle hot soup into warm bowls. Sprinkle with fresh parsley and top each serving with a slice of the warm toast. Serve at once.

More Food Plants for an Ornamental Perennial Food Garden

Rhubarb, caraway (its roots can be eaten), good- king-henry, french sorrel, and chicory could also be included in this garden. All of these but rhubarb are aggressive, so beware—deheading is compulsory!

If you want to try some of these ornamental perennial food plants but can't find them locally, the following addresses will help.

Seeds for the ground-cherry and vine peach are available from:

Thompson Morgan
P.O. Box 100
Farmingdale, NJ 07727

Nichols Garden Nursery
1190 N. Pacific Highway
Albany, OR 97321

Both nurseries will send a super catalog with all kinds of guidelines for planting times and so forth.

Amelanchier canadensis (juneberry), *Prunus besseyi* (western cherry bush), *Rosa pomifera* (rose apple), and *Shepherdia argentea* (buffaloberry) are all available from:

Farmer Seed & Nursery Company
Faribault, MN 55021

Orchard Fruits and Why I Don't Grow Them

One group of plants our garden does not include is fruit-bearing trees. My husband and I tried several kinds before surrendering the effort.

Peaches are so much juicier and more delicious if allowed to ripen on the tree. We planted four, of two different varieties. Two developed borer problems when young and never produced. Today I would try hanging a bar of Octagon soap at the fork of any affected trees. With each succeeding rain more soap would be washed down on the trunk. . . soon no borers. We are also hanging this soap on any plant that deer eat. (Good luck finding this soap. If you can't find any, use Safeguard soap instead.)

The other two lived long enough for us to harvest seven bushels of peaches, and then they suddenly died. Those peaches were so good, I still dream about them. Maybe I'll try again. If

I do, I won't put them in the same place. You must plant any new fruit tree in a new location—and do not let grass grow under your trees. I think this is what killed ours.

We also planted four plums, Burbank variety, two of them too close to a vegetable garden. Their roots were always getting chopped into by the rototiller. Two died, two lived, and one of these was loaded to the ground with plums last year. They will tolerate grass; thin the fruit, though.

Pears hate grass. One we planted, the seckel pear, lived to produce. The other three got fire blight, so we never harvested from them.

A yellow delicious apple tree is growing on the south bank.

It provides enough apples for me, bearing every year, sometimes several bushels, sometime only one.

Even the few of these trees that survived require lots of extra care and frequent sprayings to produce any quality and quantity of fruit. My long-range goals of easier maintenance and leaving the land in better condition than I found it preclude growing these in the ornamental, naturalized food garden.

Care of Your Perennial Food Garden

Your perennial food garden will need care. Composting, mulching, and fertilizing will be necessary, since once the garden is established, you can't be working up your soil or sowing a green manure crop each year. But soil quality can be readily maintained by spreading a one-inch layer of compost yearly. Gardeners do not build soil; the bacteria, molds, and earthworms do that. We provide the organic matter for them to turn into rich humusy soil. Even the poorest of subsoils can be turned into fertile topsoil by spreading a yearly layer of compost made in the classic way: 2 inches of soil to every 1 to 6 inches of dead leaves (not oak leaves), grass clippings, overripe vegetables, shredded plant material, animal manure. Compost is a magic cure-all for garden ills. Everything benefits from a 1-inch layer of compost applied each year.

All methods of composting rely on the same basic ingredients. The main differences lie in what kind of container you make and store it in and the speed with which you want the raw compost to break down. I make it by the old-fashioned, slow method, on the ground. When my pile of raw compost is about 3 feet deep, I cover it with 2 to 3 inches of good soil and moisten it well. In five to six weeks, I turn the pile with a pitchfork and cover it with another 2 to 3 inches of soil. This I leave for about six months. This slow method produces a rich, brownish-black, clean-smelling compost, free of disease organisms and weed seeds.

Not only will you be composting your perennial veggies and fruits yearly—you will need to fertilize and mulch as well.

For food crops I recommend a 10-10-10 fertilizer, 10 pounds for a 25 by 25-foot vegetable plot. The ingredients are nitrogen, phosphorus, and potassium.

Wood ashes are valuable as a fertilizer only if your soil shows a potassium deficiency. Apply 20 pounds to a 25 by 25-foot plot.

Manure, of course, is a time-honored fertilizer. Use 10 pounds of manure for a 10 by 10-foot area. Or mix an equal part of wet peat with sterilized manure for optimum results.

Whichever fertilizer you choose, use the suggested amounts three times in a season. Most American gardeners do not use enough fertilizer.

Exotics

America's eating habits certainly have changed in the last ten or twenty years. We're eating foods today that we didn't know existed a decade or so ago. Of course, new tastes in food lead to new habits in gardening. Just as the ornamental food garden was an idea that erupted in my mind during sleepless nights, so was my yen to grow "exotic" foreign fruits and vegetables.

Some years ago, magazines started printing all kinds of stir-fry recipes for unusual fresh veggies. This led to my trying more and more kinds. Locating seeds for the ones we didn't grow but had read about was quite a chore. I tried a lot of things I'd never heard of, as well. When I think how quickly these new tastes have developed, it amazes me. Today all the seed catalogs offer a large selection of "exotics."

The first thing I discovered: as with any other vegetables, some are hardier and tougher, can be planted earlier in the season, can withstand temperature changes and are tremendous for a fall garden, and like midwestern weather. Many vegetables actually do best when they mature in cooler weather. And many taste better after a good frost. Check with your county agricultural agent and determine your mean frost date. Plant cold-tolerant seeds in summer, figuring out how many days they will need to mature before the first frost.

Chinese cabbage family *Brassica rapa* chinensis group and pekinensis group

Burpee's Lei Choi Pak Choi is a versatile vegetable with choice spicy, pure white, celerylike stalks. Some are ready to be thinned and eaten in thirty days. They are very easy to clean, an important plus for me. Another one of these foods to lunch on in the garden. I use this in stir-fries or raw, cut into strips, on relish trays. Or stuff the stalks with the following cheese spread.

Cheese Spread for Raw Vegetables

> 2 cups mild cheddar cheese, grated
> 1 cup canned pimiento, minced
> Mayonnaise
> chinese cabbage or celery stalks

Blend cheese and pimiento together and add enough mayonnaise to bind. Stuff the stalks with this spread and cut into bite-size pieces.

Frozen Chinese Cabbage

Makes about 4 quarts

For the brine:

> 2 cups distilled white vinegar
> 1 cup water
> 4 cups sugar
> 2 teaspoons celery seed
> 2 teaspoons mustard seed

Bring all ingredients to a boil in a heavy saucepan (not aluminum). Boil until sugar is dissolved. Cool before proceeding.

For the cabbage:

> 2 large heads chinese cabbage, cores removed
> 2 large red peppers
> 2 large green peppers
> 6 stalks celery
> 6 large carrots, peeled
> 1 teaspoon canning salt

Chunk the cabbage and shred it in a food processor using the metal blade. Remove to a glass punch bowl or other large nonmetal bowl. Sprinkle with canning salt and cover with cold water. Let stand 2 hours, then drain, squeezing out moisture.

Return to bowl. Chunk the peppers, celery, and carrots and shred them in the food processor as above. Add these to the shredded cabbage and mix well. Pour the cooled brine over all and distribute into cartons. Freeze. Defrost and drain before using. This is good mixed into cottage cheese or, mixed with mayonnaise, as a stuffing for avocados. I often make it when I'm preparing sauerkraut, saving some of the grated cabbage from that operation.

Another Burpee exclusive that can't be beat is their Two-Season Chinese Cabbage. I start seedlings in the greenhouse in April, transplanting hardened plants to the garden in the middle of May. These are equally successful in a fall planting. Again, I start them in the greenhouse so I can control the moisture (usually in August), setting them out in September. This cabbage withstands mild frosts and is great for October harvests. Use it as you would lettuce or spinach. Great for stir-frying, adding at the last minute. Steam it or cut it in quarters for a boiled dinner. Has a milder flavor than our cabbage, and is very easy to slice or shred.

Shredded Chinese Coleslaw

Serves 6

1 head chinese cabbage, cored

1 daikon radish (optional)

½ cup salad oil (not olive)

1 tablespoon fresh ginger, peeled and minced

2 tablespoons good-quality soy sauce

2 tablespoons rice wine

1 teaspoon sugar

Wash cabbage and scrub the radish but do not peel. Shred the cabbage finely by hand or in a food processor to make 3 or 4 cups. Reserve remaining cabbage for another use. Slice or shred the radish and add to the cabbage. Combine remaining ingredients in a pint jar with a lid and shake well to blend. Pour over the shredded vegetables, toss, and serve chilled.

Chinese kale *Brassica alboglabra* 'Bailey'

Don't forget to try the new oriental leaf vegetables. They are packed with vitamins and delicious. Chinese kale (seed available from Nichols) is highly bolt-resistant. The stalks, young leaves, and buds are all pickable. Sow in August, placing boards over the rows to keep in moisture until the seeds germinate. Easy to grow; use like ordinary kale. This does not freeze well.

Daikon or oriental fall radish *Raphanus sativus* 'Longipinnatus'

Nichols offers many varieties of daikon or fall radish. We Americans tend to think of the radish as a relish, to be eaten with our fingers. Asian cooks do wonderful things with them, serving them grated raw, stir-fried, and boiled. Try them sliced thinly, then breaded and fried in a light oil, or prepare a tempura batter and deep-fry them. I like the Chinese White Celestial—very mild. Be careful not to buy the western variety. Sow the seed late in the summer (mid-August), and keep it moist. To keep your seed rows evenly moist, try covering each row with boards. Keep checking, removing the boards as soon as the seed sprouts. Fall radishes are heavy feeders, so fertilize all season. The ripe radishes will keep all winter if packed into moist sand. Do not freeze them. I dip these radishes, along with many of the other exotics, in tomatillo sauce for a quick appetizer or snack.

Melons *Cucumis melo*

Yes, we can grow melons in the North! Burpee has two, 'Ambrosia' and 'Haogen', that I've been growing for years. From three hills of each, I've picked more than I can count. 'Ambrosia' has salmon-colored flesh; 'Haogen' has green. There aren't words to describe their deliciousness. "The best melons we've ever tasted," comment friends. I've even frozen the extracted juices, adding them to apple and currant juices for a new winter taste. Mostly we just gorge on them.

Melon Chicken Salad

Serves 4

3 cups cooked chicken or turkey, cut into bite-size pieces
1 pint jar chutney, drained (reserve liquid)
Mayonnaise
Fresh lettuce leaves
1 ripe 'Ambrosia' melon

Combine the chicken or turkey with the chutney and mix well. Add a little reserved chutney liquid if the mixture seems dry. Let stand in refrigerator 3 to 4 hours. When ready to serve, halve, seed, and quarter the melon. Set the quarters on individual plates lined with fresh lettuce leaves. Combine the chicken salad mixture with enough mayonnaise to bind it and divide equally between melon quarters. Serve this gourmet treat at once.

Nichols has a cantaloupe—*Cucumis melo* var. *reticulatus* 'Honey Gold #9'—ready in 85 days after planting. It's an oriental delicacy, a small egg-shaped melon with white rind and flesh, eaten like a pear. This melon is ideal for small areas because it can be trellised or grown on a fence.

Also from Nichols, there is an excellent vine peach they call "mango melon" (MICucumis melo, chito group). This is a native American annual. Raw, it's terrible, but when cooked in preserves and chutneys, there's nothing better. We all know that the major ingredient in any chutney is mango. Where to get mangoes? If you found them, they would be expensive. This is a substitute that's cheap, delicious, very productive, and easy to grow. People really appreciate it as a gift, either the whole fruits or prepared as a condiment for meats and any curry dish.

Fake Mango Chutney

Makes 12 pints

Have your clean, sterilized pint jars ready, rims and lids standing in simmering water, before you begin.

> 5 cups sugar
>
> 4 cups cider vinegar
>
> 1 tablespoon chili powder
>
> 23 vine peaches, washed, peeled, seeded, and cut into bite-size pieces
>
> 2 cups seedless raisins
>
> 2 cups walnut meats, chopped
>
> 1 cup crystallized ginger
>
> 2 teaspoons salt (not iodized)

In a large, heavy saucepan (not aluminum), bring the sugar and vinegar to a boil. Simmer 5 minutes, until all sugar is dissolved. Add the chili powder and fold in the vine peaches, raisins, walnuts, ginger, and salt. Simmer until peaches are soft and mixture is nicely thickened. Pour into jars, seal, and process in a boiling water bath for 10 minutes. Keeps a year or two in a cool, dark place.

I like to put 2 or 3 tablespoons of this chutney into an avocado half as a quick salad, or, in winter, into the cavities of canned pear or peach halves, baking in a buttered dish at 350°F until hot and bubbly. Vine peaches can be cut into large pieces and substituted in any recipe for spiced peaches.

Chinese winter melon *Benincasa hispida* 'Doan Gwa'

These pale green round fruits with thick white firm flesh are succulent and mildly sweet. They grow on a single vine and need very warm soil, plenty of moisture, and fertilizer—the same conditions as pumpkins. Nichols carries the seeds. You'll need to start them indoors, as the 15- to 25-pound fruits need 150 days to mature. When ripe, the fruits will be covered with a heavy, waxy white coating. They store well. All parts are edible: young leaves, buds, even immature fruit. Stir-fry or use in curries. The rind can be made into watermelon pickle.

Snow peas *Pisum sativum* var. *macrocarpon*

No longer new, but what a boon. Easy to clean and prepare—no endless shelling with green fingernails afterward and few peas to show for your efforts. Snow peas are tender, crisp, and sweet and some varieties are stringless; they have half the calories of ordinary peas. A necessity for Asian cooking, try them in tempura batter for your vegetarian friends, or add them to any soup right before serving. Another plus: the plants are full of nitrogen, so as soon as they are finished producing, till them into the soil as green manure.

Pickled Snow Peas

2 cups distilled white vinegar

½ cup honey

1 large head fresh dill or 2 tablespoons dill seed

1 tablespoon mustard seed

1-inch piece fresh gingerroot, peeled and sliced

6 whole onions

½ teaspoon canning salt

6 whole peppercorns

6 whole allspice

3 pounds fresh snow peas, cleaned, trimmed, and strings removed

Combine all ingredients except snowpeas in a large saucepan (not aluminum) and bring to a boil. Boil a few moments, let cool, and let stand overnight in refrigerator.

Arrange snow peas in a medium-size crock or large glass jar with a lid. Strain the prepared brine over the peas. Cap or cover securely and let stand in the refrigerator for one week before serving. These pickled peas will keep in the refrigerator for 2 or 3 months. Shake the jar or crock now and then.

Tomatillo *Physalis ixocarpa*

A native of Mexico (seed from Nichols), this fruit grows in a husk. Pick when husks are just turning golden for eating raw. Use them green for the famous salsa verde or green sauce. I start these inside and plant outside when all frost danger is past. You will only need four or five plants, as they are very heavy producers. Have your lunch on them—they are always clean, ready to eat, and so good raw. A natural thickening agent with very few calories, they make a great dip or green sauce for fresh vegetables. They can be frozen for winter use and substitute beautifully for avocadoes in guacamole at a fraction of the price.

"Guacamole" Sauce

4 hot green peppers, chopped

1 cup onion, chopped

3 pounds green tomatillos, husked, washed, and halved

Water to cover

2 to 3 tablespoons good-quality olive oil

Salt and pepper to taste

Fill a large kettle (not aluminum) two-thirds full of water and add the peppers and onion. Bring to a boil and add the tomatillos. Simmer about 5 minutes (do not let vegetables become mushy). Drain well, cool, then process in food processor till smooth. Put back into the pan with the olive oil. Cook and stir until thick. Do not let it stick to the pan. Cool, then season with salt and pepper. Mix with cooked meat for enchiladas; use in tacos when you don't have fresh tomatoes. This sauce freezes beautifully. You can thicken runny spaghetti sauce and gravies with it or whisk it into salad dressings to prevent the dressing from separating.

Tomatillo Salsa

1 pound green tomatillos, husked, washed, and quartered

3 hot green peppers, halved and seeded

3 buds rocambole, crushed and skewered on a toothpick

¾ cup water

⅓ cup fresh coriander leaves, packed

Salt and sugar to taste

Combine all ingredients except coriander and seasonings in a saucepan (not aluminum). Bring to boil, then simmer for 10 minutes. Cool and transfer to a food processor along with the coriander leaves. Process, then transfer to a serving bowl. Add salt and a little sugar to taste. (If you want to freeze this salsa, do so before adding the coriander leaves. Chop and add fresh coriander before serving.)

This is delicious on tacos, in tortillas, or as a dip for chips. You can create a quick hot dip by laying cheese slices over the salsa in an ovenproof dish and baking or broiling until the cheese is melted and bubbly. This recipe is equally tasty substituting green tomatoes for the tomatillos.

Domestic Annual Vegetables

This chapter would not be complete without some discussion of the domestic annual vegetables we are all familiar with and long for all winter. Naturally, we tend to buy old preferred varieties from the seed catalogs, and I can recommend many of these. Still, how boring gardening would become if we didn't seek a change: a bigger tomato, for instance. If we didn't try new seeds, I wouldn't be able to recommend 'Benewah', a Canadian tomato that withstands temperatures down to 27°F, blossoms in the cold, and sets fruit that ripens long before other varieties. Nor could I recommend my favorite cucumber, Sweet Success. It's wonderful; so productive and just perfect for all our pickling and fresh salads.

Always be searching for something better, but be aware that sometimes the "better" will be worse. Too many new varieties have been created for the convenience of commercial growers, who sacrifice taste, fragrance, and texture for vegetables that ship and keep well. Strawberries that no longer have that sweet taste or smell. Green beans that are tasteless and get mushy when frozen. Hybrids that can't reproduce—what will happen if we are left with a planet of plants that can't make offspring? So be selective—enjoy the old and experiment with the new, but don't expect the new always to be best.

The following are some of my favorite domestic annual vegetables, along with my tastiest recipes for preparing them.

Beets *Beta vulgaris*

Beets are naturally sweet, high in iron, and lower in calories than apples; baking them makes them sweet as fruit. There is a new one from Nichols called Baby Beet Spinel, bred for the critical gourmet trade. The beets stay small; small enough, I hope, so that I can cook the whole plant, top and all, at the same time.

The easiest way to cook beets is to bake them. Wash and dry medium-size beets and rub them with a little safflower or olive oil. Bake them at 400°F for about an hour; cool and slip off the skins. For an unusual flavor, roll the cooked beets in powdered ginger or in a flour made from dried ground sweet potato slices.

Beet Apple Salad

Serves 4

2 cups fresh apple, peeled and grated

1 cup raw beet, peeled and grated

1 tablespoon fresh lemon juice

1 tablespoon honey

2 tablespoons walnut meats, chopped

Fresh, clean endive leaves

Combine lemon juice and honey and toss with grated apple and beet. Spoon onto bed of endive and sprinkle with walnuts.

Sounds awful? Try it, you'll like it.

Beets Vinaigrette

Tiny spring beets are yummy served in a vinaigrette. Toss hot, cooked, skin-slipped beets with the vinaigrette dressing given for Green Beans Vinaigrette, below. Let marinate for about an hour. Serve at room temperature. So much better than those rippled pickled beets you buy.

Carrots *Daucus carota* var. *sativus*

Glazed Carrots

Serves 6

8 to 10 carrots, peeled and sliced lengthwise

¼ cup honey

1 teaspoon caraway seed or 2 tablespoons fresh summer savory, minced

½ cup mild cheddar cheese, grated

Steam or simmer carrot sticks until barely tender. Cool a little and roll in the honey. Put into a buttered casserole. Sprinkle with caraway seed or minced summer savory and top with the cheese. Bake at 400°F for 10 to 15 minutes.

Apricot Glazed Carrots

Serves 6

8 to 10 carrots, peeled and sliced into rounds
3 tablespoons butter
1/2 cup apricot preserves
1/4 teaspoon nutmeg, grated
1/4 teaspoon salt
1 teaspoon crystallized ginger, minced
2 teaspoons fresh lemon juice

Steam or simmer carrot rounds in water until just tender. Drain and reserve. Melt butter in a heavy saucepan (not aluminum) and stir in all ingredients except carrots. When glaze is bubbling, add carrots and heat through. Serve hot.

Carrots Dressed to Go

18 to 20 carrots, peeled and sliced lengthwise
3 tablespoons vinaigrette dressing
(See Green Beans Vinaigrette, below)
2 ribs celery, very thinly sliced
3 tablespoons fresh orange juice
1 tablespoon fresh basil, minced

Steam or simmer the carrots until tender crisp; drain. While still hot place in a double plastic bag and add remaining ingredients. Twist-tie shut. By the time you get to the picnic, these will be ready to eat.

Corn *Zea mays* var. *rugosa*

I plant 'Tokay', from Nichols, and many others: 'Kandy Korn', 'Honey and Cream', and 'Silver Queen', to name a few. We fight the raccoons for the first harvests, but after awhile they leave the rest alone. These new hybrids are so sweet and tender, you don't even need butter on them. Have you ever roasted corn Indian style? Turn back the husks on freshly picked cobbies and strip off the silks. Replace the husks and soak cobs in water for an hour, then put the ears in a single layer on the grill over hot coals, turning often for 15 to 20 minutes. Husks will become dry and brown. Serve at once, with melted butter if you're not counting calories.

For always-tender boiled corn on the cob, put 2 tablespoons distilled white vinegar and 2 tablespoons sugar in the boiling water, add cobbies, boil 6 minutes, and drain. The corn will stay tender till eaten (if it's tender-fresh to begin with).

Green Beans *Phaseolus vulgaris*

Simple Green Beans

Serves 4

1 pound fresh green beans, washed, trimmed, strings removed

3 tablespoons garlic- or rocambole-flavored olive oil

4 tablespoons fresh mint, chopped

4 tablespoons distilled white vinegar

Salt and pepper to taste

In water to cover, blanch the green beans: bring water to a boil, add beans, and cook 3 to 5 minutes without a lid. Add ice cubes to stop the cooking. Drain beans in a colander. Return pan to stove and add the olive oil, heating until fragrant. Add the beans, stirring to coat; add the mint, vinegar, salt and pepper to taste. Continue heating a few moments until beans are hot through; do not let sauce boil. Remove from heat and pour into serving dish. Best when served at room temperature.

Green Beans Vinaigrette

Serves 4

1 pound fresh green beans, washed, trimmed, strings removed

2 tablespoons fresh lemon juice

2 tablespoons fresh summer savory, minced

2 teaspoons dijon mustard

1/3 cup olive oil

salt and pepper to taste

1 ripe tomato (optional)

Blanch the beans as described above; drain. Combine the lemon juice, summer savory, and mustard in a small bowl; whisk in the olive oil and add salt and pepper to taste. Toss the beans in this dressing. If desired, peel a ripe tomato and crush it over the beans. Serve at room temperature.

Hungarian chili peppers *Capsicum annuum* var. *annuum*

I do so many things with these bright red peppers. I like them better than green peppers. They don't bite back at me and are very productive. You can raise a bumper crop of any of the pepper family by spraying them when they are blossoming with Epsom salts, 1 teaspoon per pint of water.

I freeze lots of the chili peppers, removing the seeds first and then blanching them. If you don't blanch, the peppers are absolutely tasteless when you go to use them.

Pepper Nachos

1 cup fresh hungarian chili peppers, washed, seeded, and chopped
1 cup cheddar cheese, grated
Mayonnaise
Corn chips

Combine peppers and cheese. Stir in mayonnaise to bind. Spread the corn chips in an ovenproof dish and spoon the pepper mixture over them. Bake at 400°F until cheese is melted and bubbly. A tasty tidbit.

Stuffed Hungarian Chili Peppers

Serves 6

6 hungarian chili peppers, frozen and defrosted
2 cups seasoned cooked white rice
1 cup sour cream
6 slices monterey jack cheese
1 cup cheddar cheese, grated

Blend cooked rice with sour cream and divide between thawed peppers. Lay a slice of cheese over each rice-filled pepper and roll the peppers up. Lay the peppers seam down in a buttered baking dish. Sprinkle cheddar cheese over and cover with aluminum foil. Bake at 350°F for 30 minutes.

Lettuce *Lactuca sativa*

Lettuce is a basic in every vegetable garden—easy to grow and low in calories, too. For a sweeter, milder lettuce, enrich the soil with green manure or fertilizer. If your garden plot is small, try kitty litter made from alfalfa—clean, not used litter. Toss in a few handfuls as you work up the soil.

I grow a wide variety of lettuces, each with its own special character. Bibb produces small, cup-shaped heads, tender-crisp and buttery with a delicate sweet flavor, best with a light dressing. Boston has a similar, though larger and looser, head. Escarole, with wide flat leaves, slightly curled and slightly bitter, is best combined this with other, milder greens. Leaf lettuce comes in many varieties, with curly green or red-tipped leaves that are tender and mild, ideal for wilting with a hot dressing. Romaine has a long, loose head of firm, crisp, dark green leaves with a nutty taste; it is firm enough to stir-fry. Several varieties of homegrown lettuce seasoned with fresh old-time herbs will put the zip back in your salads. Tender baby nasturtium leaves, fennel or dill fern, lemon balm, sweet cicely, and lovage, tossed with a homemade dressing, give salads a full-of-life taste.

Summer Supper Salad

Serves 4

> 4 cups torn lettuce leaves
>
> 1 apple, cored and sliced thin
>
> 2 small cucumbers, sliced thin
>
> 1 cup cheddar cheese, cut into small cubes
>
> 1 cup peanuts, chopped
>
> 1 cup safflower oil
>
> 1 cup peanut butter
>
> 2 tablespoons milk
>
> 1 scallion (bulb and stalk), minced
>
> Salt and cayenne pepper to taste

Divide lettuce, apple, and cucumber evenly into four salad bowls. Top with cheese cubes and peanuts. In a small bowl, whisk peanut butter, oil, milk, scallion, pepper, and salt until smooth. Divide this dressing among the four salads.

Zesty Italian Supper Salad

Serves 4

For the croutons:

> 2 cups spoon-size shredded wheat squares
>
> 5 tablespoons butter
>
> 1 tablespoon parmesan cheese, grated
>
> 1 tablespoon mixed dried salad herbs

Melt butter in a large, heavy skillet (not aluminum). Remove skillet from heat. Stir in dried herbs; add shredded wheat squares and mix well. Add parmesan cheese and mix until evenly distributed. Set skillet in a preheated 350°F oven and bake for 10 minutes. Remove from oven and cool.

For the dressing:

    ½ cup peanut oil
    5 teaspoons wine vinegar
    1 tablespoon mixed dried salad herbs
    Salt and pepper to taste

Combine ingredients in a pint jar with a lid and shake well to blend.

For the salad:

    1 head romaine lettuce, cleaned and torn into bite-size pieces
    1 cup canned pimientos, drained and chopped
    1 cup black olives, pitted and sliced
    2 tablespoons fresh garlic chives
    6 ounces italian ham or salami, cut into strips

Combine in a large bowl just before serving. Toss with dressing and top with croutons.

Parsnips *Pastinaca sativa*

Parsnips taste much sweeter and milder if you leave them in the ground until after the first hard frost, or if you harvest them all winter. To cook them, peel with vegetable parer and cut into strips. Cook in equal parts milk and water till tender. Drain. Can be frozen at this point; to serve immediately, sauté in butter until golden, drizzle with maple syrup.

Potatoes *Solanum tuberosum*

Boil new potatoes, drain, cut in wedges, and while warm, toss with browned butter and chopped fresh basil. Delicious.

Skillet Potatoes with Mild Chilies

Serves 4 to 6

    4 potatoes, cooked, peeled, and grated
    ⅓ cup onion, grated
    2 tablespoons butter
    ¾ cup swiss cheese, grated
    4 mild hungarian chili peppers, seeded and chopped
    Salt and pepper to taste

In an iron skillet, melt the butter and sauté the onion until translucent. Remove the onion to a large bowl and toss with the potatoes, cheese, and salt and pepper. Place half the potato mixture in the skillet, add the chilies, and top with remaining potato mixture. Bake at 350°F until bottom has browned, about 45 minutes. Then turn the oven off and the broiler on, and brown the top. Cut in wedges and serve at once.

Supreme Twice-Baked Potatoes

Makes 10 potato halves

> 5 large idaho potatoes, baked and cooled
>
> I cup cheddar cheese, grated
>
> I cup sour half-and-half
>
> 4 tablespoons butter
>
> I tablespoon fresh chervil or parsley, chopped
>
> I teaspoon fresh thyme leaves
>
> Paprika

Halve the potatoes and scoop out the insides into a large bowl, leaving the potato skins intact. Add the cheese, butter, sour half-and-half, and seasonings and beat together until fluffy. Stuff the potato mixture back into the reserved skins, sprinkle with paprika, and bake again at 350°F until the cheese melts. (I make a lot of these at a time and freeze them.)

Pumpkins *Cucurbita pepo* var. *pepo*

You either have too many pumpkins or none. I keep frozen pumpkin on hand all winter, prepared like this: Bake a whole ripe pumpkin, skin, seeds, and all, until it's tender. Cool, cut in half, remove seeds, and scoop out the pulp. Freeze this pulp in 2-cup amounts. Add 1 cup pumpkin pulp to chile con carne; it really does something for the flavor. Or try this compote:

Pumpkin-Apple Compote

Serves 6 to 8

> 3 cups apple, peeled, cored, and diced
>
> 2 cups frozen pumpkin pulp, thawed
>
> I cup maple syrup
>
> 2 teaspoons mustard, homemade or dijon

Combine the apple and pumpkin and pour into a buttered baking dish. Blend the maple syrup with the mustard and drizzle over the fruit mixture. Bake at 350°F for 35 minutes.

Salsify *Tragopogon porrifolius*

The garden-fresh "oyster." If you like oysters, you'll think salsify is great. Prepare it like parsnips. Add to bread stuffings, soups, and, of course, fry it, dredging in your favorite coating mix and frying in butter. (If you want your salsify to really look like oysters, cut the root into 1-inch rounds before cooking.)

Squash *Cucurbita maxima*

Some year, I'm going to count all the squash offered in the seed catalogs. I'm sure I'll be stunned, just as I'm sure I am among the culprits that cause all these varieties to be developed. Every year I accept some nursery's invitation to try this or that. A favorite is 'Winter Delicata', small and delicious—a half squash is a single serving. A treasure for small gardens, it doesn't ramble all over and the fruits keep till late winter.

Do you know how to keep squash? It's very important to protect them from changes of temperature. I put them in a bushel basket and keep them in a cool closet, around 55°F. In March I usually still have a bushelful in good condition.

I always try to have baked butternut squash left over. The next evening I make this:

Butternut Squash Soufflé

Serves 4

> 3 cups cooked butternut squash
> 2 eggs
> 4 tablespoons cream
> 2 teaspoons lemon juice
> Nutmeg, freshly grated
> Salt and pepper

Whisk the eggs into the pulp along with the cream, lemon juice, and seasonings. Pour into a buttered casserole. Bake at 350°F till soufflé is puffed and firm, usually 20 to 30 minutes.

Steamed Butternut and Carrot Strips

Serves 6

½ butternut squash

6 large carrots

4 tablespoons butter

2 tablespoons fresh chervil or parsley, chopped

1 teaspoon coriander seed, crushed

Coriander leaves for garnish

Peel the squash and the carrots and cut into same-size strips. Steam till tender and remove from heat. Melt butter in a heavy skillet and stir in the chervil or parsley and the coriander seed. Toss the vegetable strips in the butter mixture until hot and evenly coated. This has lots of eye appeal served on a white platter and garnished with fresh coriander leaves.

Baked Spaghetti Squash

It doesn't taste like spaghetti. This squash's charm is its texture, which is crisp when not overcooked. Cook it whole on a foil-covered baking sheet, in a 350°F oven for 30 minutes. Make a hole in it for the steam to escape. When the squash is soft, cut it in half and remove the strings and seeds. Scoop out the pulp. To serve, flavor every 3 cups pulp with 2 tablespoons butter, ½ teaspoon powdered allspice, and 1 tablespoon honey. If you have any left over, mix it with an equal amount of leftover poultry stuffing and reheat.

Tomatoes *Lycopersicon* spp.

Did you know if you let tomato plants lie on their sides, the fruits will ripen much sooner? More people grow tomatoes than any other vegetable, and there's nothing better than a homegrown one, nor a vegetable with more by-products for winter eating. I freeze tomato juice, pulp, and sauce and make this tomato relish:

Tomato Relish

8 fresh tomatoes, peeled and chopped

2 to 3 green peppers, diced

2 rocambole or garlic cloves, minced

2 cups chinese cabbage, shredded

1 cup carrots, peeled and thinly sliced

Fresh herbs, chopped, to taste

Mix all ingredients, taste, adjust seasoning. Keep in refrigerator in a large covered jar. Eat as is, as a condiment, or use in other vegetable dishes. You can fill a buttered casserole dish half full of summer squash, green beans, fresh corn, or any other vegetable, add 2 cups tomato relish, and bake at 300F for 30 minutes, or until tender.

Fried Green Tomatoes

3 or 4 green tomatoes, washed and sliced ½-inch thick

Seasoned flour, cornmeal, or bread crumbs for dredging

2 tablespoons butter

1¼ cups plus 1 tablespoon cold milk

2 teaspoons cornstarch

1 teaspoon honey

¼ cup parmesan cheese, grated

Freshly ground pepper

Fresh coriander or oregano leaves, chopped

Heat butter in a heavy, nonaluminum skillet. Dredge tomato slices in flour, cornmeal, or crumbs and lay them into the skillet when butter sizzles. Brown on each side. As the tomato slices brown, make a paste of 1 tablespoon cold milk and the cornstarch, using a small bowl or cup. Remove the browned tomatoes to a warmed plate and set in oven to keep warm. Pour remaining milk into the skillet and cook, stirring in the cornstarch paste, on medium heat until thick. Cook 1 minute and add remaining ingredients. Pour over tomatoes and serve at once. Yummy!

Zucchini *Cucurbita pepo* var. *melopepo*

I don't like big zucchini! We pick them when they are 1½ inches through the middle and 4 to 6 inches long. I freeze grated raw zucchini in the amounts called for in my favorite recipes for winter baking, including the pancake recipe below. I'm sure you know many ways to prepare zucchini. There are whole cookbooks on this vegetable. Here are a few more ideas for your repertory.

Zucchini Sausage Bake

Serves 6

5 small zucchini, ends trimmed off

I pound good-quality pork sausage

4 cups chinese cabbage, shredded

Salt and pepper

Slice the zucchini lengthwise and lay them cut side down in a buttered baking dish. In a heavy skillet (not aluminum), brown the sausage and season to taste. Spoon it over the zucchini. Spread the chinese cabbage over this, season with salt and pepper, and cover tightly with aluminum foil. Bake at 350°F about 30 minutes, or until zucchini are tender.

Herbed Zucchini Sauce for Pasta

I pound zucchini, cut matchstick-size

$\frac{1}{2}$ cup mixed fresh herbs: basil, tarragon, and chervil, chopped

2 tablespoons garlic-flavored olive oil

I cup heavy cream

4 tablespoons butter

4 gratings fresh nutmeg

Pinch cayenne pepper $\frac{1}{2}$ cup parmesan cheese, grated

In a heavy nonaluminum saucepan, combine cream, butter, nutmeg, and cayenne. Heat and simmer for 10 minutes. Remove from heat. In a large, heavy nonaluminum skillet, heat the olive oil and sauté the zucchini for about 4 minutes. Stir in the herbs. Reheat the cream sauce and stir into the zucchini mixture.

Add the parmesan and serve immediately over any cooked pasta.

Zucchini Frittata

1 onion, peeled and chopped
1 zucchini, about 6 inches long and 1½ inches around, sliced into ⅓-inch rounds
1 teaspoon fresh thyme
4 eggs, beaten
6 tablespoons monterey jack cheese, grated

In a large, heavy skillet (nonaluminum), sauté the onion and zucchini in the olive oil until tender. Add the thyme. Pour the eggs into the pan and sprinkle on half the cheese. When eggs begin to set, sprinkle with remaining cheese and pop under broiler until brown. Eat at once. This Italian omelette is easy to fix on a hot summer evening.

Quick Summer Zucchini

2 small zucchini, sliced into ¼-inch rounds
3 to 4 tablespoons sesame oil
2 to 3 tablespoons sesame seeds, toasted in the oven until brown

Heat the oil in a heavy nonaluminum skillet and sauté the zucchini rounds until tender. Sprinkle with sesame seeds and serve at once.

Zucchini Dinner Pancakes

Serves 4 to 6

3 small onions, thinly sliced
2 small zucchini, thinly sliced
½ stick butter
½ cup milk
3 eggs
½ cup flour
½ cup parmesan cheese, grated
4 gratings fresh nutmeg
Salt and pepper to taste
Tomatillo salsa (see recipe in this chapter)
½ cup cheddar cheese, grated

Melt butter in a large, heavy nonaluminum skillet and sauté onions over low heat until limp but not brown. Raise heat to medium and add zucchini; cook and stir 3 minutes. Remove from heat and cool. Place milk, eggs, flour, and parmesan in blender container or food processor. Add the zucchini mixture and pulse on and off until well blended. Add nutmeg, salt, and pepper. Pour into an 8-cup measuring cup, brush hot griddle with clarified butter or vegetable oil, and bake pancakes about 3 inches in diameter. Be sure griddle is hot and brushed with oil every time you add more batter. Use up the batter and stack the pancakes on a round baking pan or pizza pan. Top with tomatillo salsa and grated cheddar cheese; broil until cheese is bubbly. Serve at once.

A Guideline for putting down vegetable seeds

12 weeks before frost-free date: asparagus, celery, leeks, and onions

8 to 10 weeks before frost-free date: celeriac, eggplant, parsley, and peppers

6 to 8 weeks before frost-free date: tomatoes; basil, rosemary, and other herbs

5 to 6 weeks before frost-free date: broccoli, brussels sprouts, cabbage, cauliflower, collards, and lettuce

2 to 4 weeks before frost-free date: cucumbers, melons, pumpkins, and squash

Heavy Feeders		Light Feeders	Soil Builders
asparagus	kohlrabi	carrots	alfalfa*
beets	lettuce	garlic	beans, broad
cabbage	okra	leeks	beans, lima
cauliflower	parsley	mustard	beans, green (snap)
celery	pumpkins	onions	clover*
collards	radishes	parsnips	peanuts
corn	rhubarb	peppers	peas
cucumbers	spinach	potatoes	soybeans*
eggplant	squash	rutabaga	winter rye*
endive	tomatoes	shallots	buckwheat*
kale		sweet potatoes	*Use as green manure.*
		swiss chard	
		turnips	

Planning an Annual Vegetable Garden

I plan and map my annual vegetable garden every winter, keeping all the old maps to make sure that nothing is planted where it was last year and that tomatoes are never planted where potatoes have been. Potatoes have viruses that will spread to tomatoes through the soil. Again because of those viruses, never plant sprouted potatoes from the store.

It's best to clean up the vegetable plot as soon as harvest is over. Till in the stubble and plant a green manure crop so that the soil isn't bare all winter. Bare soil erodes, wind blows away the topsoil (especially here on the plains), and, of course, weeds grow. I hope you don't use plastic mulch; soil needs air circulation and will take on a foul odor if the air doesn't circulate. Add Turface or compost if your soil is in poor condition. And by all means, companion plant; sow annual herbs, flowers, and vegetables together.

Annual herbs that do well with veggies include:

Anethum graveolens dill. Benefits all the cabbage family. Don't plant it near carrots.

Anthriscus cerefolium chervil. Likes afternoon shade; plant it on the east side of tomatoes.

Borago officinalis borage. Super with strawberries and cucumbers.

Coriandrum sativum coriander. A lacy-looking herb with pretty flowers. Plant it with any vegetable—its scent repels insects.

Ocimum basilicum kelemandscharicum camphor basil. Not for consumption. Its odor keeps mosquitoes and the cabbage butterfly away. Don't plant near rue.

Satureja hortensis summer savory. Good with beans and potatoes.

Tagetes lucida anise marigold. The leaves are tastier than french tarragon. This is another good- with-anything partner.

Tropaeolum majus nasturtium. If a vegetable has aphids, plant nasturtiums beside it. The aphids will quickly leave the vegetable, preferring the nasturtium. Nasturtium doesn't like moisture.

All of these herbs make a good green manure crop if they are turned in before they go to seed. Don't use any perennial herbs as companion plants for veggies. When you clean up your garden in the fall, you would have to transplant them. Many herb perennials have creeping root systems and your vegetable bed would be taken over. Harvested perennial herb leaves benefit vegetables, however; lay sage stems and leaves on cabbage plants. All the annuals reseed except the marigold and nasturtium. Let them grow in early spring, turning them in when you plant the veggies (instant green manure).

We like to plant any squash vine on the edges of the corn plot and pole beans by the corn; carrots, radishes, and lettuce like each other. Chives and tomatoes like carrots. Set tomatoes between early cabbage plants to deter the yellow butterfly. We planted horseradish in the corners of the potato patch once. Don't try that; you can't get rid of it. You could try *Ruta graveolens* in your raspberry and rose rows—it deters japanese beetles. So do rocambole, garlic chives, and parsley. You could try planting wormwood on the border of your garden. It is said to keep animals away. It's very aggressive, though, and may take over. Try this at your own risk.

The Nichols catalog provides a very comprehensive companion-planting chart.

A Native American Perennial Food and Medicinal Garden

There is such a haunting elusiveness in the concept of a Native American perennial food garden. Of course, agriculture ran a poor second to the hunt as far as the Plains Indians were concerned, but every tribe used some plants either for food or for medicine, and we are learning more all the time about which ones they used, and why. When I'm guiding people around Wind 'n' View, I include as much as I can about native plant foods and medicines in my talk.

The Plains Indians called the leadplant "buffalo plant" because when it bloomed, they could expect to see the buffalo herds returning; that meant fresh meat and hides for clothes and tepees. They gathered handfuls of needlegrass for brushing and cleaning their hair. Yucca, the "candle of God," was surrounded by legends and had many uses, at least in story.

A specialized native foods garden would share a good deal with a prairie garden. Its plantings would not be as aggressive as some of the herbs our ancestors brought to this country.

It could be burned for easy maintenance, or mowed and raked where burning was dangerous or illegal. And the plants would perform well, easily adjusting to individual soils and microclimates, because they are native to this country, with an inborn toughness. We could intermingle shade lovers with sun seekers. We would certainly have a horn of plenty overflowing with color.

Here is what I would plant in this native perennial food garden (some of these already grow in the restored prairies and in the Ornamental Food Garden):

Allium cernuum   nodding pink onion. The Native American name for this plant is "chicago." It is hardy, flourishing anyplace, and much too strong-flavored for our palates. The Indians used it for seasoning. Medicinally, a poultice of the crushed root was said to ease painful bruises.

Amorpha canescens   leadplant. Has ornamental value.

Anemone canadensis   canadian anemone. Esteemed highly for its medicinal roots by the Omaha and Ponca Indians.

Apios americana or *A. tuberosa*   indian potato. This vine needs rich, moist, loose soil and a trellis for support. It produces a root crop of 2- to 3-inch bulbs connected by stringy roots. Harvest in late fall or early spring, peel with a carrot peeler, boil in salted water, and serve smothered in butter. Indian potatoes have a smooth, sweet turniplike flavor. The flowers are unique, brownish-pink clusters, making this vine attractive on fences. Don't harvest this plant until you have a healthy stand of it, and don't take all the bulbs. Leave plenty to keep growing. Definitely worth the trouble.

Aquilegia canadensis   columbine. The crushed black seeds were eaten for headache and fever.

Asclepias syriaca   common milkweed. The Native Americans made use of every part of this plant: early shoots, roots, young seedpods, and flowers were all eaten.

Asclepias tuberosa   butterfly weed. So decorative, and the root was used to treat bronchial problems and coughs.

Camassia scilloides   wild hyacinth. An endangered species, this needs moisture; its bulbs were sought out and eaten as a delicacy.

Ceanothus americanus   new jersey tea. A striking shrub for background purposes, blooming in July, followed by interesting black seedpod clusters. A healthful tea full of vitamin C can be brewed from the flowers.

Cypripedium calceolus pubescens   yellow lady's slipper. Becoming more rare daily. Needs dappled moist shade and mycorrhizal soil. Called "koko koho moccasin" by the Native Americans, meaning "nerve root."

Echinacea pallida   pale coneflower. Another endangered species. Northern Plains Indians revered this plant, using it as a cure-all for burns, snakebites, and stings. It is unrivaled for relieving pain. Mine does best in a dry site.

Epilobium angustifolium   fireweed. With a lovely pink flower. Its early, asparaguslike shoots were prized as food.

Eryngium yuccifolium   rattlesnake master. Another remedy for snakebite, the early settlers certainly cast aside beauty for practicality when they named it.

Euonymus americanus   burning bush. The Indians called it "wahoo." It's native to Zone 6, but I'm trying to find seeds for it to see if I can cheat on a few zones. The root is bitter and brews a strong tea that supposedly gave good health lifelong.

Eupatorium maculatum   joe-pye weed. Will grow anyplace, not just in swamps. Beloved by the bumblebee, the Indians used it medicinally.

Eupatorium perfoliatum   boneset. Drunk as a tea to relieve all pain, and wrapped on wounds in a poultice.

Helianthus tuberosus   jerusalem artichoke or sunchoke. This native perennial was so important to the North American Indians that I've given it a whole section at the end of this chapter.

Inula helenium   elecampane. Five to 6 feet tall, tolerating droughts. A plant for sore throat and chest pain.

Iris shrevei   blue iris, wild flag. It, too, survives anywhere, not just near water.

Lespedeza capitata   bush clover. Dries perfectly for bouquets. Seeds were pounded and eaten.

Lilium superbum   turk's-cap lily. Harvested for its delicious bulbs.

Medeola virginica   cucumber root or indian cucumber. A perennial root crop like the indian potato, this needs afternoon shade. Has a pretty flower. The root is an oddly shaped oblong, a fleshy white tuber that does taste like cucumber. It will naturalize if conditions are right. As with the indian potato, let it get well established before you dig it and leave some roots behind. Best eaten raw, peeled and grated, or peeled and sliced for dipping.

Monarda fistulosa   Has many common names: bergamot, oswego tea, beebalm. By any name, it makes a good pick- me-up tea.

Oenothera biennis   evening primrose. A biennial root crop that does well in dry, sandy soils. The roots produced the first year can be dug and cooked. Good added to soups or stews, or grated and processed to make a mild horseradish-like condiment.

Opuntia compressa   prickly pear or indian fig. It is perennial for me. The Native Americans relied on its fruit, making a syrup and even a simple candy from it.

Parthenium integrifolium   wild quinine. Still another protected species. The seeds were chewed for their sweetness and brewed into tea.

Psoralea esculenta   prairie turnip. Has a nutritious root that kept many a settler alive during the winter. The Indians considered it a delicacy. It likes a hot, dry spot at the edge of a dry, sandy woods. I have not been successful with it either from seed or from plants.

Rhus   sumac. The fall color is unsurpassed. It is aggressive, though—not for city gardens. Make a pink "lemonade" tea with the fruit.

Sagittaria latifolia   arrowhead or wapato. For stream banks. The tuber is choice baked, mashed, or steamed.

Sambucus canadensis   elderberry. A shrub for the background. It suckers! The fruit was eaten fresh or dried for winter. Birds like it, too.

Sassafras albidum   Another background shrub. All parts are fragrant. The root and bark make a tasty, but some say carcinogenic, tea.

Silphium laciniatum   compass plant. People ate the seeds, and the buffalo enjoyed the enormous leaves.

Sporobolus heterolepis   dropseed. With arching graceful fronds. The seeds were mashed, made into cakes, and dried for winter eating.

Stipa spartea   needlegrass. These sharp inflorescences could even penetrate hides.

Thalictrum dasycarpum   meadow rue. The seeds were used, this time for perfume! The leaves were fed to horses, to stimulate them.

Tragopogon pratensis   goatsbeard. Often called meadow salsify. This has a great big puff of a seed head, like a giant dandelion. A biennial, it can't be harvested until the second year, before the flower stem develops. Pull the roots, peel, slice, and boil them, season them, and sing their praises.

Trillium   squaw's plant. Used during childbirth.

Typha latifolia   cattail. This plant grows anyplace, not just in water. It actually seeded itself in a dry scree for me! A native all over the globe. The Indians ate the roots, young shoots, and made a porridge of the pollen. They made baskets from the swordlike leaves.

Viola pedata   birdsfoot violet. The young leaves were eaten as a green, the flowers as a treat.

Yucca filamentosa   indian needle or soapweed. The roots, flowers, and pulp of the pod were eaten. The leaves used for thatching and pounded for fiber. Not very long ago, I had potato chips made from the root!

All these remedies are pretty much unsubstantiated, as far as I know. They are fascinating and fun, but let's not doctor ourselves. Many of the plants are aggressive. Don't let them go to seed unless you want them to take over. Deheading is an easy remedy. Seeds are like paratroopers, windborne and all set to conquer any empty space. Watch out especially for common milkweed, joe-pye, boneset, inula, bush clover, compass plant, meadow rue, the grasses, and yucca. Most can be bought from the Prairie Nursery, Box 365, Westfield, WI 53964.

A Native American Staple: *Helianthus tuberosus*

No Native American food garden would be complete without the jerusalem artichoke or sunchoke. It was a favorite of the Indians across the North American continent. Easily cultivated from seed or tuber, its slender stalks are rough and hairy, branching into a ray of yellow sunflowerlike bloom late in summer. It has no disease or insect problems and should not be neglected as a vegetable. I admit it could become very aggressive. All the more reason to keep it harvested. Harvest it before the ground freezes and store as you would potatoes. It can also be dug in the early spring. (It grows 5 to 10 feet tall.)

With a slightly sweeter flavor than the potato, it can be used in all the same ways. Better yet, it's good raw, and makes an excellent substitute for water chestnut. It can be served in cream sauce, pureed for soups, pickled, stir-fried, made into pancakes, grated for slaw—cooked or raw, they are delicious.

Much of the flavor is in the skin, and the tuber is bumpy. I use a carrot peeler to peel it, or you can just brush it well if you don't mind the skin-on look. There are only 22 calories per pound in jerusalem artichokes if used freshly dug. Cooked whole and unpeeled (10–15 minutes), you can rub off the skins as soon as they can be handled (don't let them get cool or the skin won't come off).

When peeling and slicing, put the chokes in lemon or vinegar water (they darken if not treated). I add a little milk to the cooking water.

To me, jerusalem artichokes seem very similar in taste and texture to the Japanese root vegetable jicama. I use them interchangeably.

Jerusalem Artichoke Salad

Serves 6

3 cups hot cooked chokes, quartered
½ cup good olive oil
¼ cup currant or other vinegar
Dash cayenne
Salt and pepper
Fresh tarragon or parsley, chopped

Mix well. Serve warm.

Chiffonade Salad

Serves 6

1 head leaf lettuce, preferably homegrown
2 cups fresh spinach leaves
1 cup raw chokes, shredded or grated
2 tablespoons chives, minced
4½ teaspoons fresh lemon juice
1 teaspoon dijon mustard
1 teaspoon lemon rind, grated finely
4½ tablespoons good olive oil
Salt and pepper

Clean and dry lettuce and spinach and tear into bite-size pieces. Toss with chokes and chives. Shake remaining ingredients in a small jar with a lid. Pour over the salad and toss well. Serve at once.

Jerusalem Artichokes Tempura

Scrub, peel, and slice chokes about 1/5 inch thick. Dip in tempura batter and fry in hot oil (not olive oil) in a heavy frying pan or wok.

Sautéed Jerusalem Artichokes

Serves 4

1 ½ pounds chokes, scrubbed, peeled, and thinly sliced

1 small onion, minced

2 tablespoons butter

1 teaspoon soy sauce

A few drops sesame oil

Melt the butter in a heavy nonaluminum skillet and sauté the onion until limp. Add the chokes and sauté until brown. Season with soy sauce and sesame oil. Serve hot.

Quick Cream of Vegetable Soup

Serves 6

2 cups raw chokes, peeled and grated

2 carrots, peeled and grated

1 teaspoon onion, grated

4 tablespoons butter

4 tablespoons flour

4 cups milk

1 teaspoon soy sauce

Fresh coriander leaves or parsley, minced

In a heavy-bottomed 2-quart pan, not aluminum, melt butter and stir in flour. Cook until bubbly. Gently whisk in the milk and bring to boil. Add vegetables and cook until soup is slightly thick. Add soy sauce, cover, and simmer 20 to 30 minutes, or until vegetables are tender. Serve garnished with coriander or parsley.

Vegetable Chip Patties

1 ½ cups carrots, peeled and shredded

1 ½ cups chokes, peeled and shredded

1 ½ cups cabbage, shredded

¼ cup onion, minced

¼ cup pimiento, minced

¼ cup mild green chilies, minced

2 cups potato chips or taco chips, crushed

1 teaspoon fresh oregano

1 teaspoon fresh chervil

½ teaspoon celery seed

2 raw eggs, slightly beaten

Salt and pepper

1 stick butter (for frying patties)

Combine shredded and minced vegetables and mix well. Add remaining ingredients except butter and mix well. Let stand 15 minutes. Melt butter in large, heavy skillet (not aluminum) and fry patties when butter is hot. Be careful; they burn easily. Brown nicely and serve at once.

Baked Vegetable Casserole

Serves 6

3 cups celery, washed and cut into 1-inch lengths

1 ½ cups chokes, peeled and grated

⅓ cup pimiento, diced

1 cup white sauce

1 cup almonds, sliced

½ teaspoon mixed dried herbs

Cook celery in boiling water until just tender. Drain. Add the chokes, pimiento, and white sauce and pour into a buttered baking dish. Top with almonds and herbs. Bake at 350°F for 30 minutes, or until bubbly and golden brown.

Roasted Chokes

Jerusalem artichokes, washed and peeled
Preserved grape leaves (available at specialty foodstores)

Wrap each choke in a grape leaf. Place on a baking sheet and bake at 350°F for 1 hour. Test for doneness with a toothpick. These make great appetizers, 1 or 2 per person.

Fresh Pickled Choke Relish

1 medium onion, thinly sliced
1 cup water
1 cup distilled white vinegar
1/2 cup sugar
1/2 teaspoon canning salt
1/2 teaspoon mustard seed
1/2 teaspoon dry mustard
Pinch celery seed
1-inch piece hot pepper
2 pounds chokes, peeled

In a heavy nonaluminim kettle, combine all ingredients but chokes. Bring to a boil. Slice the chokes thinly, directly into the boiling liquid to keep them from darkening. Simmer about 15 minutes, until chokes are tender-crisp, stirring 2 or 3 times. Pour into jars. Let set overnight in refrigerator before using. Keeps 1 week in refrigerator.

Canned Pickled Chokes

Makes 7 pints

First day:

> 6 cups purified water
> 1/3 cup canning salt
> 2 pounds chokes, peeled
> 3 cups onion, sliced
> 2 cups peppers, sliced (a combination of green, red, and/or
> yellow peppers works well)
> 2 cups cauliflower, broken into florettes

In a large glass punch bowl or other large glass or ceramic container, mix water and salt. Slice the chokes thinly, directly into the brine. Add remaining vegetables. Mix well and let stand in the refrigerator overnight.

Second day:

Have 7 pint jars sterilized and ready, rims and lids waiting in a boiling water bath.

> 2 cups plus 1/3 cup cider vinegar
> 1 1/3 cups sugar
> 2 tablespoons dry mustard
> 2 teaspoons mustard seed
> 1 1/4 teaspoons celery seed
> 1/2 teaspoon turmeric
> 1/4 teaspoon cayenne pepper

Drain and reserve the vegetables that have been standing in the brine overnight. Pour 2 cups of cider vinegar into a large nonaluminum kettle. In a small bowl, mix the remaining 1/3 cup vinegar with the sugar and seasonings. Add this mixture to the cider vinegar in the kettle and bring to a boil, stirring constantly. When the mixture thickens, add vegetables and cook, stirring, for 5 minutes. Transfer the pickle to the sterilized jars and put on the lids. No processing is necessary. This pickle will keep in a cool, dark place for a year.

$\boxed{8}$

Propagation and Maintenance

THESE gardens we are constantly planning and planting need accessories—decorative embellishments ranging from paths, statues, fences, benches, and rock walls to arbors, pergolas, and even small buildings. If you, like me, find the expensive ones from catalogs unaffordable, devise your own. We burned large tree stumps, contrived statues from concrete silo staves and concrete rounds, and set fencing attractively for vines to grow on.

Buildings as Accessories

AS a focal point for our landscape design and as a major step toward producing our own plants for the gardens, we eventually built a greenhouse. Each gardener goes through the stage of hungering for one of these, and I was no exception. My greenhouse prompted a tremendous growth period for me.

This 12 by 20-foot, double-walled, acrylic panelled, semisolar installation faced south, with a direct entry from the house. On a sunny winter day, no additional heat was required to keep the greenhouse warm. The inside temperature fluctuated from 42°F at night to over 90°F, ideal for potted cacti and succulents. It had a sink, working tables, and lots of shelving—a great spot to retire to and beat those winter blahs.

When this was a new plaything, I tried to keep other kinds of houseplants in it over the winter, but not all did well, including episcias, hoyas, boston fern, and african violet. They could not tolerate the radical changes of temperature.

One of my central goals for the greenhouse was to raise small winter crops of lettuce, tomatoes, and cucumbers. I even tried beets and carrots successfully. And I wanted to be able to put down flats of seed for both annual vegetables and perennial flowers, and to start seedlings of shrubs, trees, and exotics. For several years I happily met the daily demands of the greenhouse, adjusting temperature, watering, and attending to my seeds and seedlings, and it was a great satisfaction to walk my land knowing I had grown almost everything from scratch. But after several years of excitement there was a letdown. That greenhouse was a lot of work! We sold it along with our first house, and today it functions as a sauna and exotic plant room for the new owners.

Just outside the greenhouse we built a lathing house to provide the shade and wind protection so necessary for flats of seedlings that have to be hardened off before they are planted in the ground. The lathing house enabled me to indulge another fancy—hanging baskets of gorgeous fuchsias, zebrinas, variegated coleus, geraniums, and ferns in the more shaded areas. In summer, all the greenhouse plants moved into the lathing house for sun and air.

We also built a root cellar into the side of our hill, with two small barns or sheds, one for my husband and one for me, above. I use mine for drying plant material and for storing all my gardening tools, sprayers, and hoops, and I have a worktable in it, as well.

Even though I did my homework before we built the root cellar, I still goofed. It was unsatisfactory for years because it held too much moisture inside. Things molded and rotted until we hit on a way to provide better air circulation. We drilled two holes through the ceiling in opposite corners. Into those holes we inserted plastic pipes, each one 6 feet long and 3 inches in diameter, so that they extended from the ceiling to a foot above the floor. The pipes allowed fresh air from my barn, above, to reach the root cellar. Voilà! No more mold or rotting.

Inside my barn I mounted several round hanging poles at a height I could easily reach. Plants to be dried are bunched, tied, and hung on the poles. The barn is dark with good air circulation, so things dry well. To preserve color, I harvest plant material to be dried when it is in peak condition. If I am going to be making wreaths, I wire *artemisias* and dictamnus to their frames while they are fresh—otherwise, they break. Then I hang them to dry, decorating them afterward.

I put culinary herbs and dictamnus (gas plant) in paper bags before hanging them, so their seeds don't scatter all over the floor. Gas plant seedpods explode when they're dry, making a terrible mess. And remember, any dried material must be brought into the house before freezing weather.

Between the two barns is a potting area containing a large table and, at table height, four metal tubs containing all the different ingredients used for soil mixes: wet peat, rotten granite gravel, sand, and topsoil. This makes it easy to prepare the right mix for any plant's needs.

Flanking the entrance to the root cellar stand bleacherlike steps, 12 feet apart and two on each side. They make an ideal display accessory for container-grown plants. Such steps can be used to create privacy and display on a small deck, patio, balcony, or in any situation where the wind isn't a crucifier. The containers can be shifted into more or less visibility depending on what plantings look best at the moment. They could even be tucked underneath for complete concealment. (Plastic pots are a temptation to be resisted. They capsize too easily.)

Such a concentrated garden will definitely need extra watering and fertilizing. If you choose to plant annuals and vegetables, you can change the display every year, even the color scheme. You will want to empty these pots in the fall. If you have no storage space for them, they can stay on the bleachers, upside down. The soil could be reused if it is refortified.

Plant Propagation from Seed

A greenhouse is not a necessity for propagation. Now I convert my drying barn or my garage into a propagating room every winter. I set up a simple table of a sheet of fireproof plywood on top of two sawhorses, with a fluorescent shop light above and heating cables taped onto the plywood surface. This table is inexpensive and can be put away when not in use.

Whether you have a greenhouse or just a propagating table, midwesterners should plant their perennial seeds in January or February and their annual seeds between April 7 and 14. An equal mixture of Turface, builder's or sharp sand, and sterilized potting soil is a very successful medium. Pack your soil into the containers, wet thoroughly, and firm well. If your seed is fine, mix it up in wet sand first. Distribute as evenly as possible and dust the seed with milled sphagnum to reduce damping-off (mildew). Label the flats or containers. If you are using the table method, cover the plantings with a sheet of clear plastic, or put individual planted containers inside clear plastic bags. For a few seeds, use a small container; for many seeds, use a flat.

Bottom heat is necessary for germination. The ideal temperature is 60°F to 70°F. If you are setting seeds out in cold frames or on windowsills, water heater, or furnace, check first for temperature and be sure it stays even. Check often for germination. When it occurs, remove your plants at once to a cooler location: 55°F to 60°F.

Remember, too, south windows are nice but there is no way you are going to get fourteen to sixteen hours of daylight from them during the winter months. Special grow lights are no more effective than ordinary fluorescents. It is the amount and placement of the lights, just a few inches above the plants, that will give you the best results.

Make sure you keep your soil moist, and thin the seedlings by cutting off the extras with scissors. Don't attempt to pull them out, as this will disturb the remaining root systems.

We midwesterners suffer from the lack of imagination shown by our local nurseries. For the rare, unusual, and unavailable we must grow our own. The American Rock Garden Society has a remarkable seed exchange. Each year a seed list of thousands of varieties is published. Trees, shrubs, conifers, perennials— every kind of seed is available for a nominal sum. If you desire treasures, join this group. Many of the seeds I propagated in the greenhouse originated from this source.

Many growers use sterilized soil mediums, and these are effective if you intend to transplant right away. If you don't transplant immediately, you will need to use booster fertilizers at least once a week to keep your seedlings growing. The type of growth encouraged by these fertilizers often transplants poorly, sometimes dying because it is too dependent on the fertilizer.

Why I harvest and plant my own seeds

1. Seeds are at least a dollar a packet, and each packet contains just a few seeds.

2. I can trade seeds with people who want to share.

3. Seed saving is easy: perennial seed can be put in paper bags and hung in the garage. Annual seed must be stored inside and never allowed to freeze. I put these seeds in jars of dry sand or in paper bags, never plastic, because plastic prevents water from evaporating, and damp seed will mildew.

4. Even hybrid flower seed (snapdragon, zinnia, marigold, columbine, and delphinium) will germinate. The new plants won't be true to the parent, but they will still be worthwhile. (This won't work with hybridized vegetable seed, however. These seeds will produce fruits with bitter or no flavor, if they germinate at all.)

5. By saving seed, you can have bagfuls for direct seeding instead of just a pinch. This is surely the way to go whether you have a small area or acres.

6. Seed you harvest yourself will be fresh. Store-bought seed is often old or stored improperly, so germination is poor. Remember, though, to harvest your seeds at top viability, when pods are starting to burst or are shattered and blowing. If you let your seed get old, it isn't going to germinate well.

Working with Seeds

Seeds! Some are microscopic, others only small. Some are good sized. Many are tricky, needing to be sown instantly for germination: among these are *Angelica*, many natives previously discussed, and also *Cheiranthus, Corydalis, Delphinium, Dicentra, Lavatera, Lunaria, Oenothera, Papaver,* and *Perovskia.*

Still other perennial seeds need changes of temperature (stratification) in order to germinate.

Some seeds will germinate in the dark but need to be moved to light at the instant of germination. Broccoli, brussels sprouts, cabbages, kale, kohlrabi, leeks, and peppers must be moved to a cool-nights-but-sunny-days place once germinated. This will develop stocky stems and healthy bodies.

Tree and shrub seeds often take a long time (six months to a year) to germinate. Sow them inside, in October or November. Many tree and shrub seeds have a complex dormancy period. If chilling and moisture are necessary for germination, place this seed in wet sand in the refrigerator. Plant the seedlings where they will stay permanently by June 1 to give them five months to prepare for the next winter. If you're really keen on something that isn't supposed to stand our winters, try this technique.

Remember, too: All plants grown inside will have to be hardened off before transplanting outdoors. Stop fertilizing two weeks before outdoor planting and cut down on watering. Place the containers in the lee of a building so they are shielded from the wind for an hour each day for three days, then increase exposure to three hours a day for a week. You will have to carry them in and out if you don't have a cold frame that you can close the lid on. Cold frames protect from below-freezing temperatures and can also be used as seed beds. Anything you plant in there will have to be transplanted, though, and the more you transplant your seedlings, the less hardy they become. This plays havoc with any attempt to cheat a hardiness zone or two. I try to resist the temptation to plant in cold frames.

Propagating by Direct Seeding

In fact, these days I start fewer and fewer seeds indoors. My gardens are so large that I need to get into them as early as possible in the spring, and caring for many seed flats is time-consuming once I am working outdoors. I have had my greatest successes when I just pat the seeds around directly where I want them to grow. With passing years, each of us devises methods that save time and energy. My biggest time-saver is direct seeding.

I actually plant seeds all year round. This works well for most perennials and self-sowing, self-germinating annuals and biennials. I collect seeds all summer long, paying careful attention to the seed that needs to be planted instantly. Those that will wait till winter, I let wait. There is absolutely nothing more rewarding than patting seeds around the garden during those cold, bleak winter days. I keep a mix of wet peat and sand ready in a tub and mix the seed up in it, 1 pint of seed to 5 pints of mix. I take this mixture to the garden along with a bucket of small gravel and written labels. Put down a couple of handfuls of gravel and then a teaspoonful of the seed mix. Mess it around. If the ground is frozen and you can't get the label in, just lay it alongside and put some of the gravel on it to hold it down. Go on to the next spot.

This is just as much fun to do in the summer. Then you can tell exactly where you need a certain plant, and how many.

Each year my propagating techniques have convinced me again of the value of direct seeding. Seeding in place eliminates the traumatic experience of transplanting. Plants that are sold by garden centers and nurseries have been transplanted several times without the benefit of root pruning. All too often these plants are over-fertilized. This over-fertilization makes them too dependent on fertilizers and weakens the root system. Weak roots do not develop winter hardiness. When you seed directly in the garden, the roots cope with a natural situation from the beginning. Plants grown directly will catch up to a root-bound purchased tree or shrub within three to four years. They will be healthier and happier, with well-shaped branches and trunks, surviving all that nature decrees.

This gardening naturally technique has proven itself time and time again over the years. I urge you to try it. You won't have to be intimidated or afraid to swindle on climate zones. Few of my treasures would be in the gardens today if I hadn't cheated. If you do start from seed inside, plant the seedlings out as soon as possible. Many growers keep their seedlings in pots for years. Not me! Don't keep them on hold. I feel they need to be planted where they're going to live early in their lives. Put a hoop around them for protection.

Many times I have asked a fellow gardener for permission to collect seeds or to save seed for me, and I have never been refused. Don't turn aside even if that seed you're longing for takes six months to germinate. Become intimately involved with your seeds. It's the best way of learning identification in a hurry. Once you have grown something from seed, recognizing it in the future is easy.

An Informal Flowerbed from Seed

Here is a new and amusing way of making a flowerbed. Work up the soil, then form an area up with stone to about a foot high in whatever shape you desire, in sun or shade. Fill this raised bed with a 3-inch layer of hay or grass clippings packed down, then top with 6 inches of sharp sand, wet peat, and pea gravel (equal parts of each mixed together). There will be no weeds to contend with. Select the type of seed you want: from shade-loving plants if your bed is in the shade, from sun lovers if your new bed is in the sun. Mix like seeds together with some of the mixture, then pat it around in colonies. Some possible combinations: for shade, tall-growing choices are *Corydalis, Gentiana, Lunaria, Monarda*; lower-growing choices are *Myosotis, Campanula, Primula*, and *Geum*. For sun, tall growers are *Aquilegia, Allium, Coreopsis, Echeveria, Liatris*; lower growers are *Aubrieta, Armeria, Arabis*, and *Dianthus*. This garden would have a very natural look and would be such fun to create. I've always had the feeling that many people get turned off with gardening because of the grim soil they are dealing with. This mix is so super and feels so good to the touch, you will want to play in it. It smells good, too.

Seeds are tougher and smarter than people. Seeds know when to germinate. You can impersonate nature by planting in these colonies. Do not disturb and you will have a long-term, weed-free perennial bed as a reward. Don't waste your time with cheap seeds. Cheap seeds are no bargain, for you pay dearly with their poor results: little germination, weed seeds,incorrect labeling, and inferior directions. Buy the best. You are worth it and so are they. Many seeds have a short viability time, so rather than take chances, you are better off planting all perennial seeds as soon as possible.

If your *perennial* seeds do not germinate, set the containers outside in a protected place and let them freeze. Bring them back inside and put them on the heating cable. Many times this trick will wake up the seed. Another trick to try with delphinium, lupinus, and other shell-like flower seeds, as well as many vegetable seeds: start them on moist paper towels in covered pans in the refrigerator. Once sprouting takes place, use tweezers to remove the seeds and place in small pots that have been filled with a soaked soil mixture.

Other times, the only way you can get little corms like those of windflower and *Aconitum* to germinate is to soak them in warm water overnight. How do you keep that water warm for so long? Put the seeds or corms in an empty tea bag and staple it shut. Then put the tea bag in a thermos filled with almost hot water. (Good seeds swell. The others stay dark and withered.)

Other Ways to Propagate

Cuttings, layering, and even rooting in water are all good ways to propagate plants. Cuttings are a bit difficult but worth the trouble. I do this in June when the new growth has hardened but is still pliable. Cut off a 6-inch twig or stem at an angle near a leaf. Remove any leaves from the cutting, being careful not to tear any bark or sheathing from the stem, and place it 4 inches deep in a sand-filled container with drainage holes in the bottom. Wet the sand thoroughly and never let it dry out. Provide bottom heat of 60°F to 70°F and keep the container loosely covered with clear plastic, or place it inside a clear plastic bag. Many people apply a rooting hormone to the cutting, but it's not necessary. I've rooted *Cotoneaster* 'Tom Thumb', *Genista tinctoria*, and many varieties of dwarf conifers using this method.

Layering is easy. Bend a branch or stem low and scratch off a little of the sheathing along the side that will lie on the ground. Leave the stem attached to the mother plant, press the scratched area to cleared earth, and cover it with wet soil, leaving the tips of the plant exposed. Put a stone on top of the soil to weigh the stem down. Again, don't let it dry out. *Hydrangea anomala* subs. *petiolaris*, *Forsythia*, and most other shrubs or trees will root using this technique.

The ancient Romans propagated trees using a type of layering I find fascinating. "To make shoots take root while on the tree, make a hole in the bottom of a pot and push the branch you wish to root through it. Fill the pot with earth, press it down thoroughly and leave it on the tree. When it is two years old, cut off the branch, shatter the pot and plant the branch in a pit together with the pot." These are Cato's instructions. Propagation methods haven't changed all that much over the centuries.

Rooting in water is the easiest propagation method of all. Use a clear glass jar and pure water. Change the water often and in no time you will have roots growing. Your plant material must be cut when the sap is coming up in the spring, when the little buds are just starting to swell. I've rooted corkscrew, fantail, and french pink pussy willows, mexican tarragon (*Tagetes lucida*), dittany of crete, salvias, and much more in this fashion. Just remember, these are "water roots," so when you plant your new shoots, don't let them dry out. Water often enough that the soil stays soaked until you see new growth.

Willow can be rooted directly from a cutting. Take an 18-inch-long cutting from a branch. Cut it straight across at the bottom. This causes callusing and balanced rooting. Cut at an angle at the top so moisture is cast off. Bury the lower 9 inches of the cutting in a deep container filled with wet sand. Keep the sand moist and presto, you'll have a new tree.

Division is another means of propagation for perennials such as *Achillea*, *Echinops*, *Papaver*, *Verbascum*, *Sedum*, succulents, and many others. Simply lift the clump, cut or gently pull it apart, and replant the divisions, making sure to water frequently until they show new growth.

Garden Maintenance

There is no question that gardening is labor intensive. Watering, weeding, pruning, thinning, harvesting, deheading—all must go on, season after season, whether one is planning and planting a new bed or simply encouraging the existing ones to look their best. As I get older, I find myself grappling constantly with the need to keep maintenance manageable. My preference is for a specimen garden, where individuals are highlighted and given space to look their best, rather than for the cottage garden, where species grow almost on top of each other and the eye sees only a mass of color, everything stuffed in to the hilt. But a specimen garden requires great control, and I am sometimes hard-pressed to provide it.

More and more, naturalizing seems to be an answer. Prairies, meadows, the shaded sanctuary of naturalized specie bulbs and shrubs, the miniforests of conifers and shade-loving perennials I have begun in place of the vegetable gardens that claimed so much of my time—if some of my gardens are allowed to naturalize, I will be able to maintain the character of others,

17. Layering

like the alpine berm and my formal herb garden, where "naturalizing" would simply mean one or two aggressive species overwhelming the rest.

But naturalizing is only part of my maintenance strategy. Raised beds of boulders or stone are economical to build and a big energy-saver planted with herbs, perennial flowers, or vegetables. Weeding is easier; it's contained and you can sit to do it. Small sprinklers can be moved from bed to bed for watering. Raised beds are not walked in, so the soil does not become compacted, requiring tilling or spading. Harvesting involves less bending and reaching.

A raised vegetable bed could be built right on top of a lawn or an existing garden. I would make it 18 inches high and fill it up to 3 inches from the top with repeating 2-inch layers of dead leaves and hay sprinkled with 10-10-10 fertilizer. Wet well and top with 2 inches of compost or good topsoil. In the fall, all disease-free crop residue can be turned back into the beds. Cover with hay for the winter; this will decompose down. In the spring, dress again with soil or compost, and plant—no waiting to cultivate. Cover the seeds with lightweight fibercloth. They will germinate under it. The cloth will keep the soil four degrees warmer than unprotected soil, and it can be left on until the seedlings start to raise it. Then fold it up and store it for next season.

There is no way to escape weeds completely, even in a naturalized garden. The best ways to deal with them: get them out when they're infants. If you have a large weed growing so close to a treasure that you're afraid to pull it, cut it off at the ground and jam a tin can over it. Put a rock on top to hold the can down and wait until the root is dead.

Never let weeds go to seed. One year when weed seed escapes means ten years of weeding to get rid of the babies. Dehead all season long, not just weeds but also annuals and perennials that threaten to take over. There is no way your soil or your space can support them all. Some rampant reseeders, like *Phacelia, Gaillardia, Centranthus*, and dahlberg daisy, are so hard to control that you should save them for desperate situations where nothing else will grow. You may need to apply Preen, an inhibitor of germination, around the parent plant, or surround it with fibercloth barriers.

Soilless mixes are another way to keep weeds down. A combination of sharp sand, Turface, pea gravel, and sifted compost or finely shredded leaves is an excellent substitute for soil. For shady areas that need a richer mix, add more compost or leaves. I use this mix in all my new beds. Older beds get a 2- to 3-inch topdressing of it, or a mulch of pea gravel.

Weeds in the lawn are probably the hardest to deal with. For years I resisted treating my lawns with chemicals—I didn't want that poison in the air, in the soil, or in my vegetables. But gradually dandelions and crabgrass were smothering my lawns and seeding into the gardens, and I couldn't stand it any longer. But I don't treat as often as the lawn service tells me to! After the first year, they came out twice and now only once, in crabgrass season. Why did our ancestors bring over these insidious, naturalizing aliens?

Other pests in the garden include slugs, ants, and other insects. Don't build raised beds or paths with wooden logs or landscape timber. Slugs and bugs love them. Some natural pesticides: try setting out dishes of beer for slugs to drown in, or sprinkle a 3-inch barrier of ashes or coffee grounds around the plants you want to protect. Some say that a concoction of orange peel, thrown into the blender with a little water, can be poured onto anthills to get rid of ants. To reduce mildew, spray your plants frequently with a solution of 1 teaspoon baking soda to 1 quart of water. Cutting out the centers of your phlox and watering late in the evening, not all day, will also help.

To get rid of insect pests, spray your ornamental shrubs and fruit trees with dormant oil early in spring before insect larvae hatch. To be effective, dormant oil must be applied when the temperature has been above freezing (preferably above 40°F) for twenty-four hours.

If your gardens are being encroached upon by suckering shrubs like elderberry, chokecherry, plum, artemisia, or raspberry, you will appreciate this easy way to control them. Gently lift up the suckers and leave them exposed to the air, or tie them up to stakes or to the mother plant so they can't travel. Believe me, this works.

For a flourishing garden, you must fertilize. Each square yard of your ornamental growing area needs a three-ounce application of fertilizer at least twice during the growing season. But remember, too, that every botanical has a life span, and the day will come, no matter how carefully you have fed, weeded, and watered, when it will go into a decline. Get rid of it then; don't wait until it's bare and brown. By the same token, realize that trees and shrubs have a useful life span, too, and then they become oversized, scraggly, and past their prime. Get rid of them. Your garden, like your home, needs redecorating every now and then. Foundation plantings rarely look good for more than fifteen years; then they are overgrown, and it's time to start again.

Always think ahead to next spring. If you leave a mess in your gardens in the fall, you'll find yourself dreading spring cleanup. As winter approaches, I cut many perennials back to the ground, especially those that are mildew-prone or need all their strength to develop good root systems, like *Anthemis*, *Artemisia*, and yarrow. Use wintertime to prune your trees, make hoops, clean and repair tools, and order plantings for the new season. It helps to stagger delivery times, so you aren't suddenly buried under your new treasures.

With organization and planning, maintenance chores can be kept to a minimum, but they can never be eliminated. There is no status quo for very long. We must keep recreating, redeveloping, rethinking our gardens for as long as we keep them, always striving for new harmonies of color, foliage, and setting and for an equilibrium that the gardener can maintain.

Epilogue

LATE on a hot afternoon a few summers ago, I was weeding in the bottom terrace, decided that I'd had it, and came into the house to start supper. Only a few minutes later, I heard an awful noise. Going out on the deck, I saw all kinds of activity down by the road. A landscaping truck with a carrier had been coming up the road when the coupling broke and the carrier, like some mad thing, tore through the lower fence and an ornamental rock cluster and plowed up two terraces, throwing off the tractor it was hauling exactly where I had been weeding just a short time before.

Late last spring in the same garden, I was gutting the bulb beds, naturally on my haunches, when a terrible screech made me start to get up. The deer that a car had braked to stop from hitting sailed over my head, missing me by inches; it fell, stumbled up through the terraces, and bounded across the road with me watching open-mouthed. I turned to sit again and not four feet from me stood a big buck, as startled by all this as I was.

Other adventures are quieter. On the native prairie, so peaceful and still in the early morning or at dusk, I've often seen a mother fox with her kits—usually three, but one year she had six of them. She's wary, but they are exuberant. Of course, the woodchucks are fearless. I watch them rear up, their noses twitching in complete unconcern.

Pheasants, ducks, Canada geese migrating northward in spring, flocks of sandhill cranes stopping in a nearby marsh—they are all old friends. One pair of cranes has been nesting in the river marsh near me for many years. I hear their raucous mating call around daybreak. No matter how many eggs she lays, they only seem to raise one chick. Last year, the surrounding acres were planted in winter wheat. After this was harvested, I could see them feeding on the stubble every day.

Deer, mice, and raccoons bring adventures of another sort. The deer have been especially wicked in the past two years. They have cropped all the new arborvitae in the sanctuary. We didn't harvest any beets, peas, or lettuce last summer and only the fourth crop of beans came in. The mice gird the new trees unless I hoop them all with hardware mesh. Raccoons and woodchucks feast on the sweet corn despite care traps, cayenne pepper sprinkled liberally on the new ears, and noise generated to drive them away.

Weeds are vegetable adventures. Do their seeds live forever? A century ago, the famous botanist William Beal buried bottles containing seeds from twenty common weeds. One bottle was to be exhumed every five years, and the seeds planted in sterilized soil. According to *Weed Science of America*, plants from the seeds exhumed in 1980 are flourishing.

Often I feel I have every weed ever viable right here on River Road. I spend more time on my knees weeding than doing anything else. I make myself comfortable and contemplate and dream. Hoeing, planting, moving stones, and watering are hard; weeding happens when I get too tired to do those things. I am never at a loss for words when people ask me, "Where do you get your ideas?" I respond, "While weeding."

Sometimes summer, that rich and bountiful season, is swallowed up by the rush and pressure of gardening tasks. I try to steal back some appreciation of the season as I weed. My mind drifts to childhood summers: the creek that flowed by our door, a muddy, rushing, noisy thing overspilling its banks in spring; then later, in the hot, hazy days of August, murmuring a different melody as we waded and paddled and tried to keep cool. Then thoughts of the school years that seemed to drag by at the time, marriage and my own children to raise, and now my gardens.

I continually redesign my gardens in my mind, and in the evenings and winter I redesign on paper. I try to stroll through my gardens weekly with pen and notebook in hand, noting ideas and problems. In winter I grapple with all of them, trying to pull them into some kind of sequence or plan for spring. I review my scrapbook, bringing it up to date with magazine pictures that have tantalized me, and I read gardening books that share my enthusiasms.

My students always accuse me of trying to brainwash them. They're right. Gardeners see the world with different eyes. We are intimate with each season of the year: its colors, foliage, backdrop of rocks, water, clouds, and shadows. In winter we see the shapes of trees and the shape of the earth under them.

I try to convince my students to plant a walnut, an acorn, a butternut, a hickory nut. Is anyone planting these trees anymore?

And why are we limiting the kinds of ornamentals we plant?

We can't let our gardens be limited by what nurseries want to sell. They sell what is easy to propagate, easy to plant, and easy to maintain. You and I must insist on what we want. Let's demand *Abeliophyllum* instead of forsythia, *Paeonia suffruticosa* instead of *P. officinalis*, *Buddleia alternifolia* 'Argentea' instead of lilac.

Let's visit other gardens and share our treasures with other gardeners, not try to keep them to ourselves. When enthusiasm wanes at midsummer, stopping at someone else's garden always sends me home reinvigorated and inspired. Let's learn from the Europeans, who have created and visited public and private gardens for centuries. We have many splendid ones right here in our own country; we don't need to travel abroad to find gardens to admire. Make it a point to visit them often, and encourage others to do the same.

I want to leave you with a bouquet of wishes: for inspiration, hope, humility, patience, tranquility, love of nature, and, most of all, the time you need to grow a real bouquet. Regardless of how busy your garden keeps you, always take the time to appreciate it, and to dream.

Where to Buy Plants and Seeds

ALL these suppliers provide mail-order services, and many will send you a catalog at little or no cost.

Bulbs

McClure & Zimmerman
108 West Winnebago, Box 368
Friesland, WI 53935
414-326-4220

Bulbs and Perennial Plants

White Flower Farm
Litchfield, CT 06759-0050
203-496-9600

Perennial Plants

Canyon Creek Nursery
3527 Dry Creek Road
Oroville, CA 95965
916-533-2166

Milaegers
4838 Douglas Avenue
Racine, WI 53402
414-639-2040

Siskiyou Rare Plant Nursery
2825 Cummings Road
Medford, OR 97501
503-772-6846

Wayside Gardens Company
910 Garden Lane
Hodges, SC 29695
800-845-1124

Rhododendrons and Shrubs

Greer Gardens
1280 Goodpasture Island Road
Eugene, OR 97401-1794
503-686-8266

Trees, Shrubs, Perennial Plants

Forest Farm
990 Tetherow Road
Williams, OR 97544-9599
503-846-7269

Tropical and Subtropical Plants

Logee's Greenhouses
55 North Street
Danielson, CT 06239
203-774-8038

Full-Service Nurseries

Seeds, bulbs, annuals, perennials, shrubs, trees, gardening tools

Farmer Seed & Nursery Company
Faribault, MN 55021
507-334-1623

Gurney Seed & Nursery Company
Yankton, SD 57079
605-665-1671

Seeds

W. Atlee Burpee Company
Warminster, PA 18974
215-674-4900

Nichols Garden Nursery
1190 SW Pacific
Albany, OR 97321
503-928-9280

Park Seed Company
909 Cokesbury Road
Greenwood, SC 29647
803-223-7333

Prairie Nursery
P.O. Box 365
Westfield, WI 53964
608-296-3679

Shepherd's Garden Seed
7389 W. Zayante Road
Felton, CA 95018
408-335-6910

Stokes Seeds, Inc.
U.S. Box 548
Buffalo, NY 14240
716-695-6980

Thompson & Morgan, Inc.
P.O. Box 100
Jackson, NJ 07727
908-363-2225

Index